BIG NOTE PIANO LEVEL 1–2

M000105164

FUN-TO-PLAY Christmas Songs

Arranged by RICHARD BRADLEY

Richard Bradley is one of the world's best-known and best-selling arrangers of piano music for print. His success can be attributed to years of experience as a teacher and his understanding of students' and players' needs. His innovative piano methods for adults (Bradley's How to Play Piano – Adult Books 1, 2, and 3) and kids (Bradley for Kids – Red, Blue, and Green Series) not only teach the instrument, but they also teach musicianship each step of the way.

Originally from the Chicago area, Richard completed his undergraduate and graduate work at the Chicago Conservatory of Music and Roosevelt University. After college, Richard became a print arranger for Hansen Publications and later became music director of Columbia Pictures Publications. In 1977, he co-founded his own publishing company, Bradley Publications, which is now exclusively distributed worldwide by Warner Bros. Publications.

Richard is equally well known for his piano workshops, clinics, and teacher training seminars. He was a panelist for the first and second Keyboard Teachers' National Video Conferences, which were attended by more than 20,000 piano teachers throughout the United States.

The home video version of his adult teaching method, How to Play Piano With Richard Bradley, was nominated for an American Video Award as Best Music Instruction Video, and, with sales climbing each year since its release, it has brought thousands of adults to—or back to—piano lessons. Still, Richard advises, "The video can only get an adult started and show them what they can do. As they advance, all students need direct input from an accomplished teacher."

Additional Richard Bradley videos aimed at other than the beginning pianist include How to Play Blues Piano and How to Play Jazz Piano. As a frequent television talk show guest on the subject of music education, Richard's many appearances include "Hour Magazine" with Gary Collins, "The Today Show," and "Mother's Day" with former "Good Morning America" host Joan Lunden, as well as dozens of local shows.

Project Manager: Zobeida Pérez
Art Design: Ken Rehm & Lisa Greene Mane

Contents

Here Comes Santa Claus
(Right Down Santa Claus Lane)

Words and Music by
GENE AUTRY and OAKLEY HALDEMAN
Arranged by Richard Bradley

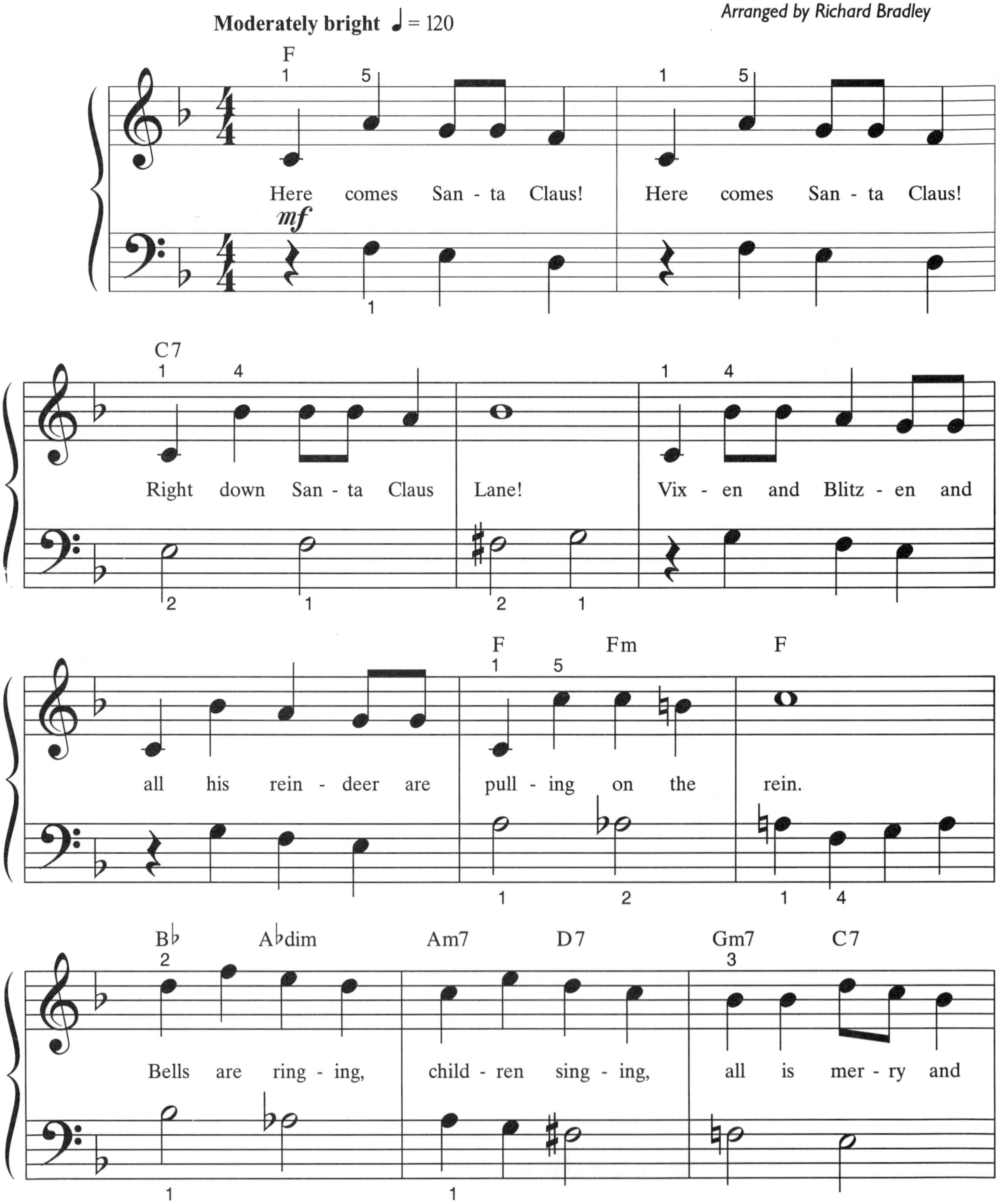
Moderately bright ♩ = 120
F
Here comes San - ta Claus! Here comes San - ta Claus!
mf
C7
Right down San - ta Claus Lane! Vix - en and Blitz - en and
all his rein - deer are
F Fm F
pull - ing on the rein.
B♭ A♭dim Am7 D7 Gm7 C7
Bells are ring - ing, child - ren sing - ing, all is mer - ry and

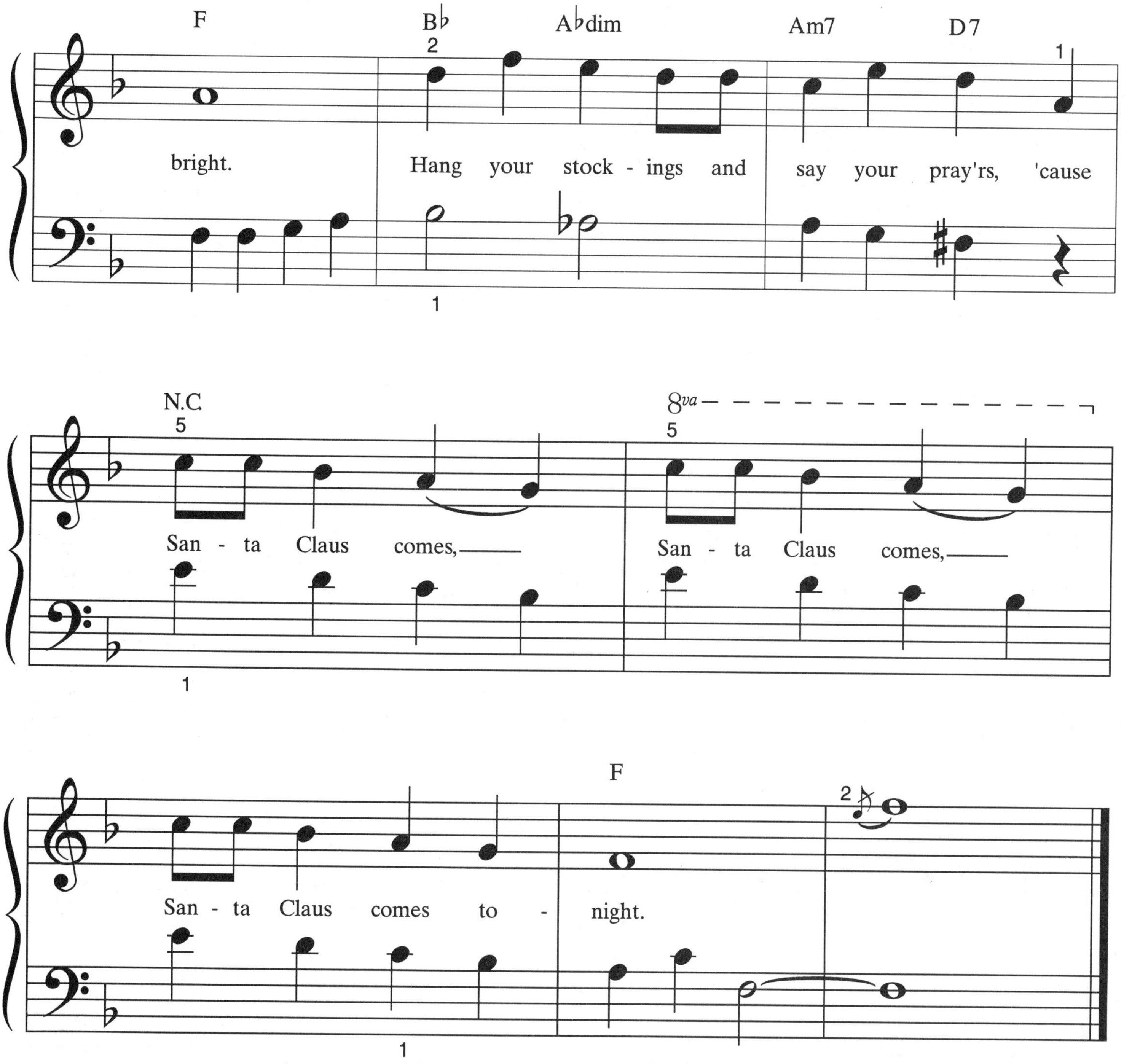
F
B♭
A♭dim
Am7
D7
bright.
Hang your stock - ings and say your pray'rs, 'cause
N.C.
8va
San - ta Claus comes,
San - ta Claus comes,
F
San - ta Claus comes to - night.

Verse 2:
Here comes Santa Claus!
Here comes Santa Claus!
Right down Santa Claus Lane!
He's got a bag that is filled with toys
For the boys and girls again.
Hear those sleigh bells jingle jangle,
What a beautiful sight.
Jump in bed, cover up your head,
'Cause Santa Claus comes tonight.

It's the Most Wonderful Time of the Year

Words and Music by
EDDIE POLA and GEORGE WYLE
Arranged by Richard Bradley

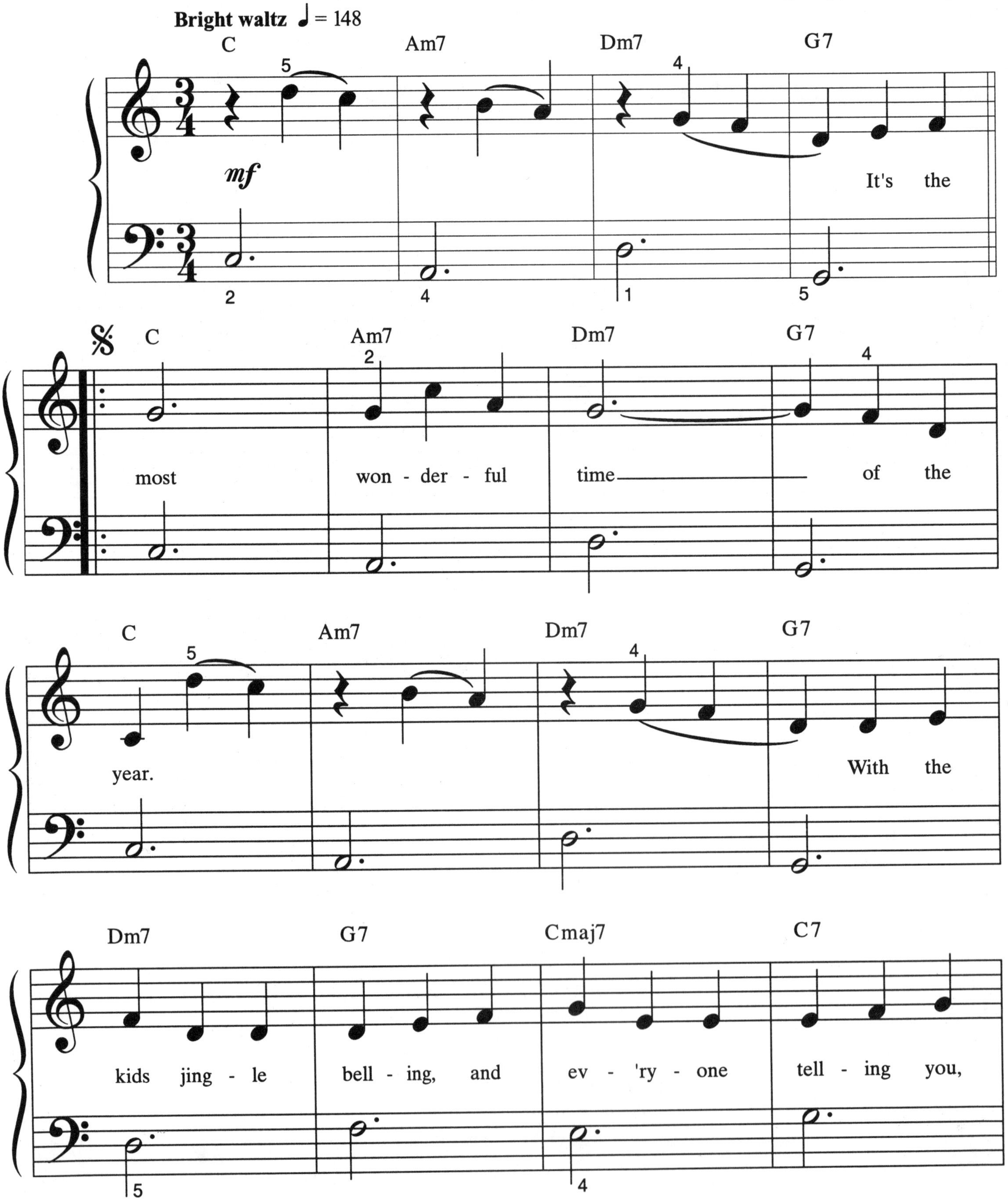
Bright waltz ♩ = 148
C Am7 Dm7 G7
mf
It's the
C Am7 Dm7 G7
most won - der - ful time of the
C Am7 Dm7 G7
year. With the
Dm7 G7 Cmaj7 C7
kids jing - le bell - ing, and ev - 'ry - one tell - ing you,

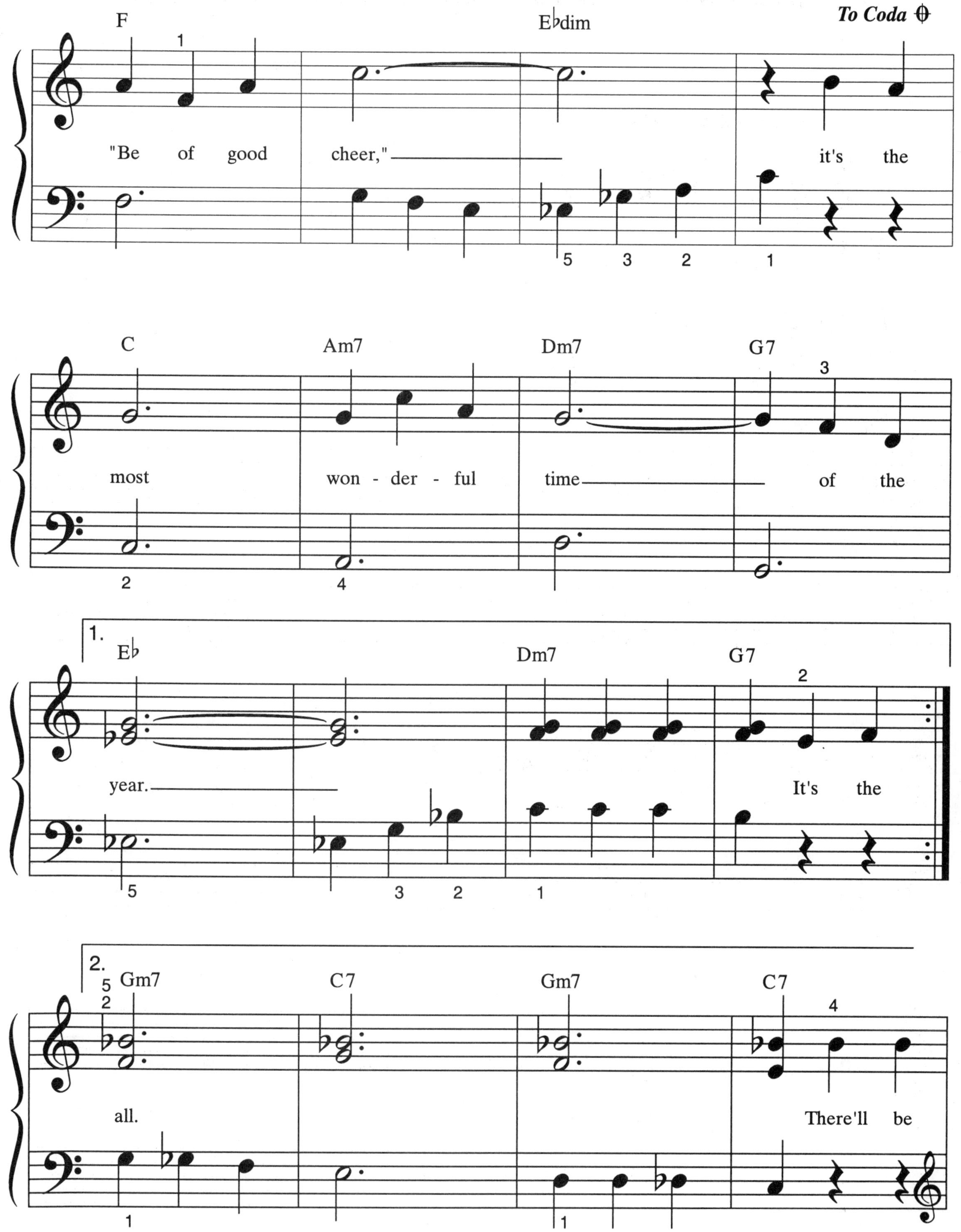
To Coda
F
Eb dim
"Be of good cheer," it's the
C
Am7
Dm7
G7
most won - der - ful time of the
1.
Eb
Dm7
G7
year. It's the
2.
Gm7
C7
Gm7
C7
all. There'll be

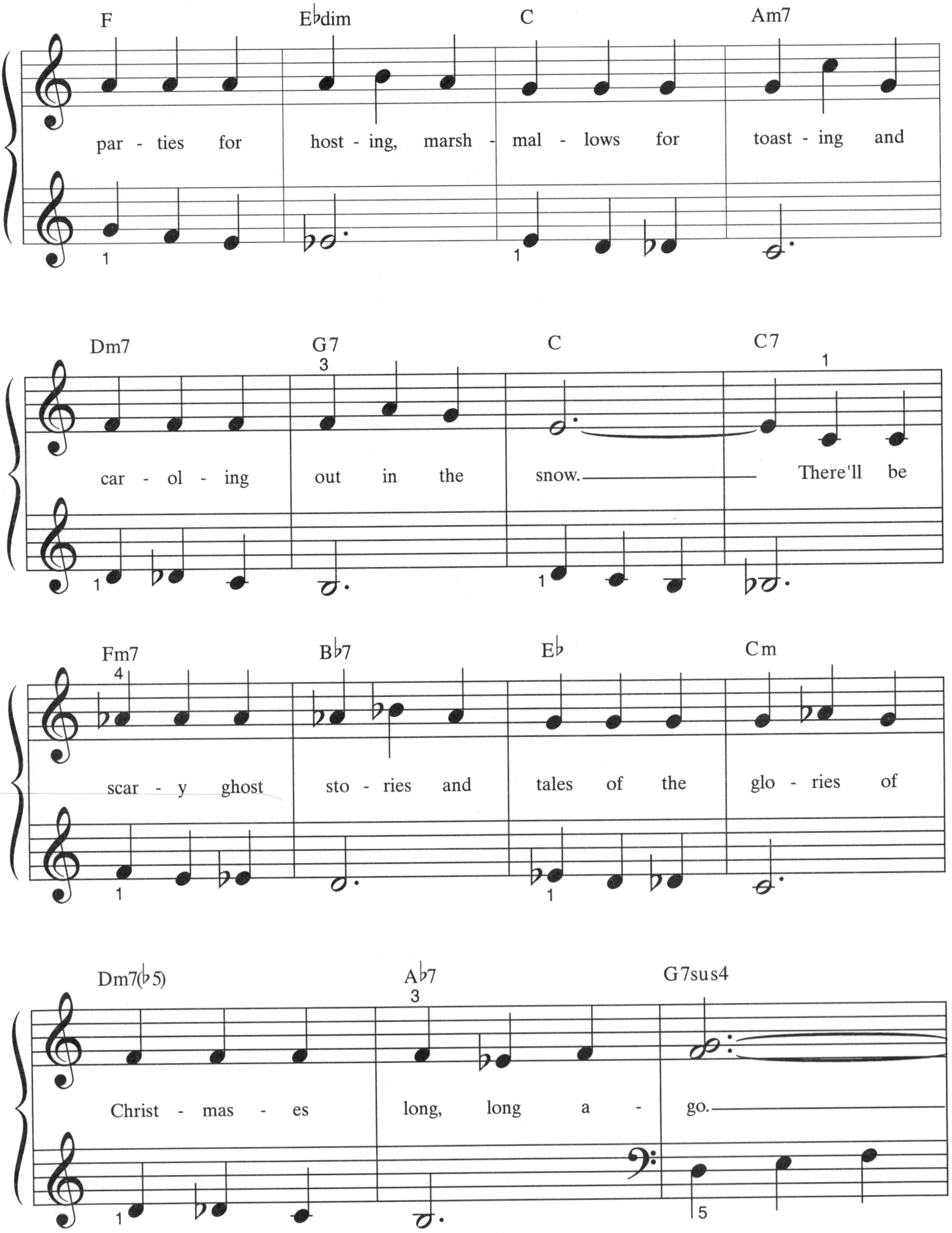
F
E♭dim
C
Am7
par - ties for host - ing, marsh - mal - lows for toast - ing and
Dm7
G7
C
C7
car - ol - ing out in the snow.
There'll be
Fm7
B♭7
E♭
Cm
scar - y ghost sto - ries and tales of the glo - ries of
Dm7(♭5)
A♭7
G7sus4
Christ - mas - es long, long a - go.

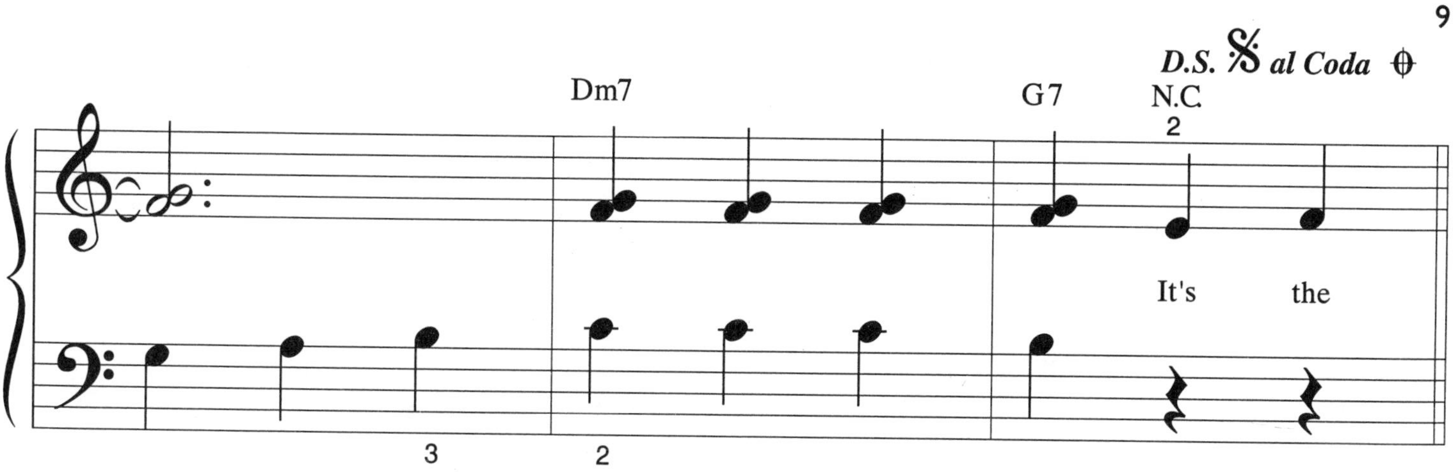

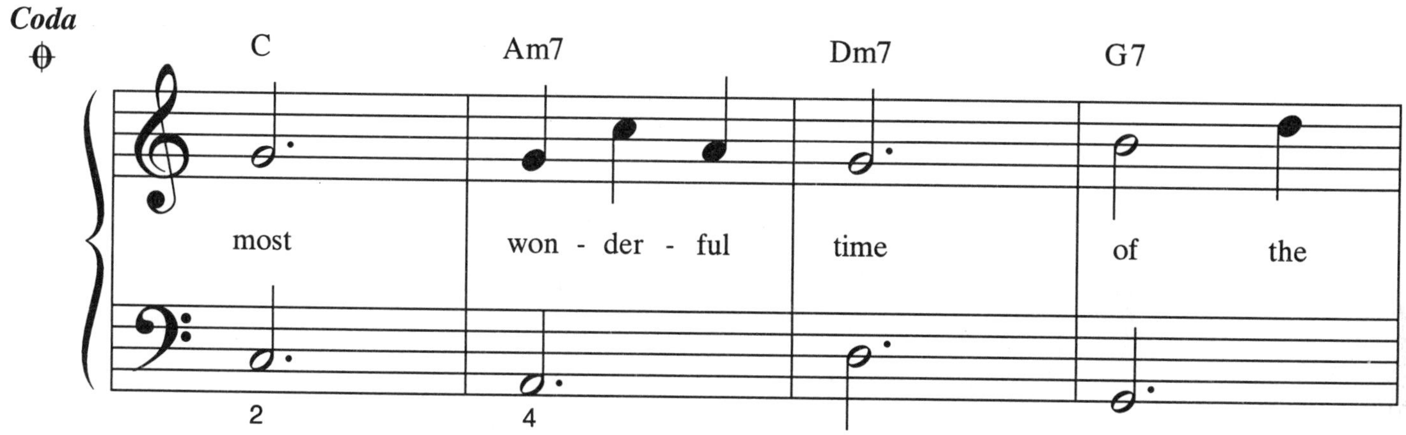

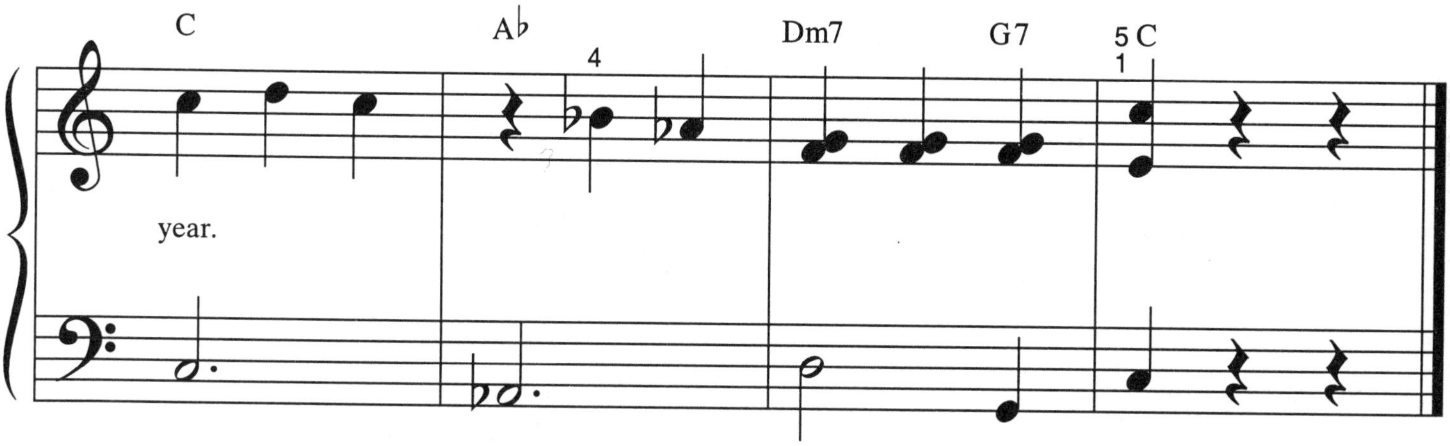

Verse 2:
It's the hap-happiest season of all.
With those holiday greetings,
And gay happy meetings
When friends come to call,
It's the hap-happiest season of all.

Verse 3:
It's the most wonderful time of the year.
There'll be much mistletoeing
And hearts will be glowing,
When loved ones are near.
It's the most wonderful time of the year.

The Twelve Days of Christmas

TRADITIONAL
Arranged by Richard Bradley

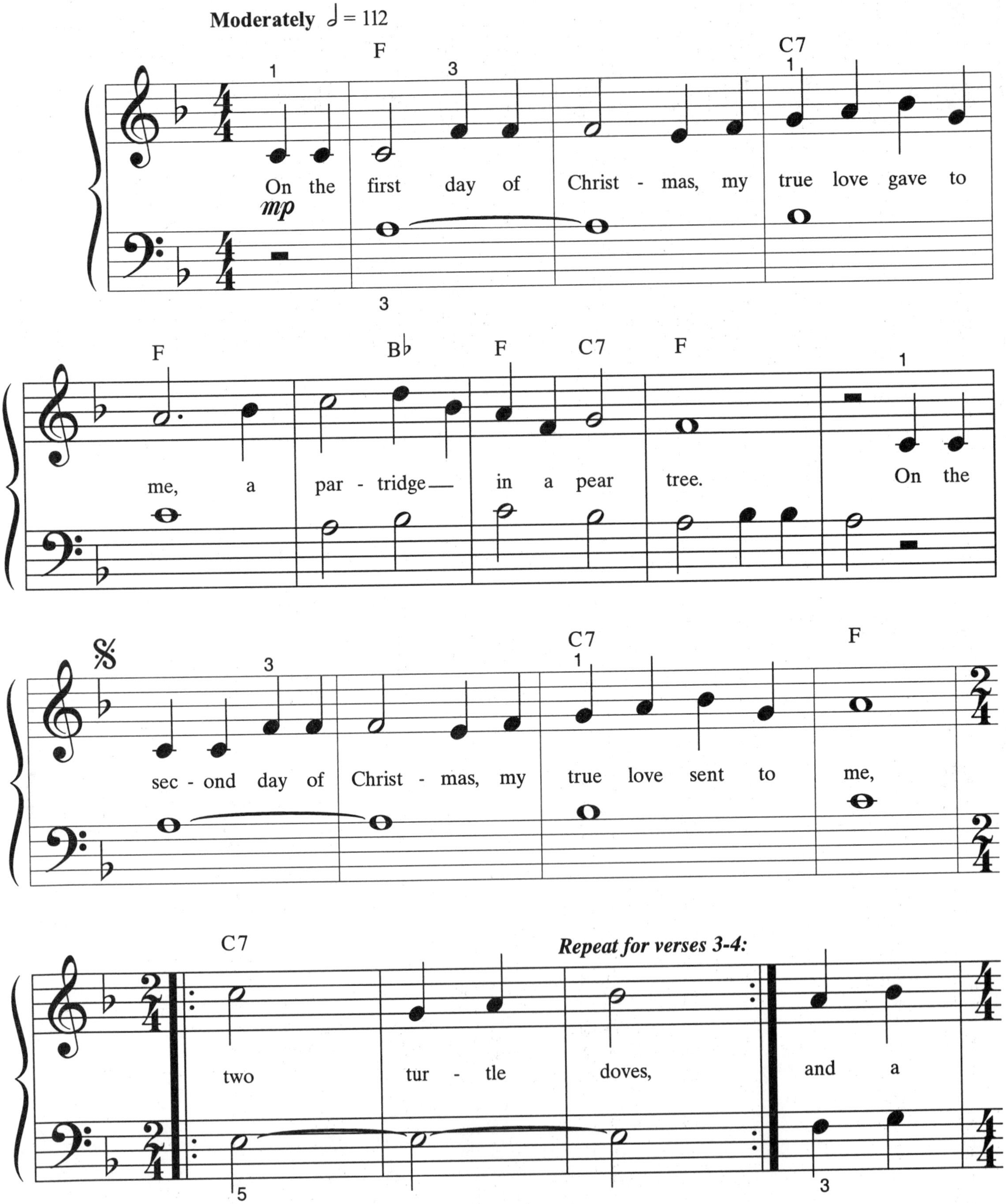
Moderately ♩ = 112
F
C7
On the first day of Christ - mas, my true love gave to
mp
F
B♭
F
C7
F
me, a par - tridge— in a pear tree. On the
C7
F
sec - ond day of Christ - mas, my true love sent to me, the
C7
Repeat for verses 3-4:
two tur - tle doves, and a

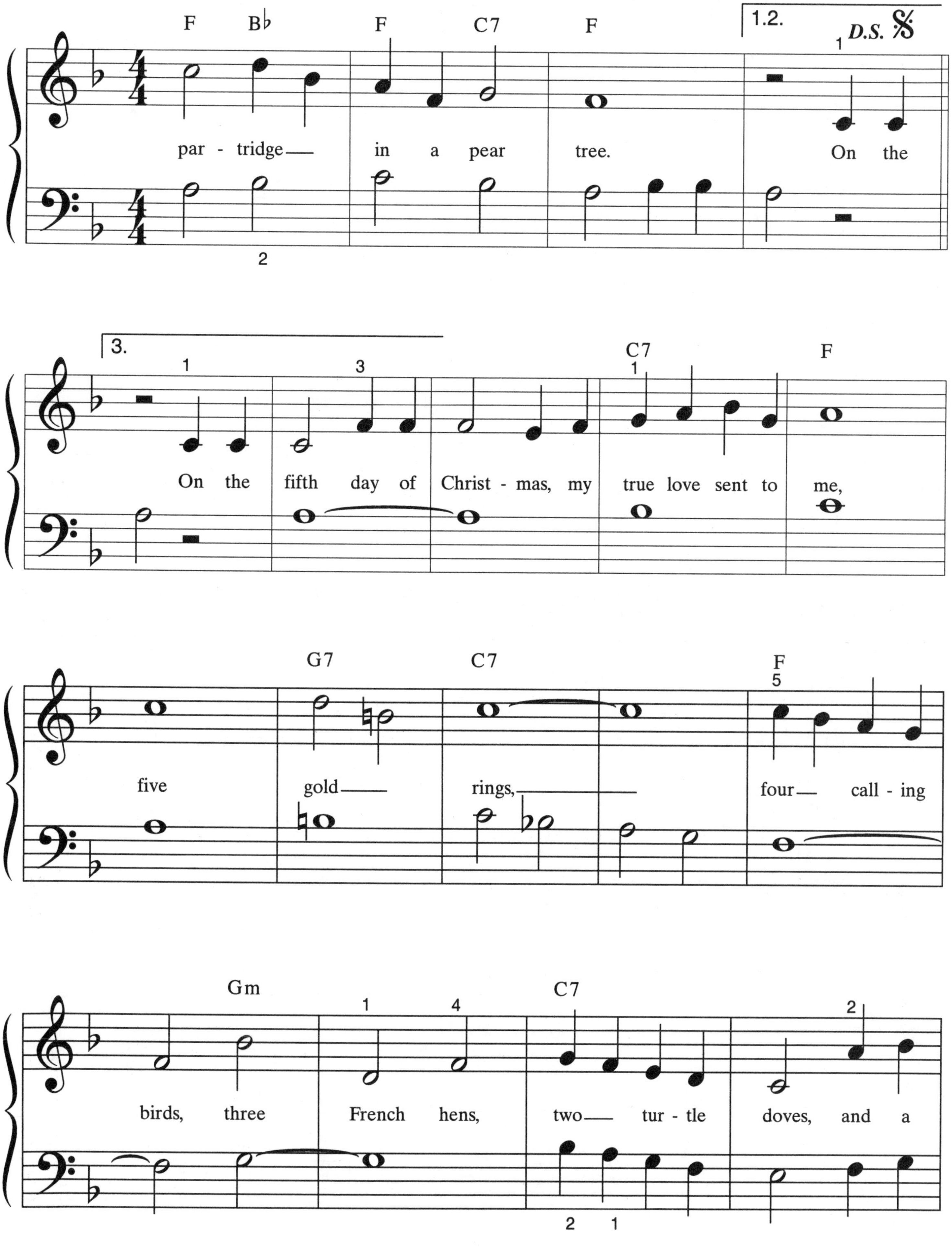
F Bb F C7 F
par - tridge in a pear tree.
1.2.
D.S.
On the
3.
On the fifth day of Christ - mas, my true love sent to me,
C7 F
five gold rings,
G7 C7 F
four call - ing
birds, three French hens, two tur - tle doves, and a
Gm C7

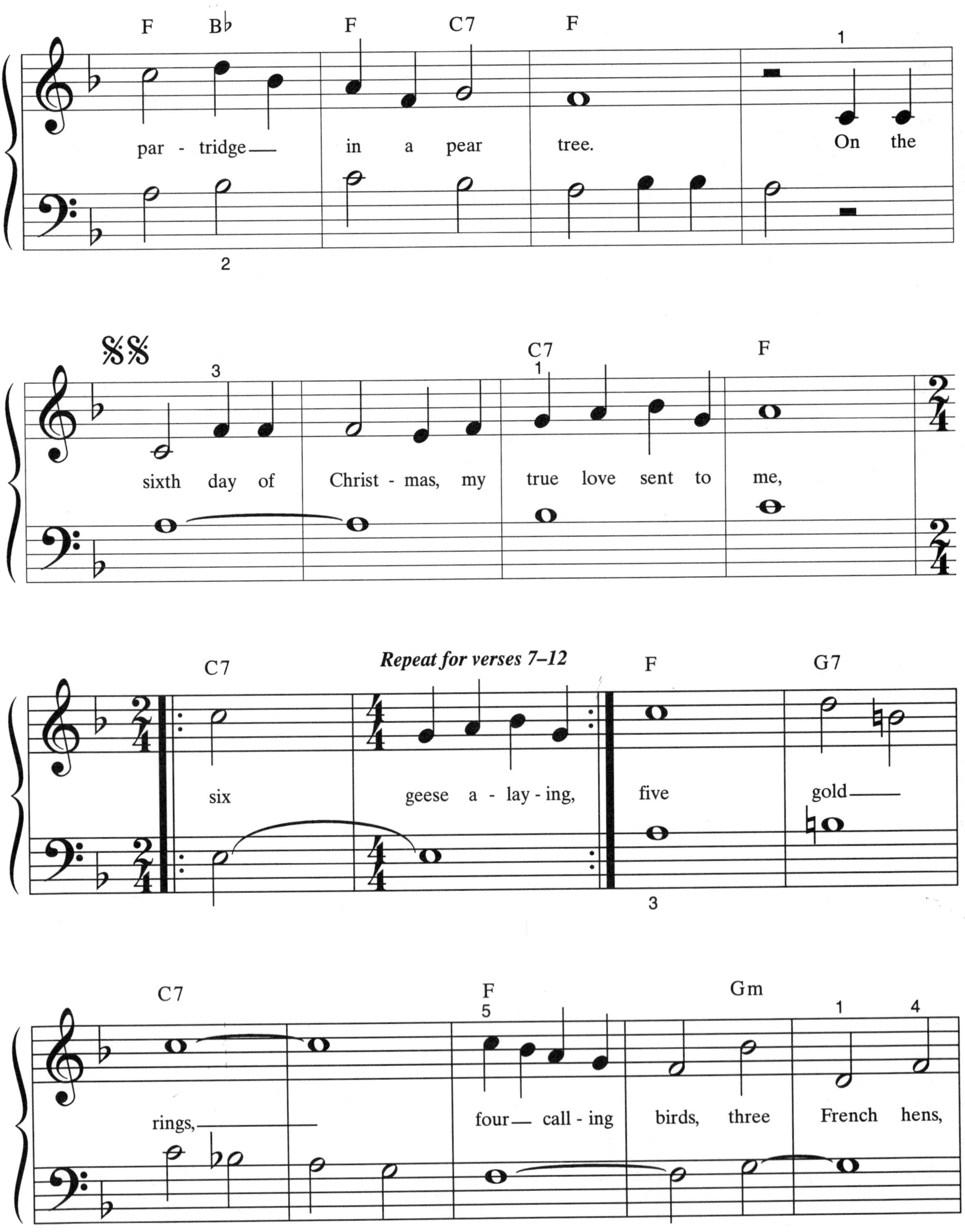
F B♭ F C7 F
par - tridge in a pear tree. On the
C7 F
sixth day of Christ - mas, my true love sent to me,
C7 Repeat for verses 7–12 F G7
six geese a - lay - ing, five gold
C7 F Gm
rings, four call - ing birds, three French hens,

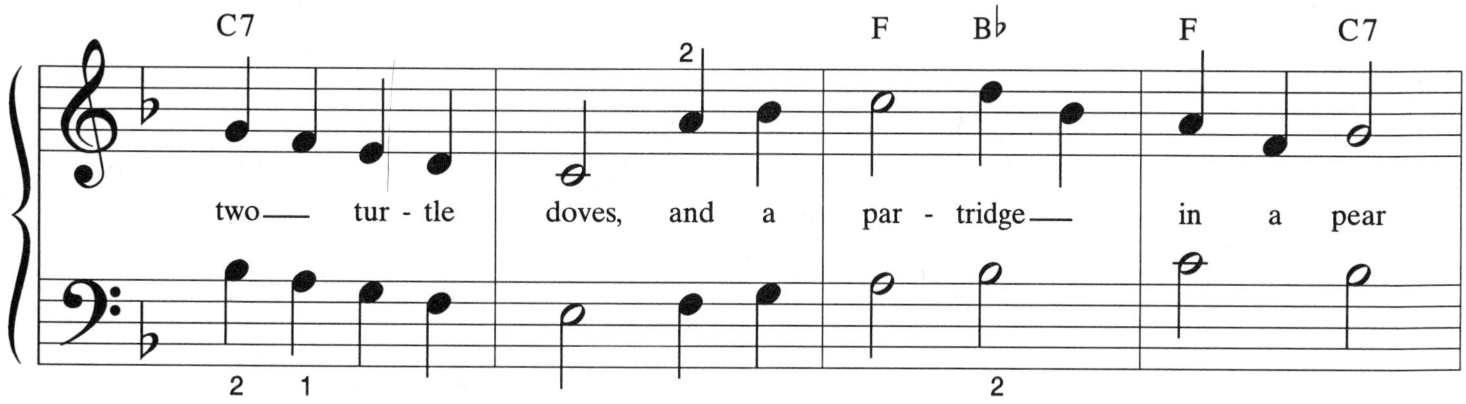
C7
F
B♭
F
C7
two— tur - tle
doves, and a
par - tridge—
in a pear

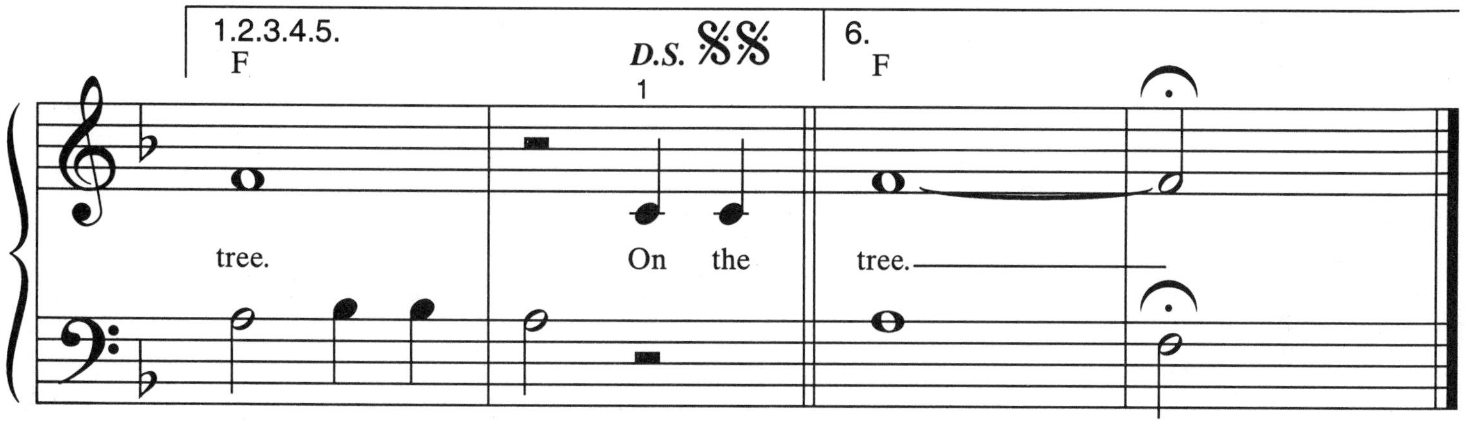
1.2.3.4.5.
F
D.S. 𝄋𝄋
6.
F
tree.
On the
tree.

3. Third day of Christmas, my true love sent to me, three French hens,

4. Fourth day of Christmas, my true love sent to me, four calling birds,

7. Seventh day of Christmas, my true love sent to me, seven swans a-swimming,

8. Eighth day of Christmas, my true love sent to me, eight maids a-milking,

9. Ninth day of Christmas, my true love sent to me, nine ladies dancing,

10. Tenth day of Christmas, my true love sent to me, ten lords a-leaping,

11. Eleventh day of Christmas, my true love sent to me, eleven pipers piping,

12. Twelfth day of Christmas, my true love sent to me, twelve drummers drumming,

Joy to the World

By
ISSAC WATTS and G.F. HANDEL
Arranged by Richard Bradley

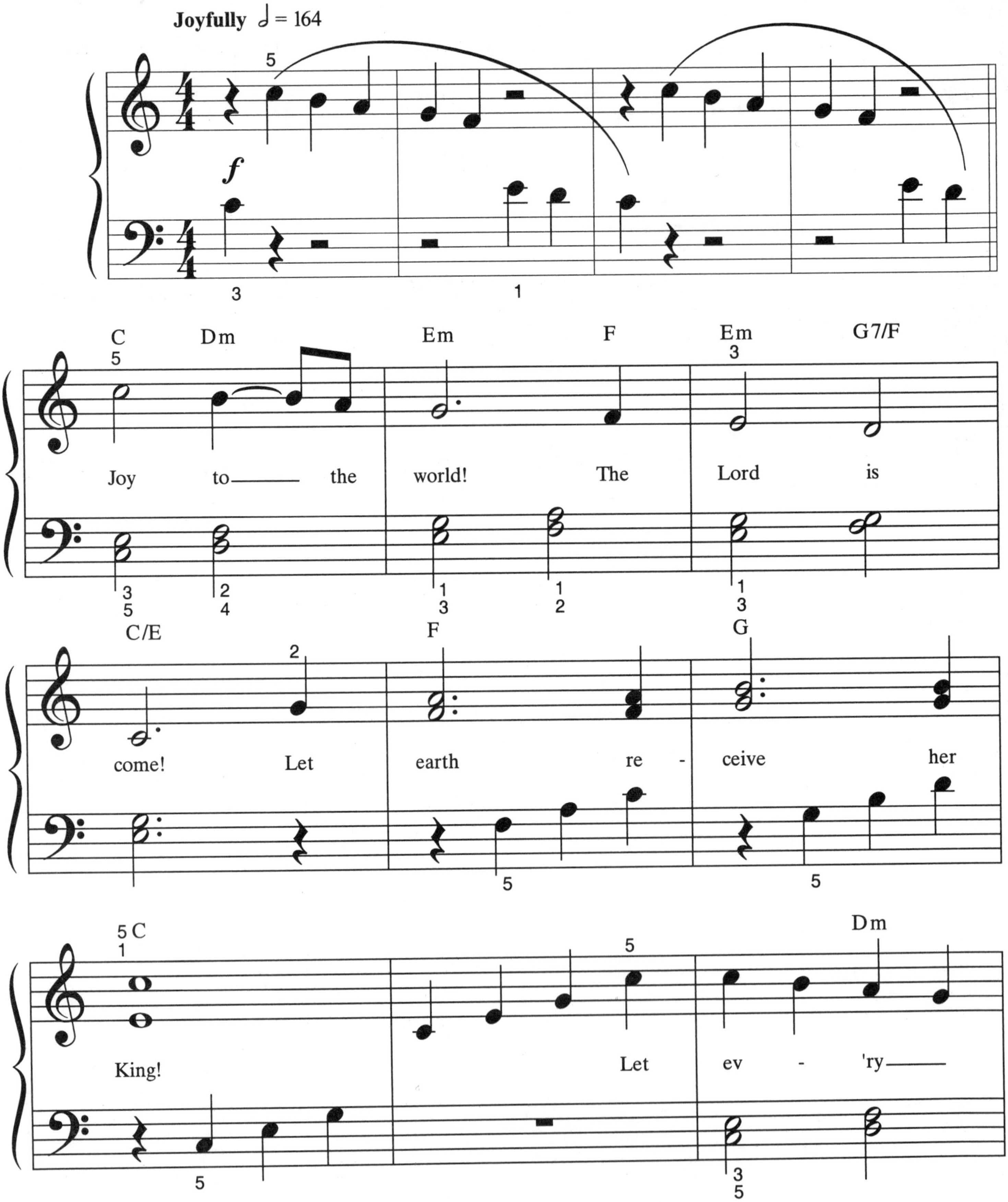
Joyfully ♩ = 164
C Dm Em F Em G7/F
Joy to the world! The Lord is
C/E F G
come! Let earth re - ceive her
C Dm
King! Let ev - 'ry

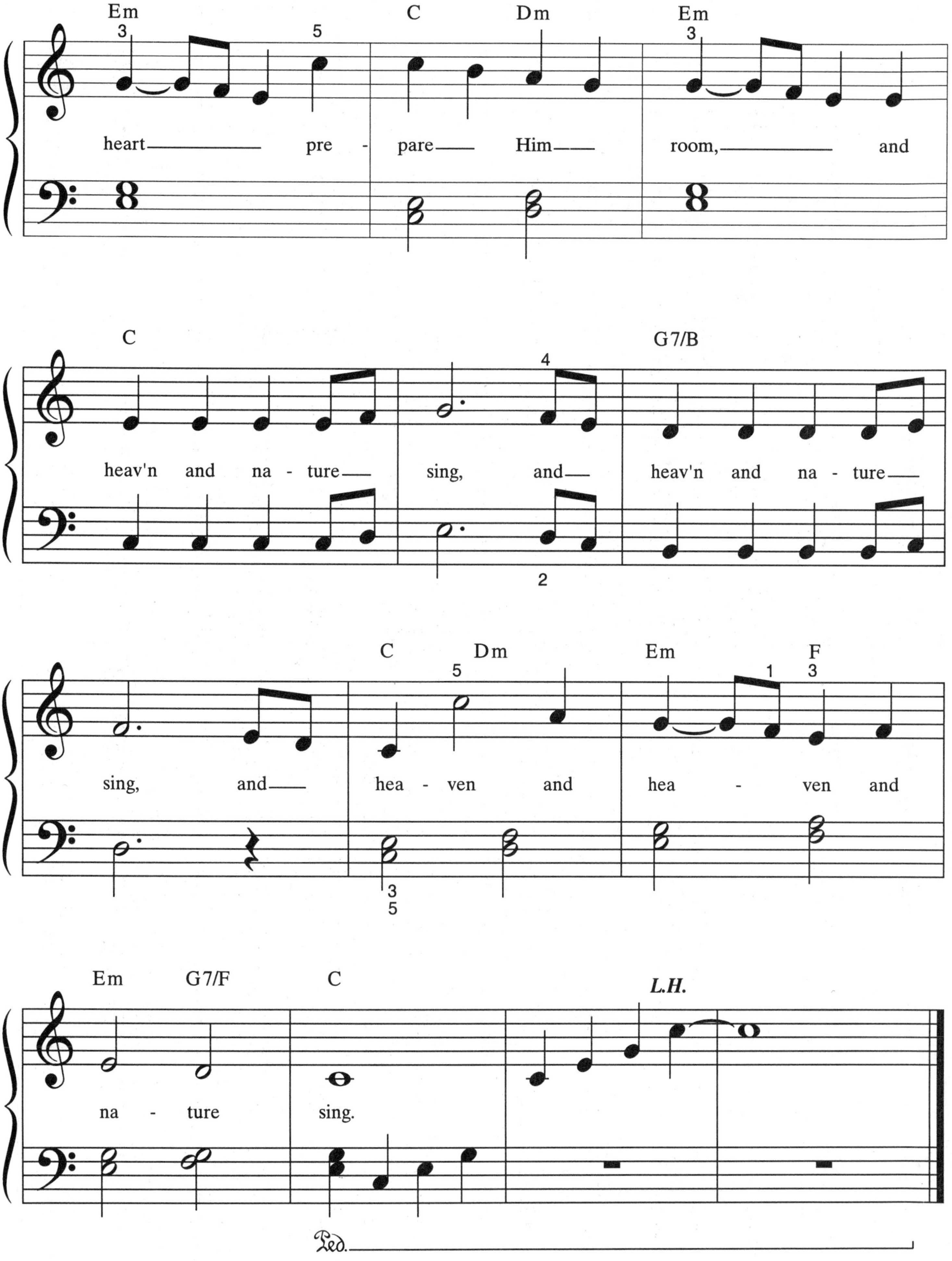
Em C Dm Em
heart pre - pare Him room, and
C G7/B
heav'n and na - ture sing, and heav'n and na - ture
C Dm Em F
sing, and hea - ven and hea - ven and
Em G7/F C
na - ture sing.
L.H.
Ped.

Silent Night

Words by
JOSEPH MOHR

Music by
FRANZ GRUBER
Arranged by Richard Bradley

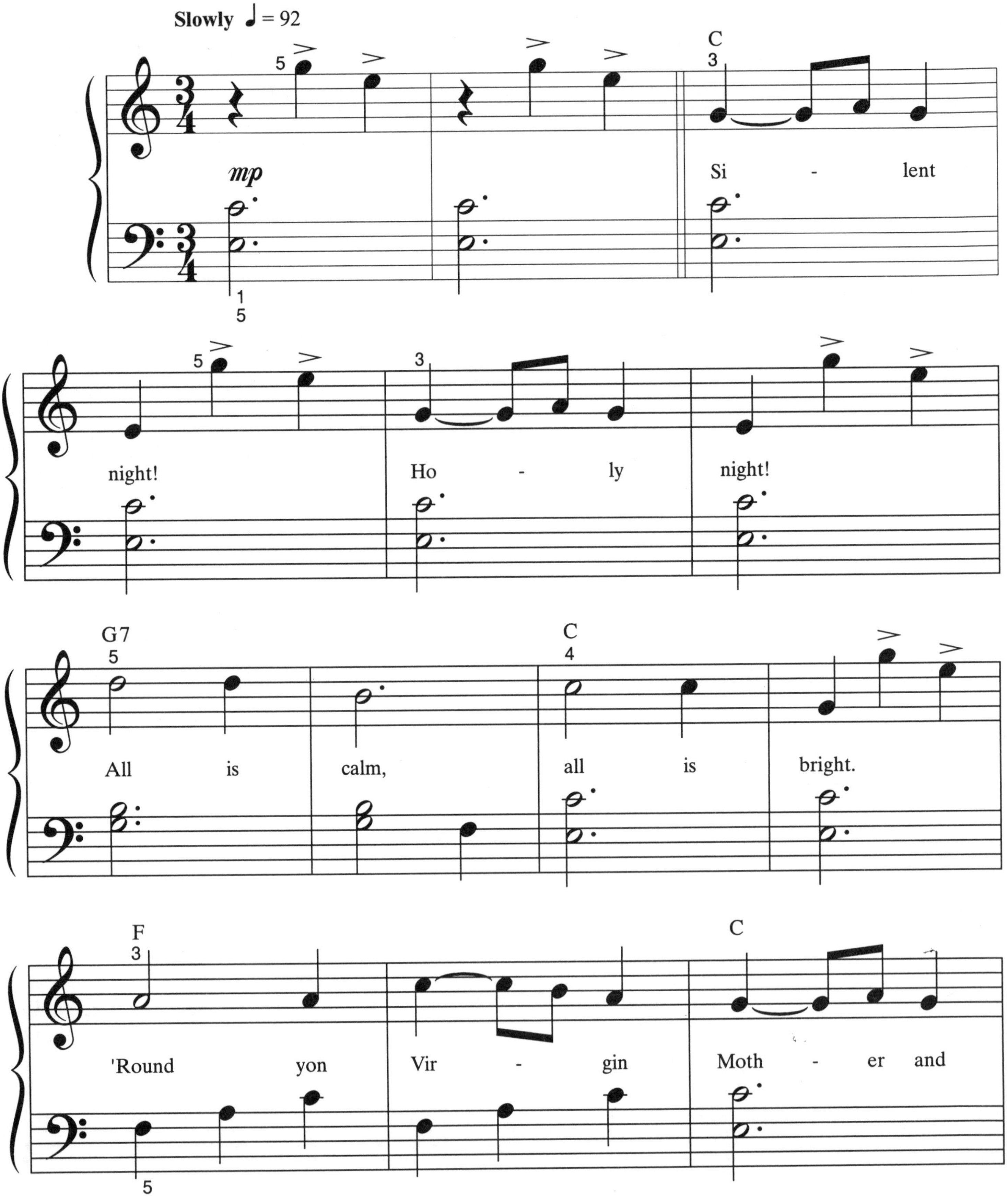
Slowly ♩ = 92
mp
C
Si - lent
night!
Ho - ly
night!
G7
All is calm,
C
all is bright.
F
'Round yon Vir - gin
C
Moth - er and

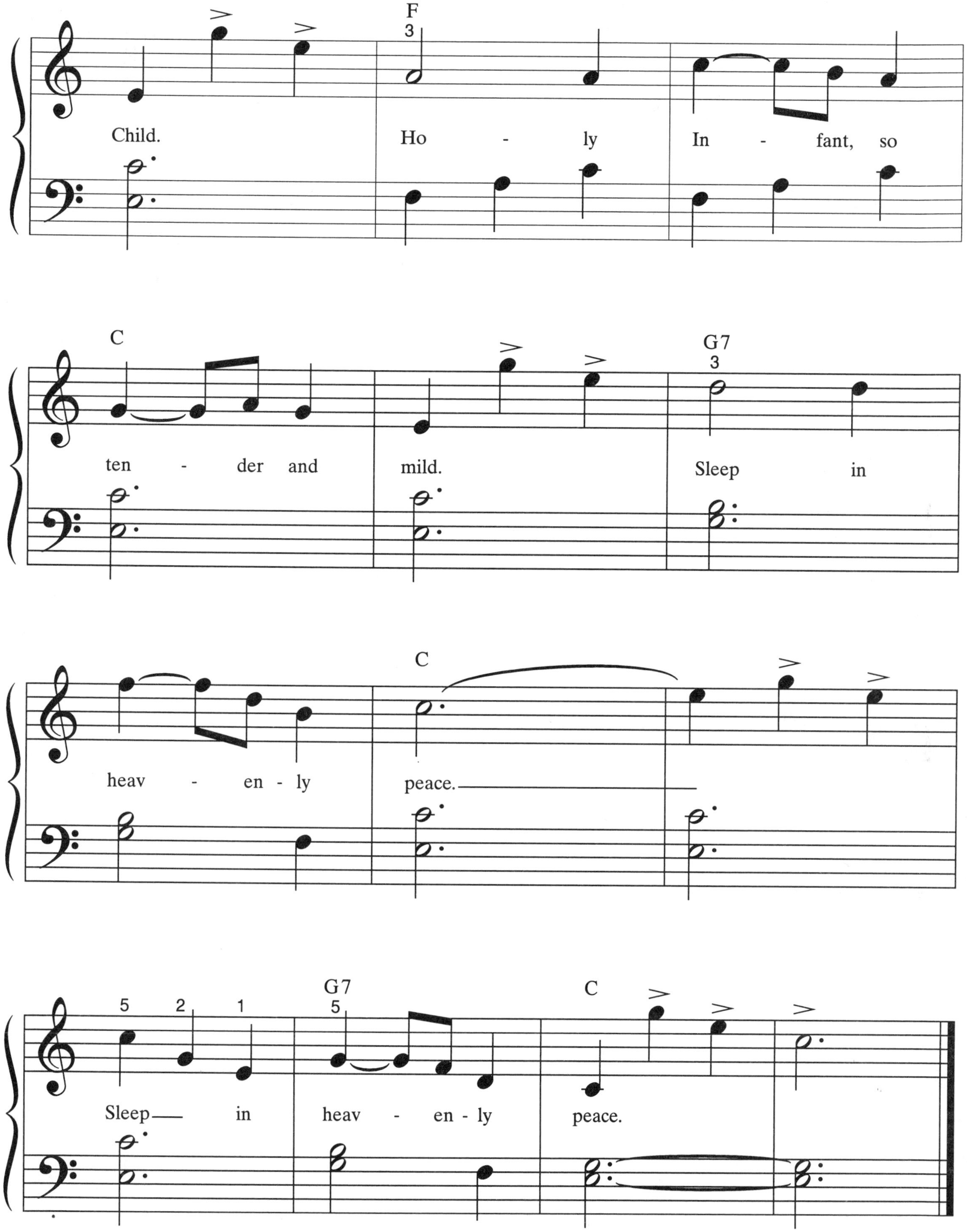
F
3
Child.
Ho - ly
In - fant, so
C
ten - der and
mild.
G7
3
Sleep in
heav - en - ly
C
peace.
5 2 1
Sleep in
G7
5
heav - en - ly
C
peace.

O Christmas Tree

TRADITIONAL
Arranged by Richard Bradley

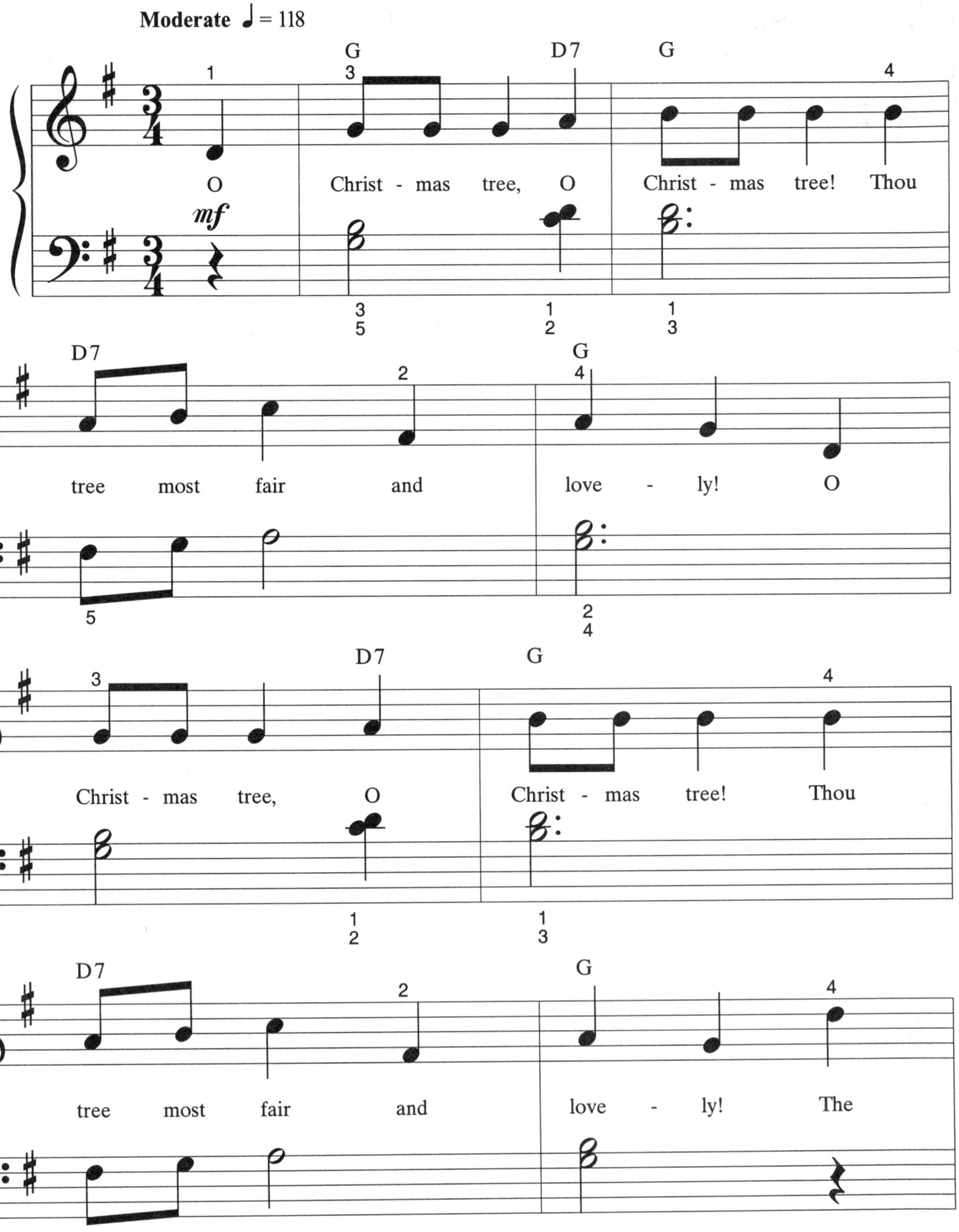
Moderate ♩ = 118
G D7 G
O Christ - mas tree, O Christ - mas tree! Thou
mf
D7 G
tree most fair and love - ly! O
D7 G
Christ - mas tree, O Christ - mas tree! Thou
D7 G
tree most fair and love - ly! The

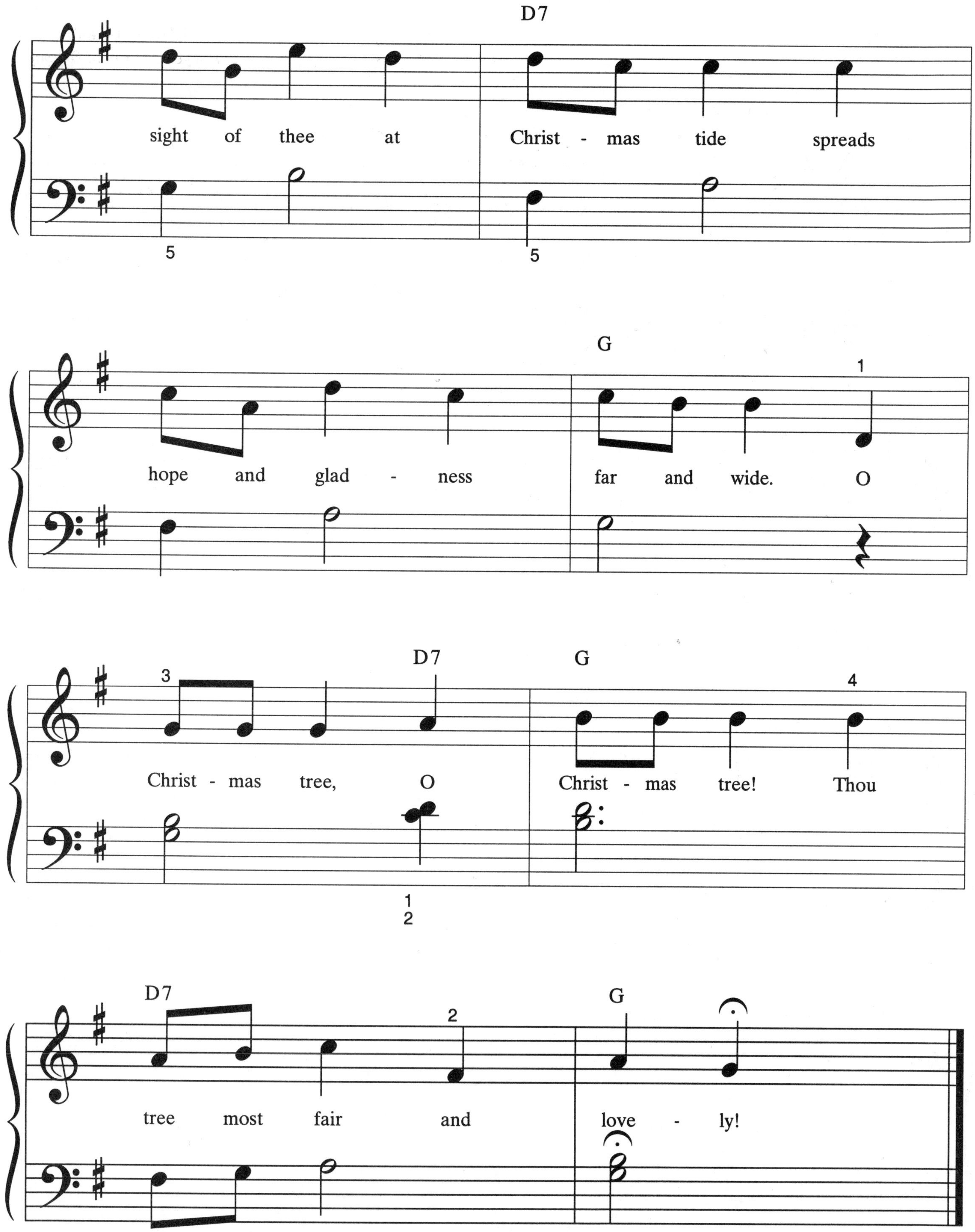
D7
sight of thee at Christ - mas tide spreads
G
hope and glad - ness far and wide. O
D7 G
Christ - mas tree, O Christ - mas tree! Thou
D7 G
tree most fair and love - ly!

Frosty the Snowman

Words and Music by
STEVE NELSON and JACK ROLLINS
Arranged by Richard Bradley

Moderately ♩ = 72

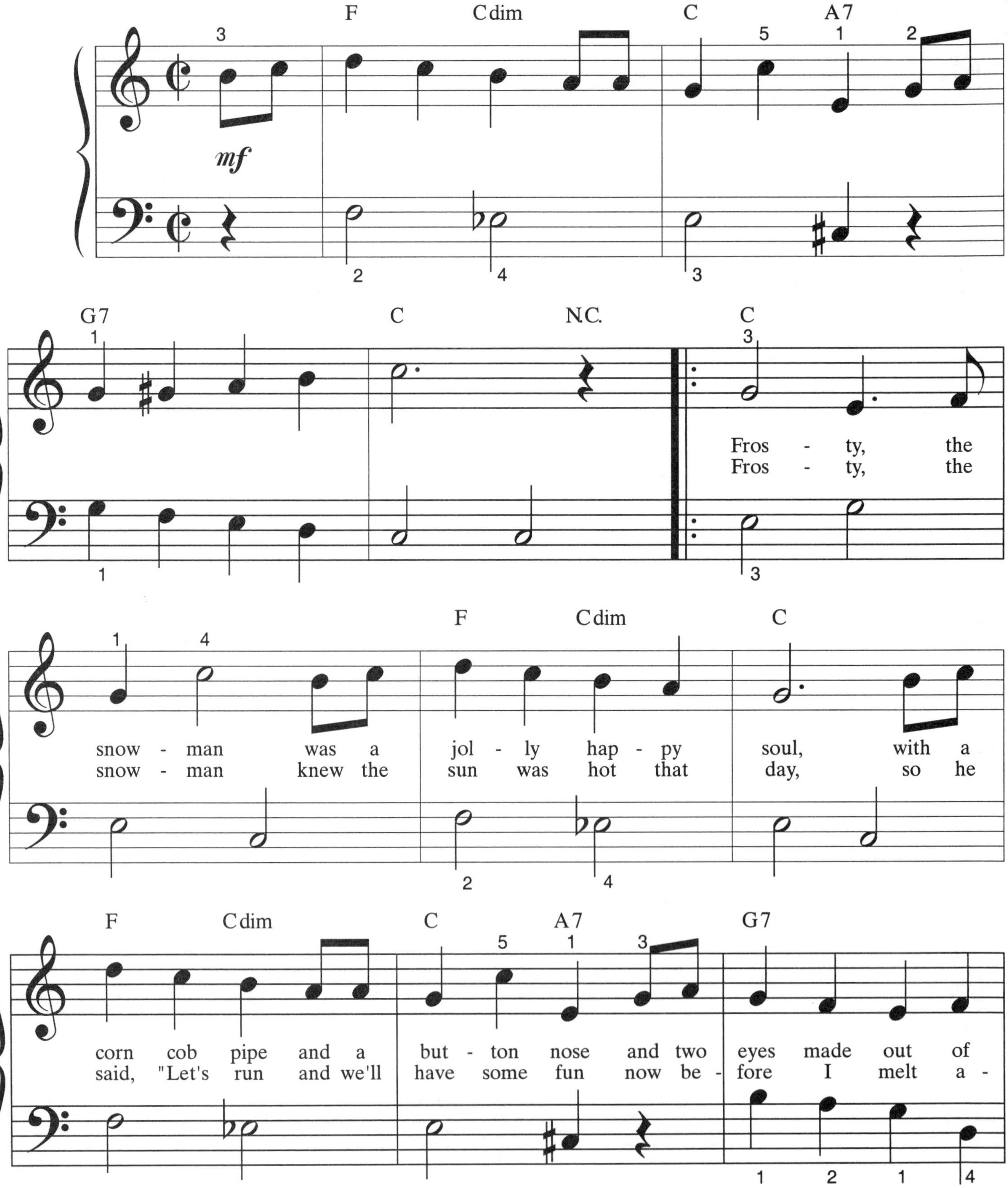
F Cdim C A7
G7 C N.C. C
Fros - ty, the snow - man was a jol - ly hap - py soul, with a corn cob pipe and a but - ton nose and two eyes made out of
Fros - ty, the snow - man knew the sun was hot that day, so he said, "Let's run and we'll have some fun now be - fore I melt a -
F Cdim C
F Cdim C A7 G7

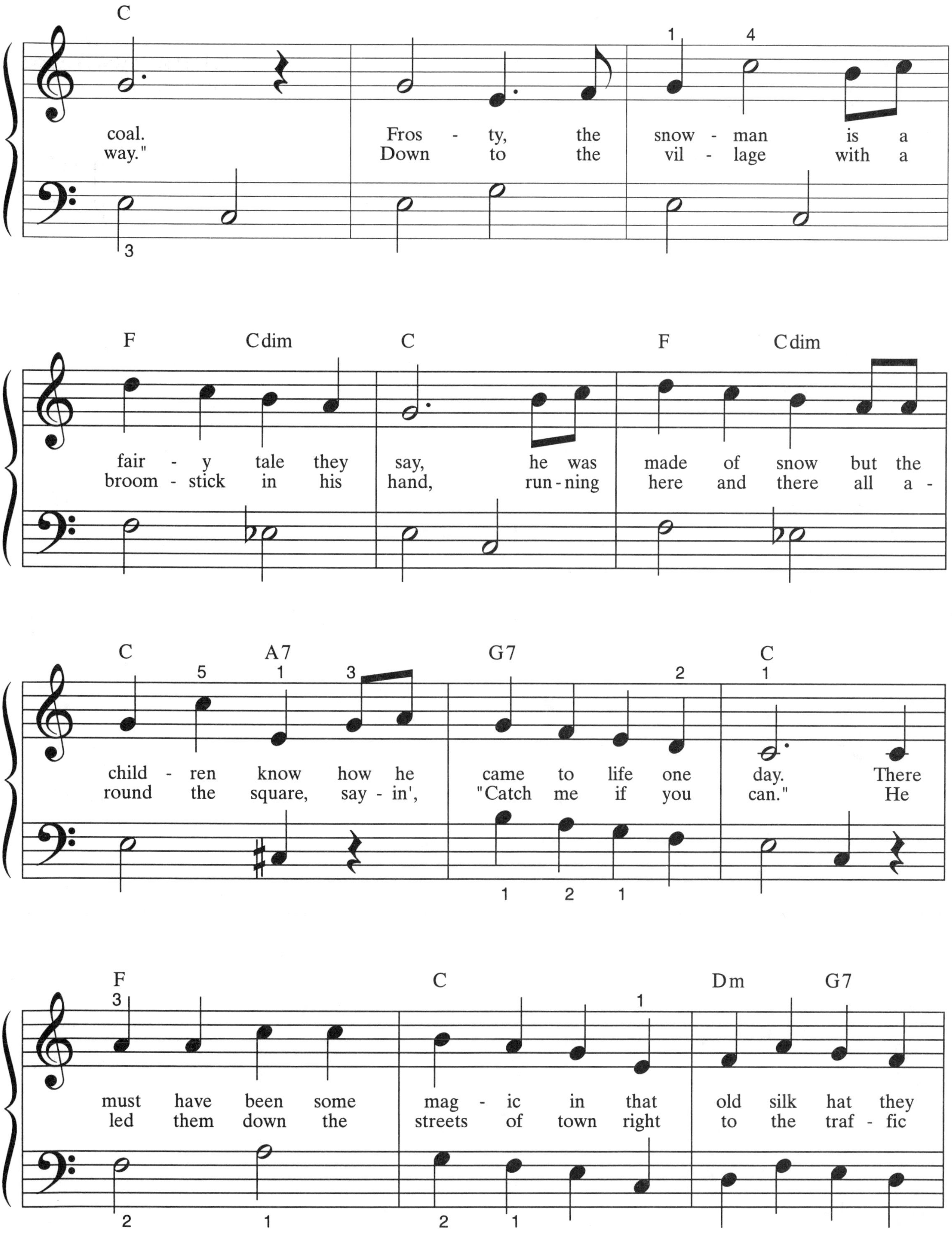
C
coal. Fros - ty, the snow - man is a
way." Down to the vil - lage with a
F Cdim C F Cdim
fair - y tale they say, he was made of snow but the
broom - stick in his hand, run - ning here and there all a -
C A7 G7 C
child - ren know how he came to life one day. There
round the square, say - in', "Catch me if you can." He
F C Dm G7
must have been some mag - ic in that old silk hat they
led them down the streets of town right to the traf - fic

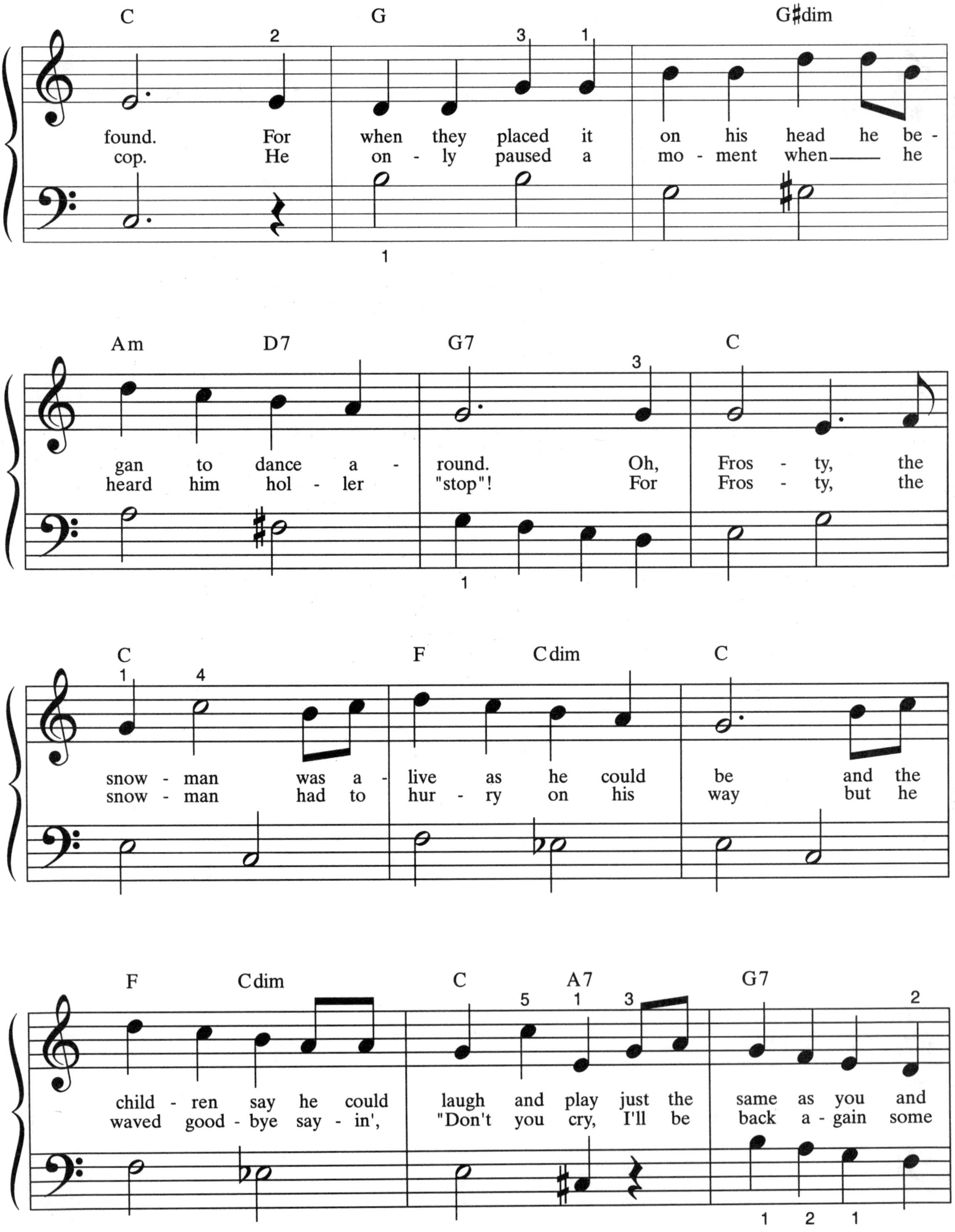
C G G♯dim
found. For when they placed it on his head he be -
cop. He on - ly paused a mo - ment when he
Am D7 G7 C
gan to dance a - round. Oh, Fros - ty, the
heard him hol - ler "stop"! For Fros - ty, the
C F Cdim C
snow - man was a - live as he could be and the
snow - man had to hur - ry on his way but he
F Cdim C A7 G7
child - ren say he could laugh and play just the same as you and
waved good - bye say - in', "Don't you cry, I'll be back a - gain some

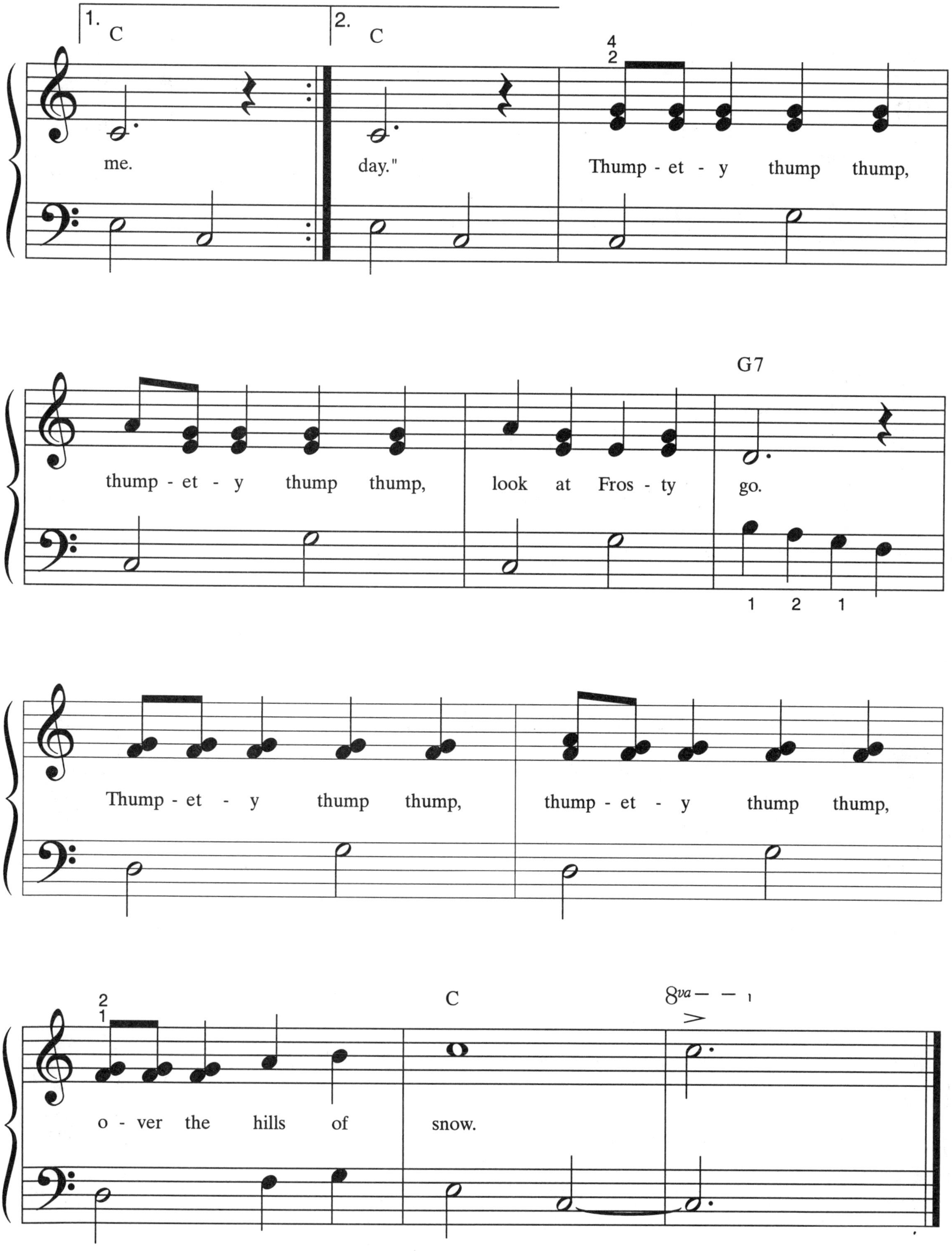
1. C
2. C
me.
day."
Thump - et - y thump thump,
thump - et - y thump thump,
look at Fros - ty
G7
go.
Thump - et - y thump thump,
thump - et - y thump thump,
o - ver the hills of
C
snow.
8va

Santa Claus Is Comin' to Town

Words by
HAVEN GILLESPIE

Music by
J. FRED COOTS
Arranged by Richard Bradley

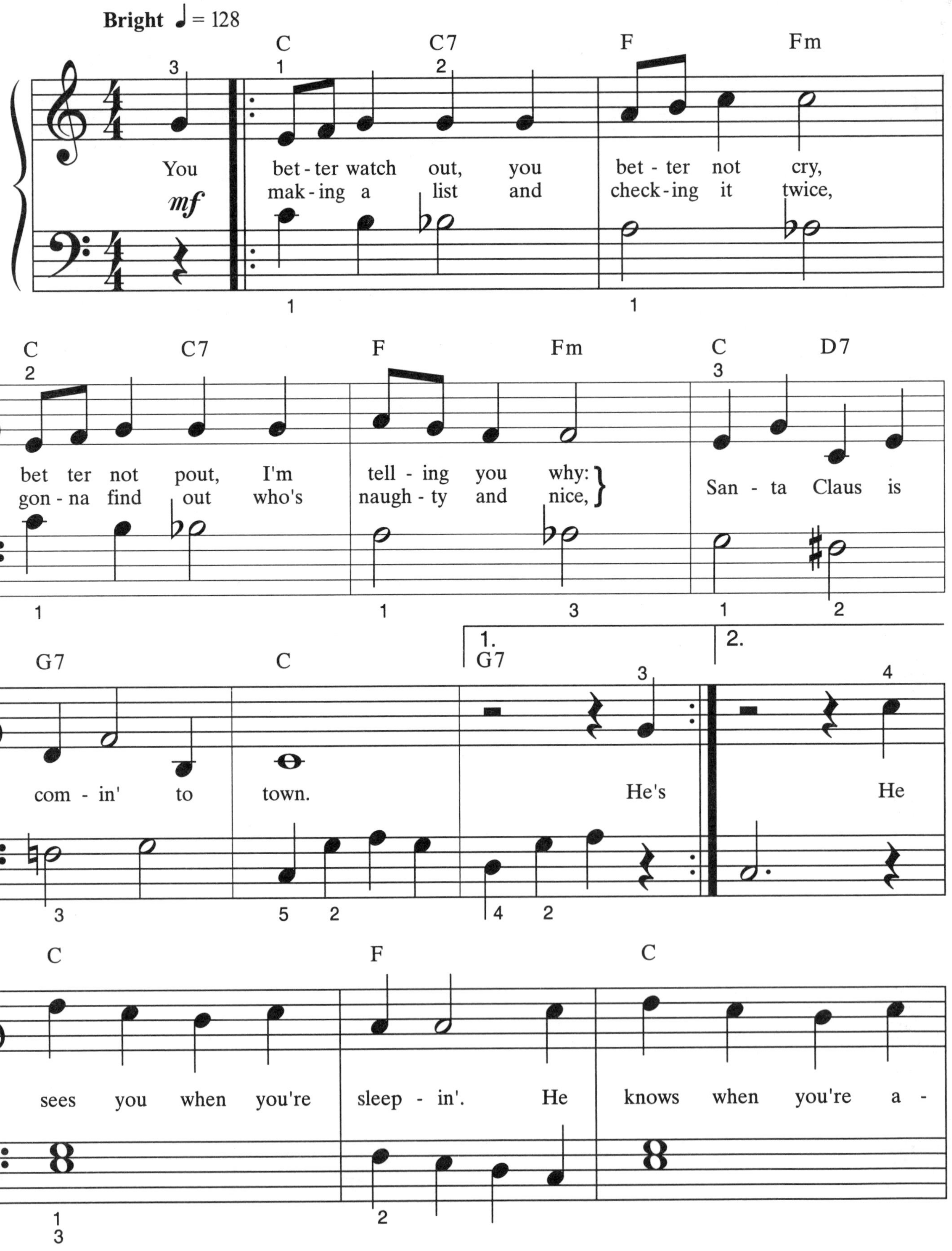
Bright ♩ = 128
C C7 F Fm
You better watch out, you better not cry,
making a list and checking it twice,
mf
C C7 F Fm C D7
better not pout, I'm telling you why:
gonna find out who's naughty and nice,
Santa Claus is
G7 C 1. G7 2.
comin' to town. He's He
C F C
sees you when you're sleepin'. He knows when you're a -

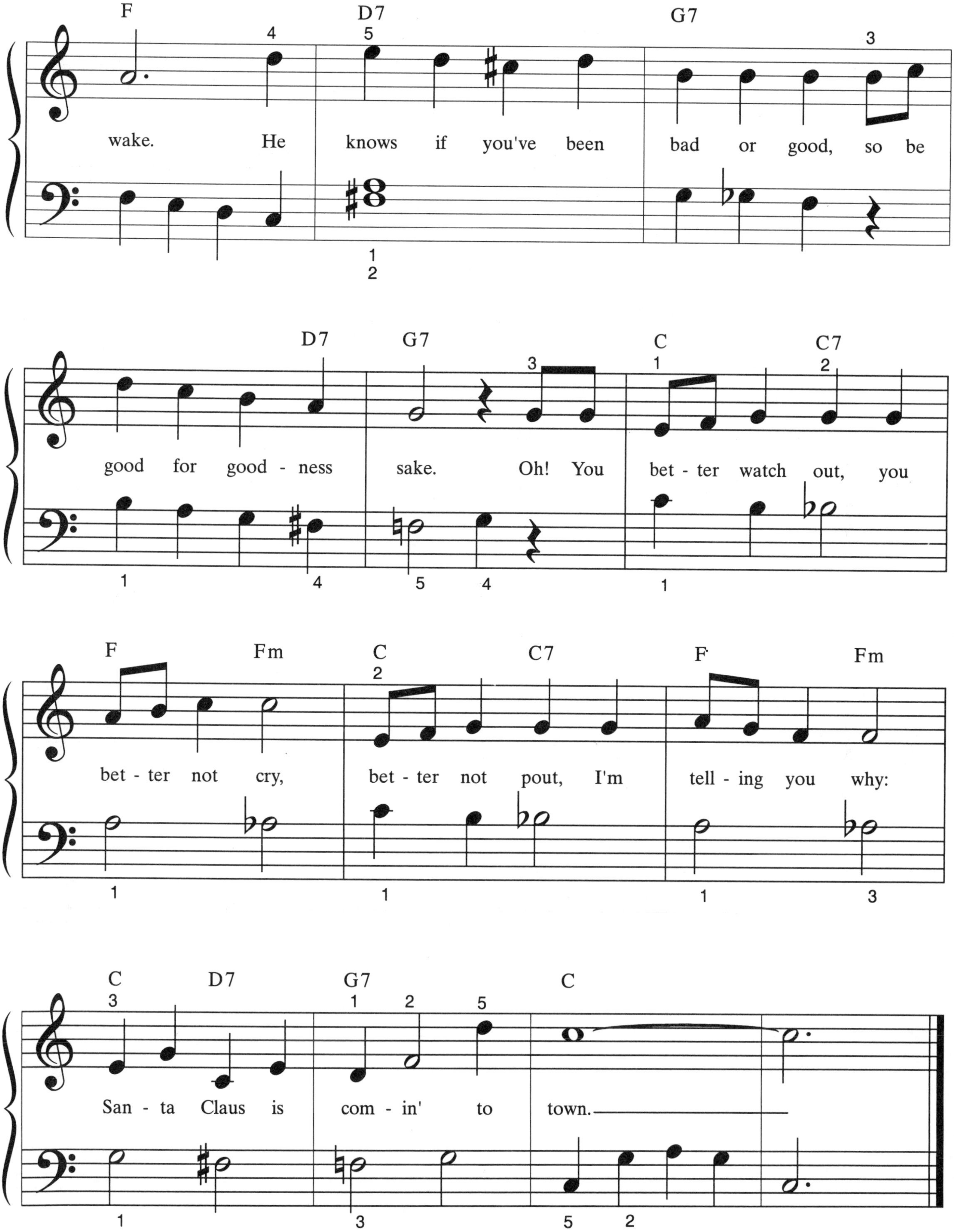
F D7 G7
wake. He knows if you've been bad or good, so be
D7 G7 C C7
good for good - ness sake. Oh! You bet - ter watch out, you
F Fm C C7 F Fm
bet - ter not cry, bet - ter not pout, I'm tell - ing you why:
C D7 G7 C
San - ta Claus is com - in' to town.

What Child Is This?

WILLIAM CHATTERTON DIX
Arranged by Richard Bradley

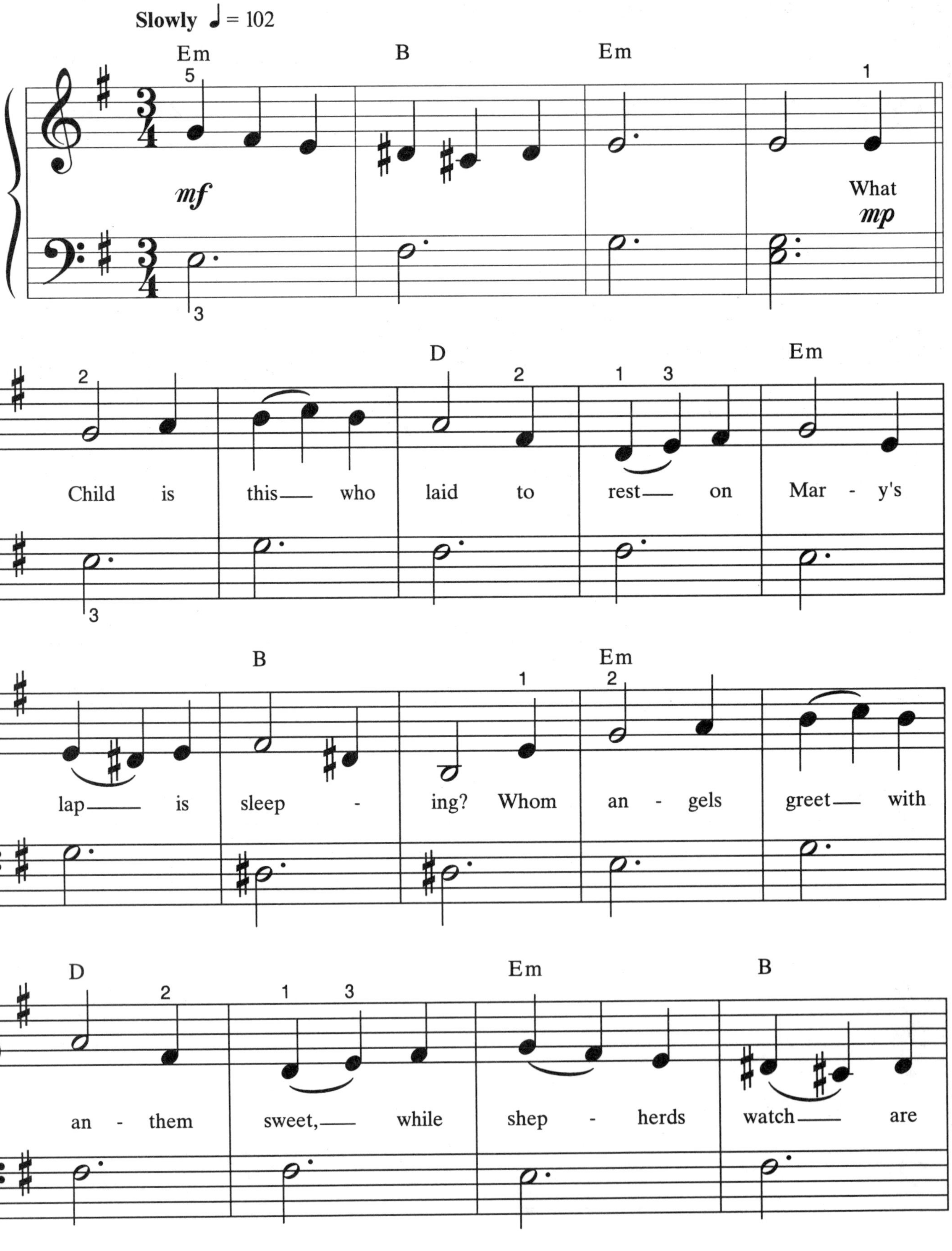
Slowly ♩ = 102
Em
B
Em
mf
What
mp
D
Em
Child is this — who laid to rest — on Mar - y's
B
Em
lap — is sleep - ing? Whom an - gels greet — with
D
Em
B
an - them sweet, — while shep - herds watch — are

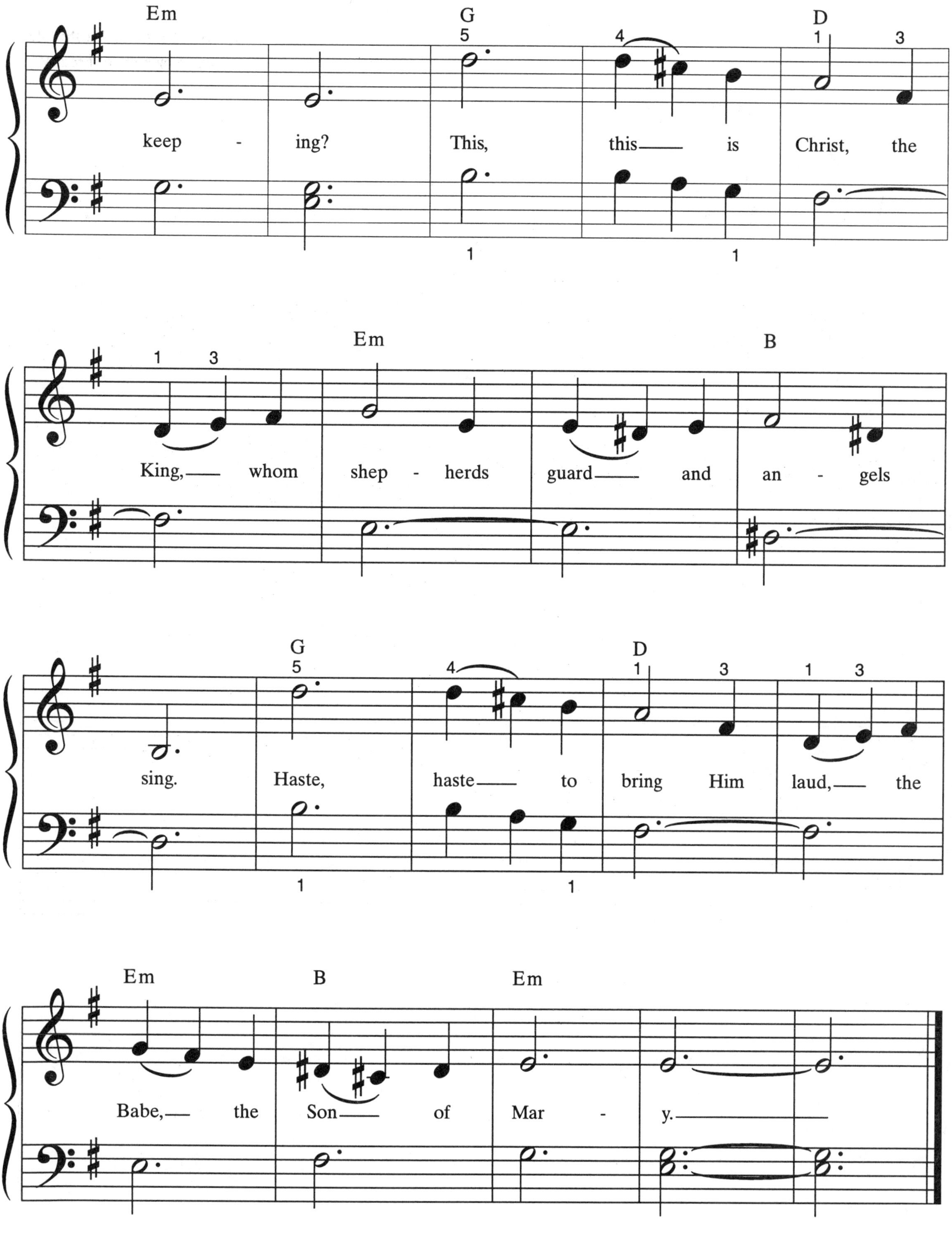
Em G D
keep - ing? This, this is Christ, the
King, whom shep - herds guard and an - gels
Em B
sing. Haste, haste to bring Him laud, the
G D
Babe, the Son of Mar - y.
Em B Em

Carol of the Bells

TRADITIONAL UKRAINIAN CAROL
Arranged by Richard Bradley

Brightly 𝅗𝅥. = 54

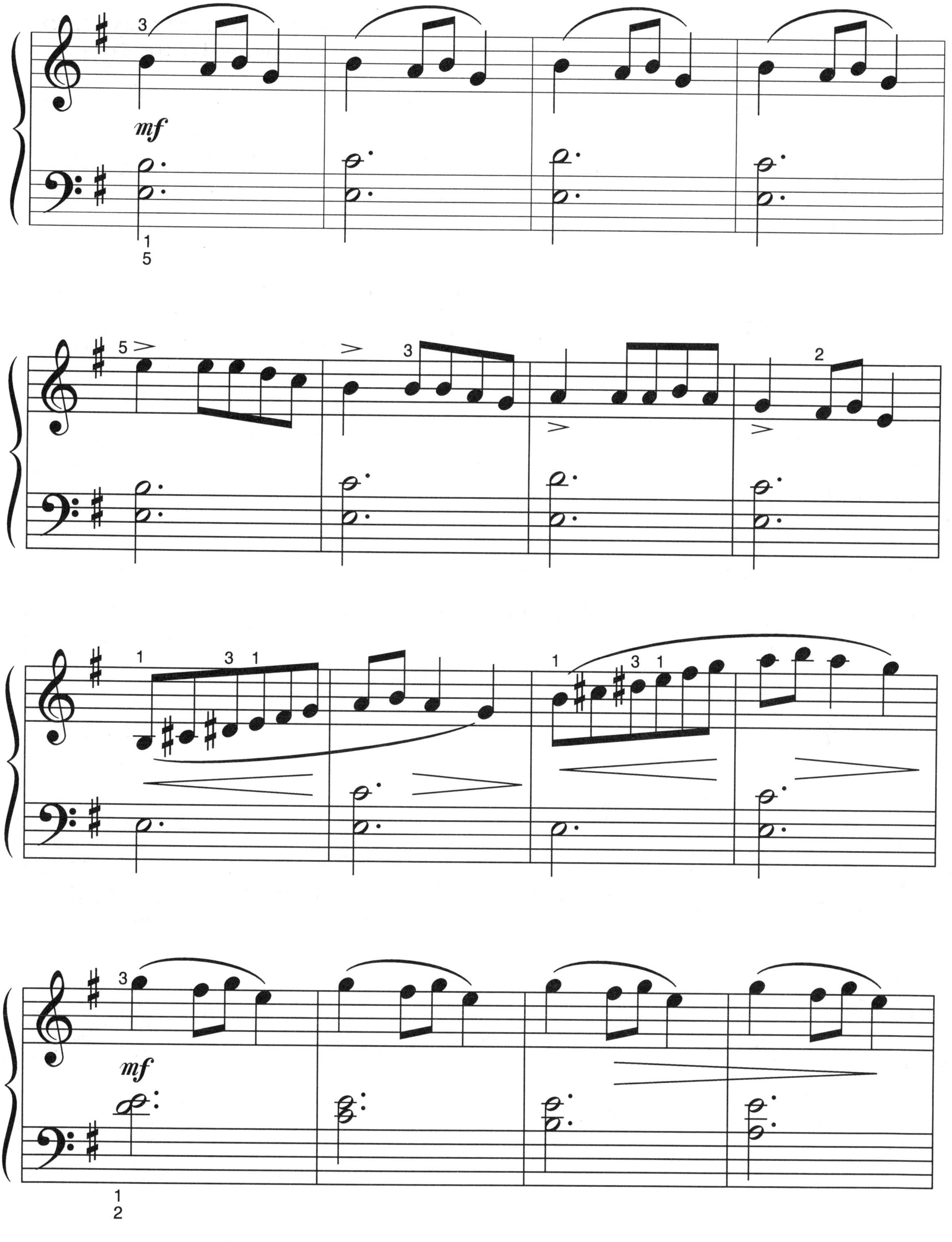

mf
mf

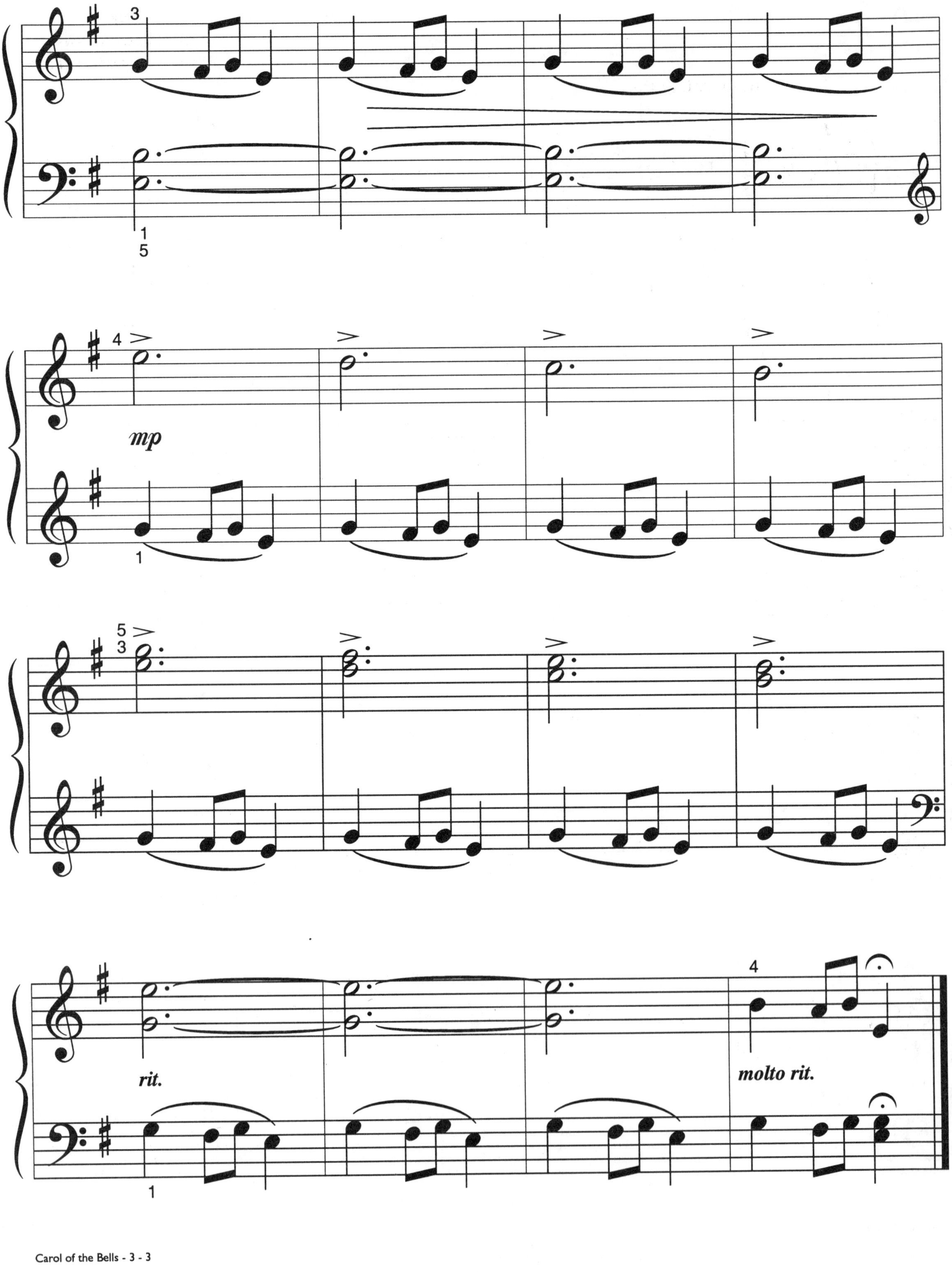
mp
rit.
molto rit.

Away in a Manger

By
JAMES R. MURRAY
Arranged by Richard Bradley

Moderately slow ♩ = 92
F
B♭
A - way in a man - ger, no crib for His
mp
F
C7/E
C7/G
F
bed, the lit - tle Lord Je - sus laid down His sweet
B♭
head. The stars in the sky looked down where He
F
C7/G
F/A
Gm/B♭
C7/B♭
F/A
lay, the lit - tle Lord Je - sus, a - sleep on the hay.

Grown-Up Christmas List

Words and Music by
DAVID FOSTER and
LINDA THOMPSON JENNER
Arranged by Richard Bradley

Moderately slow ♩ = 164
E♭
B♭/D
Cm
Do you re - mem - ber me? I
mp
Gm/B♭
A♭
E♭/G
sat up - on your knee. I wrote to you with
Fm7
1. B♭sus4
B♭
child - hood fan - ta - sies. Well,
2. B♭sus4
B♭
3. B♭sus4
B♭
dream. So
need.

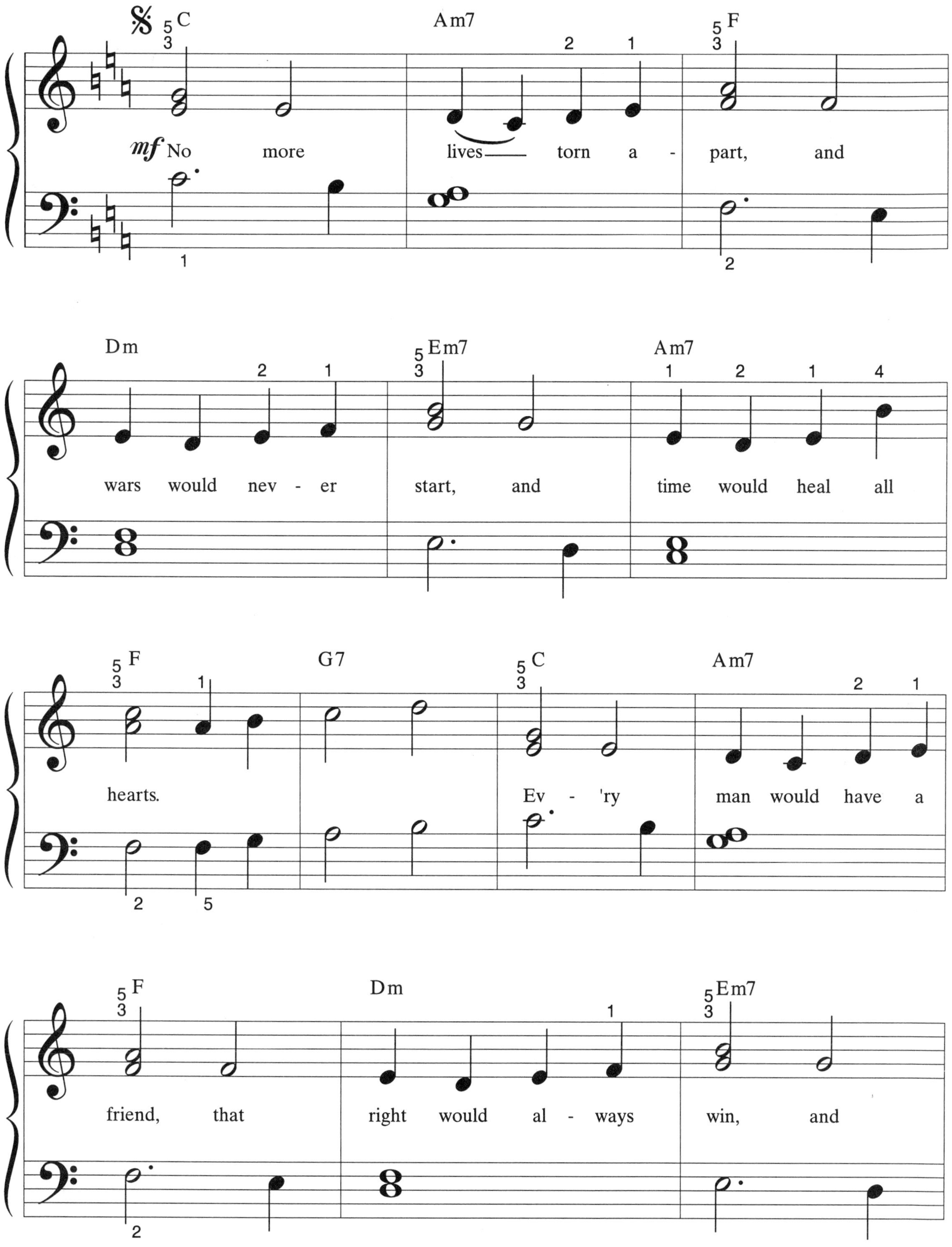
C Am7 F
mf No more lives torn a - part, and
Dm Em7 Am7
wars would nev - er start, and time would heal all
F G7 C Am7
hearts. Ev - 'ry man would have a
F Dm Em7
friend, that right would al - ways win, and

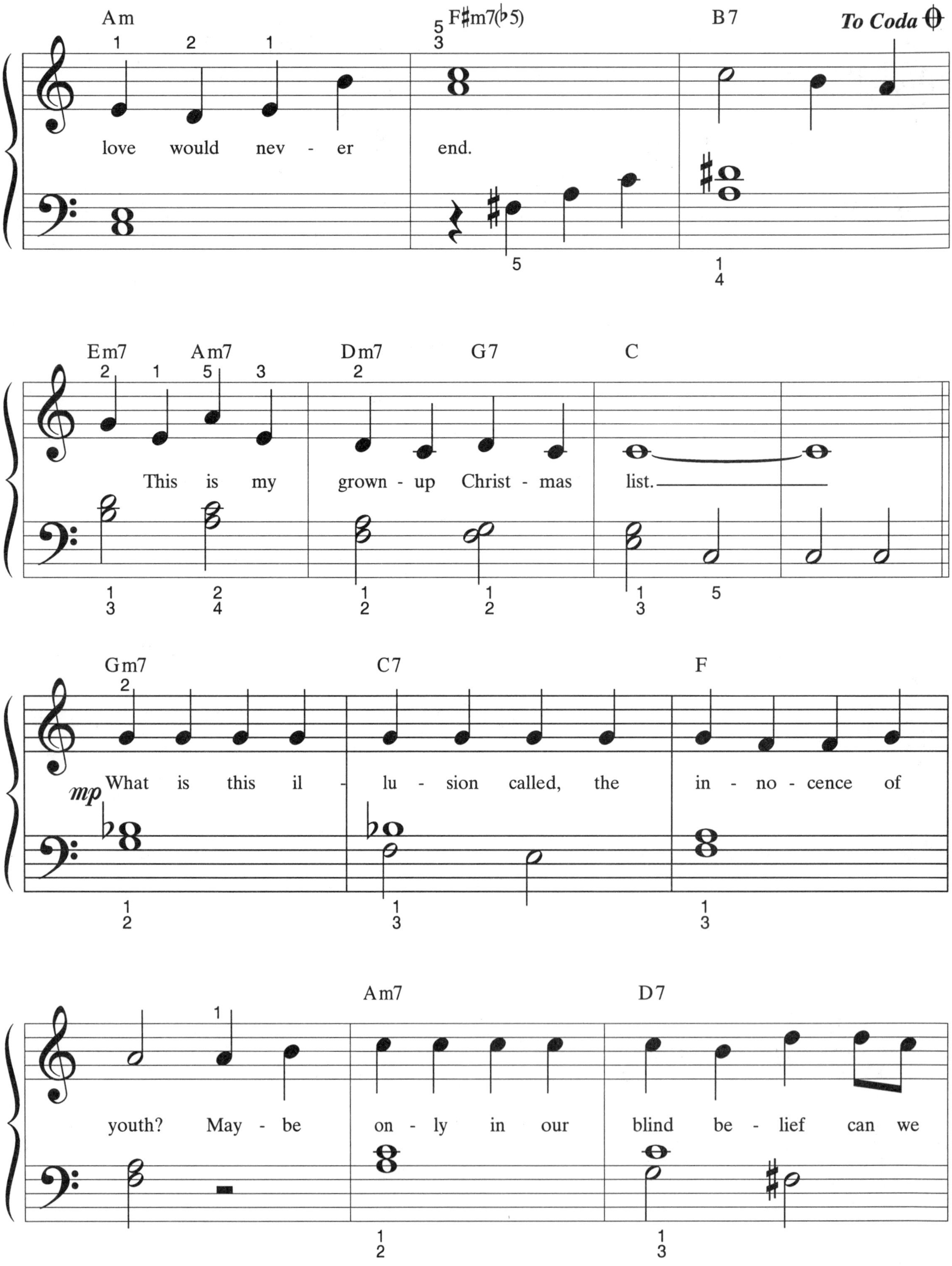
Am
F♯m7(♭5)
B7
To Coda
love would nev - er end.
Em7 Am7 Dm7 G7 C
This is my grown - up Christ - mas list.
Gm7 C7 F
mp
What is this il - lu - sion called, the in - no - cence of
Am7 D7
youth? May - be on - ly in our blind be - lief can we

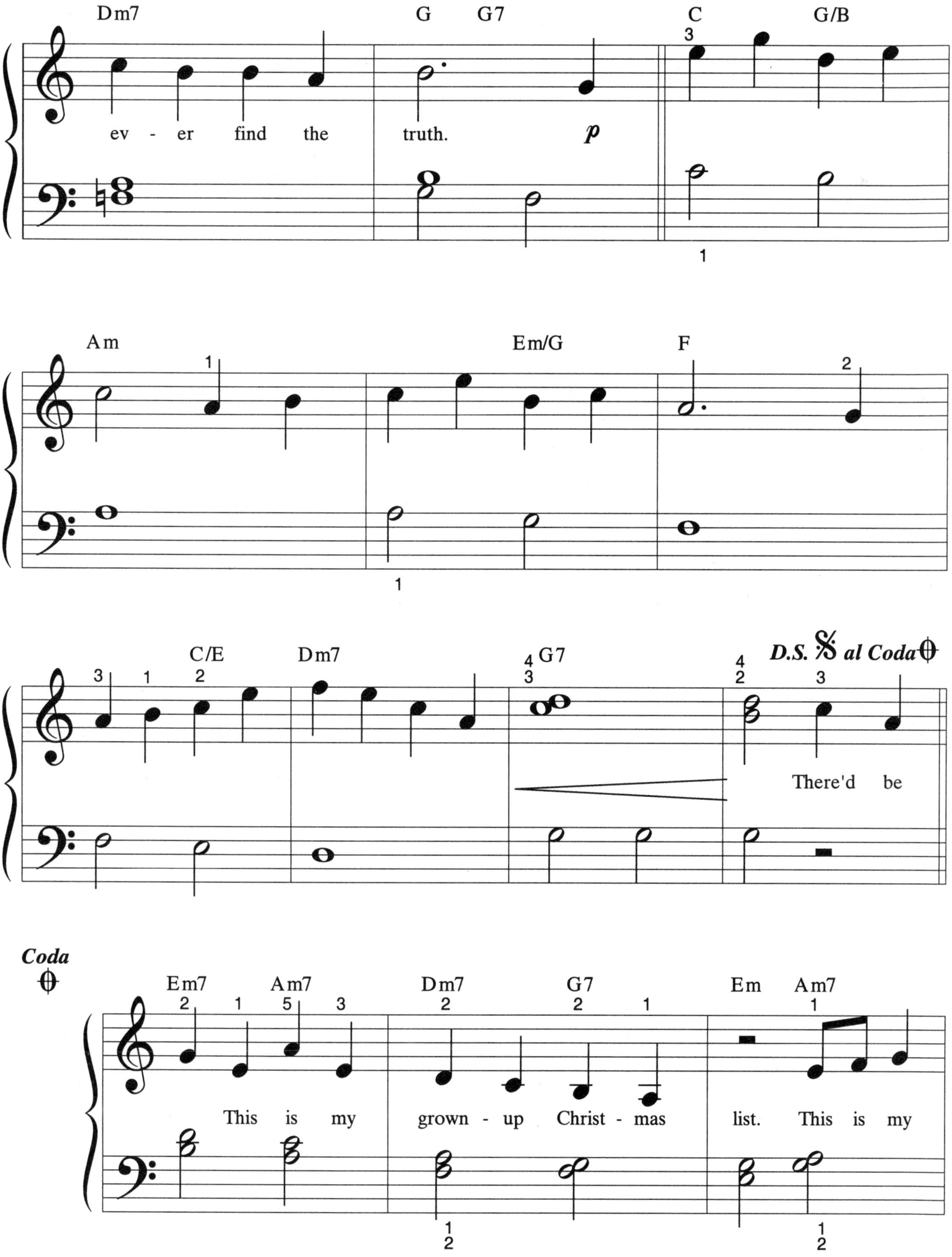
Dm7 G G7 C G/B
ev - er find the truth.
p
Am Em/G F
C/E Dm7 G7
D.S. al Coda
There'd be
Coda
Em7 Am7 Dm7 G7 Em Am7
This is my grown - up Christ - mas list. This is my

Verse 2:
Well, I'm all grown up now.
Can you still help somehow?
I'm not a child but
My heart still can dream.

Verse 3:
So here's my lifelong wish,
My grown-up Christmas list,
Not for myself but
For a world in need.

All I Want for Christmas Is My Two Front Teeth

Words and Music by
DON GARDNER
Arranged by Richard Bradley

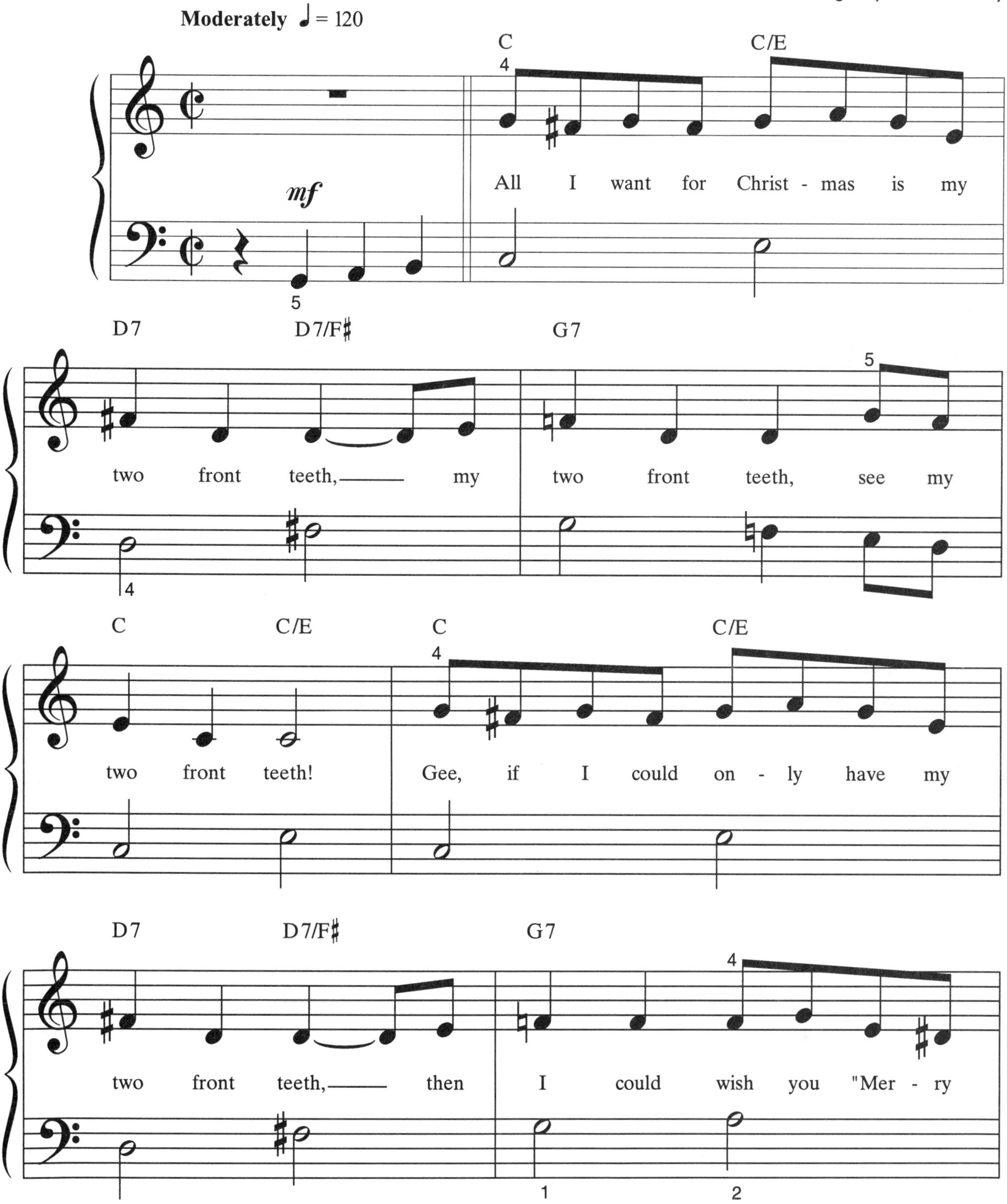
Moderately ♩ = 120
mf
C
C/E
All I want for Christ - mas is my
D7
D7/F♯
G7
two front teeth, my two front teeth, see my
C
C/E
C
C/E
two front teeth! Gee, if I could on - ly have my
D7
D7/F♯
G7
two front teeth, then I could wish you "Mer - ry

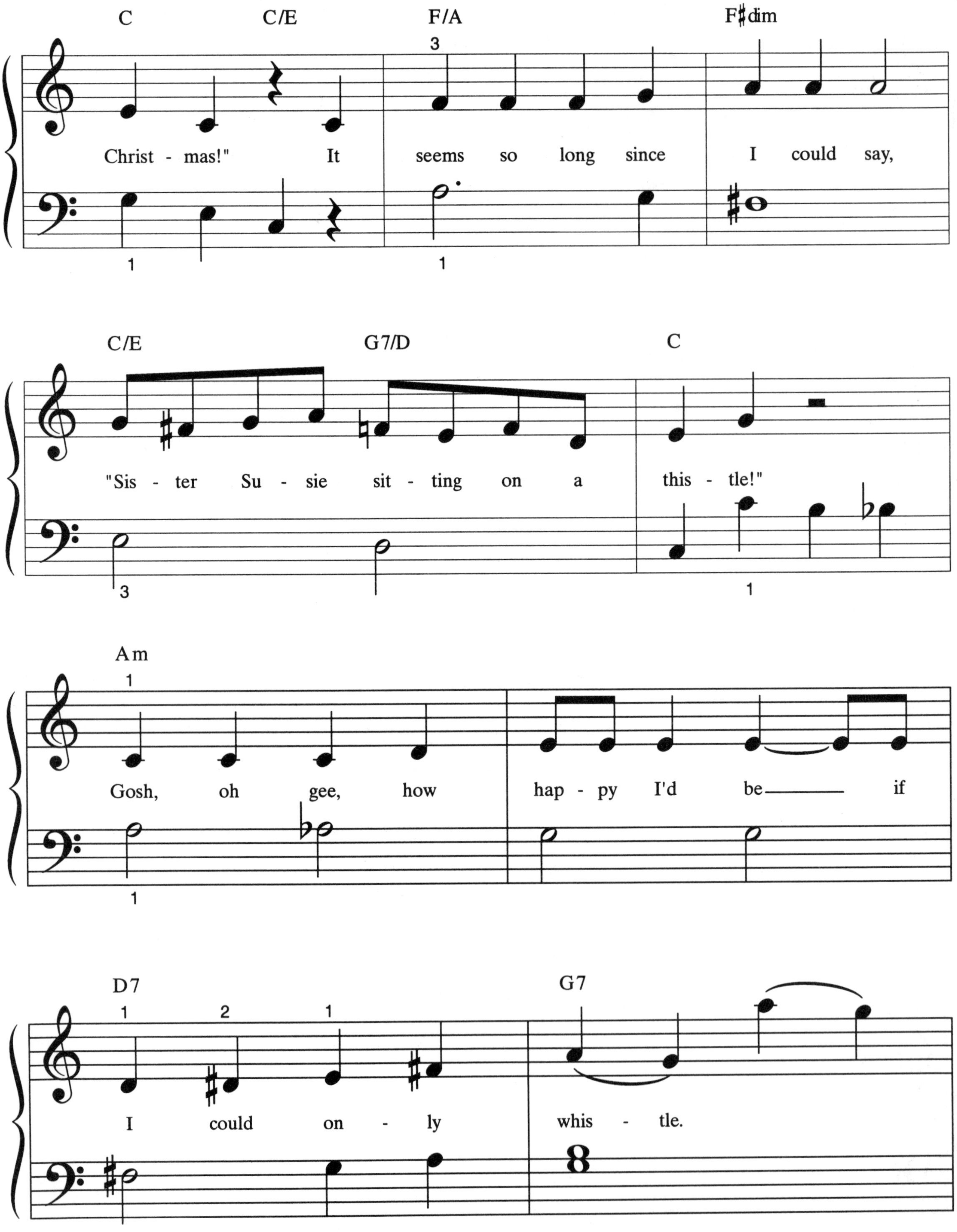
C C/E F/A F♯dim
3
Christ - mas!" It seems so long since I could say,
1 1
C/E G7/D C
"Sis - ter Su - sie sit - ting on a this - tle!"
3 1
Am
1
Gosh, oh gee, how hap - py I'd be if
1
D7 G7
1 2 1
I could on - ly whis - tle.
8

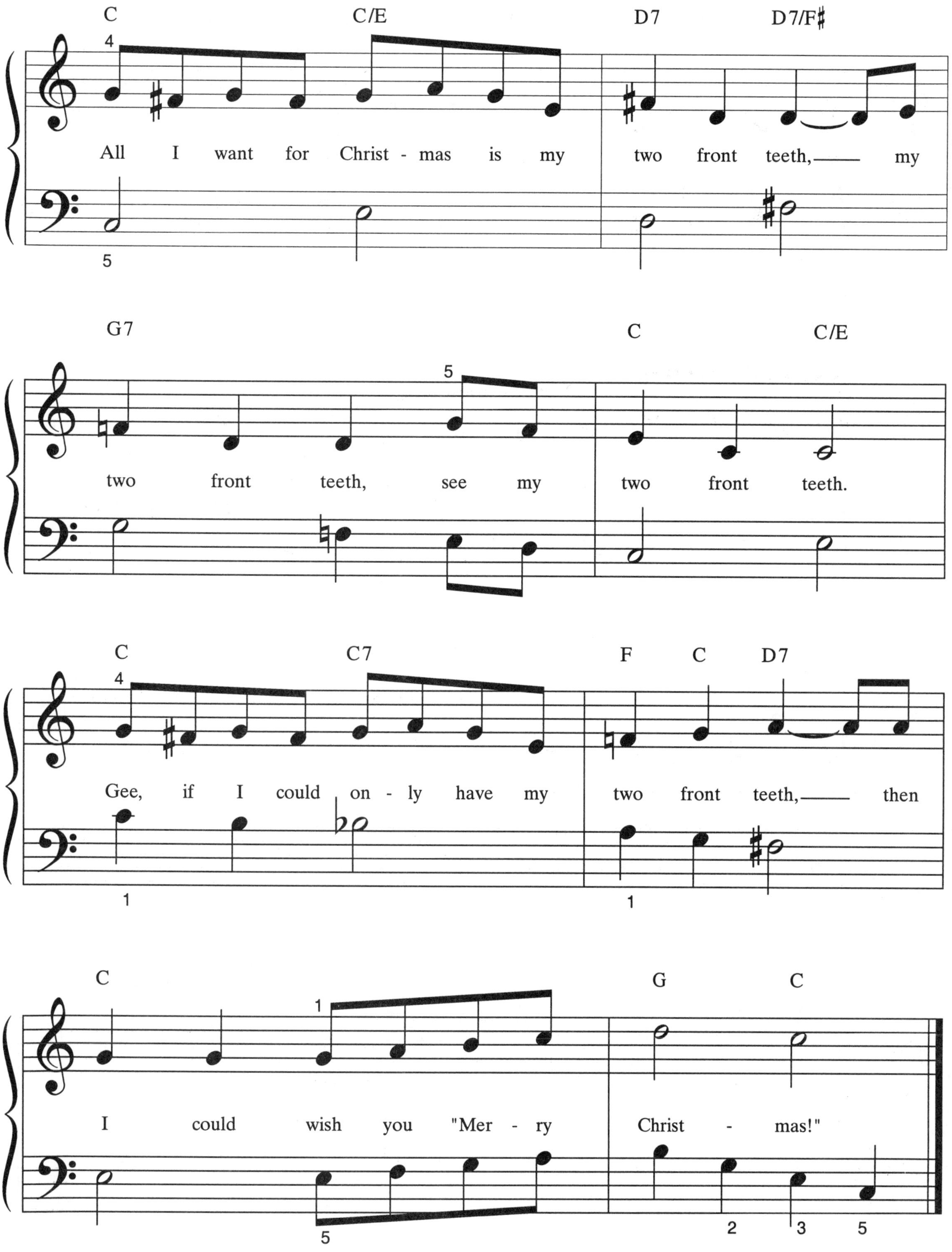
C C/E D7 D7/F♯
All I want for Christ - mas is my two front teeth, my
G7 C C/E
two front teeth, see my two front teeth.
C C7 F C D7
Gee, if I could on - ly have my two front teeth, then
C G C
I could wish you "Mer - ry Christ - mas!"

Nuttin' for Christmas

Words and Music by
SID TEPPER and ROY C. BENNETT
Arranged by Richard Bradley

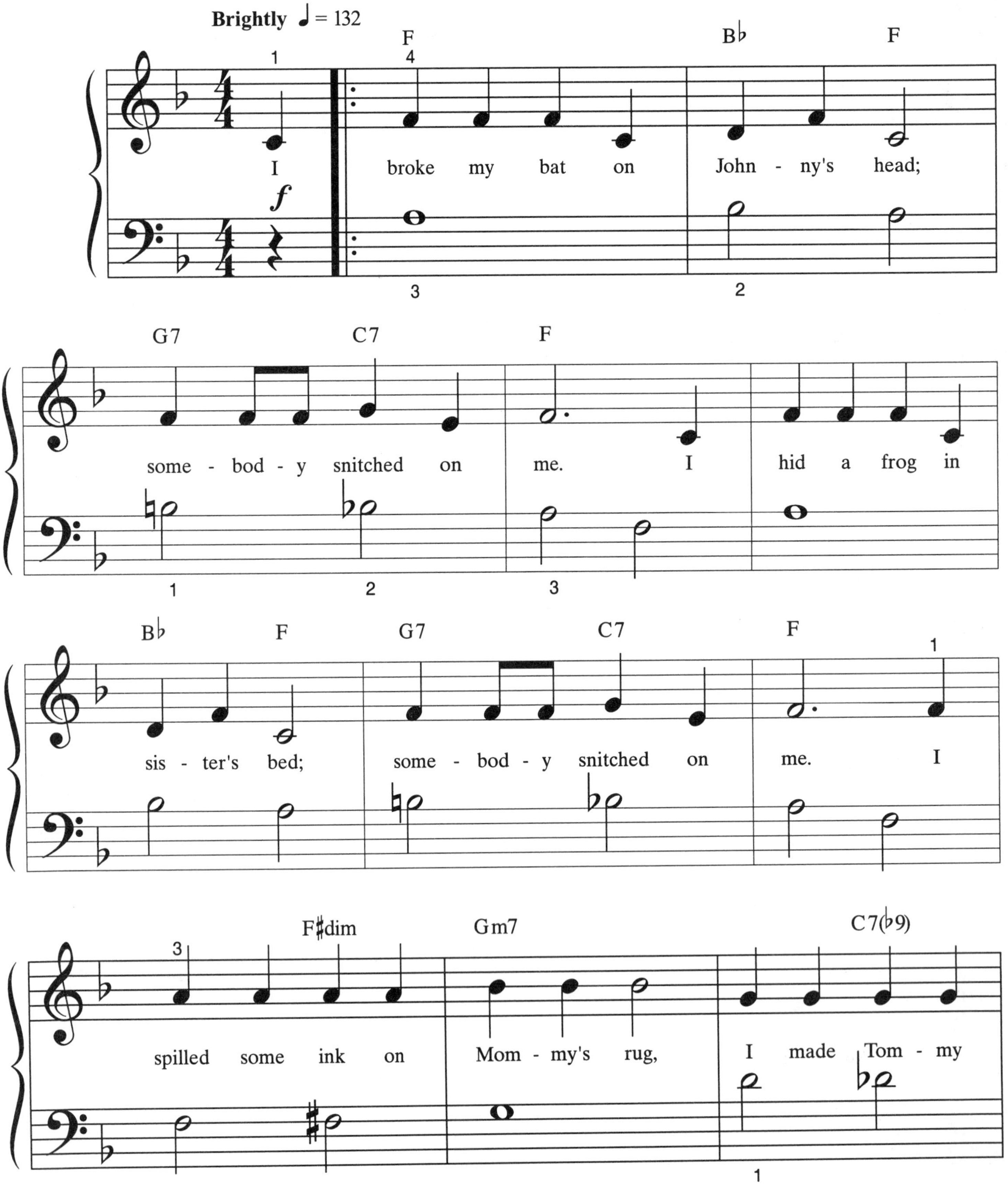
Brightly ♩ = 132
F
B♭
F
I broke my bat on John - ny's head;
G7
C7
F
some - bod - y snitched on me. I
hid a frog in
B♭
F
G7
C7
F
sis - ter's bed; some - bod - y snitched on me. I
F♯dim
Gm7
C7(♭9)
spilled some ink on Mom - my's rug, I made Tom - my

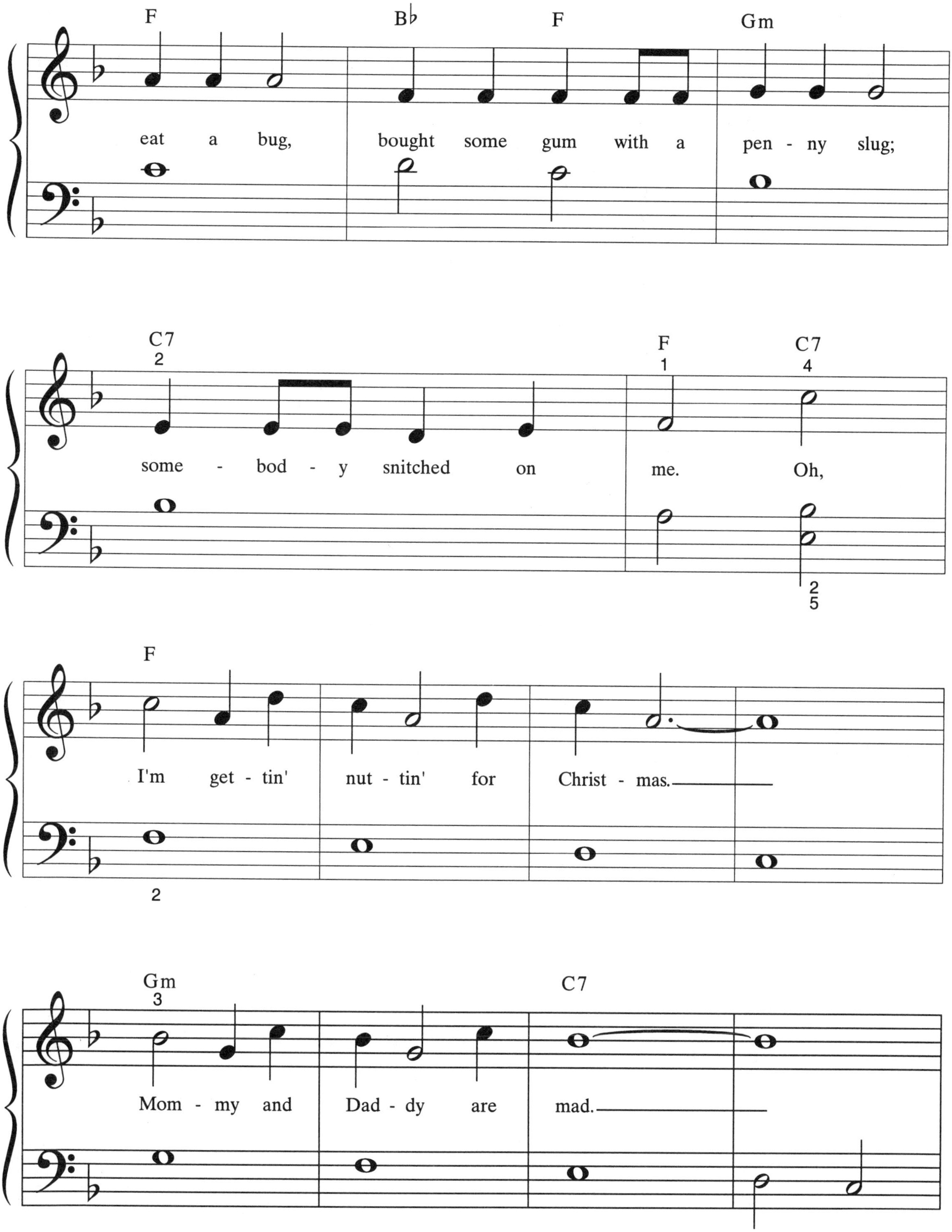
F
B♭
F
Gm
eat a bug, bought some gum with a pen - ny slug;
C7
F
C7
some - bod - y snitched on me. Oh,
F
I'm get - tin' nut - tin' for Christ - mas.
Gm
C7
Mom - my and Dad - dy are mad.

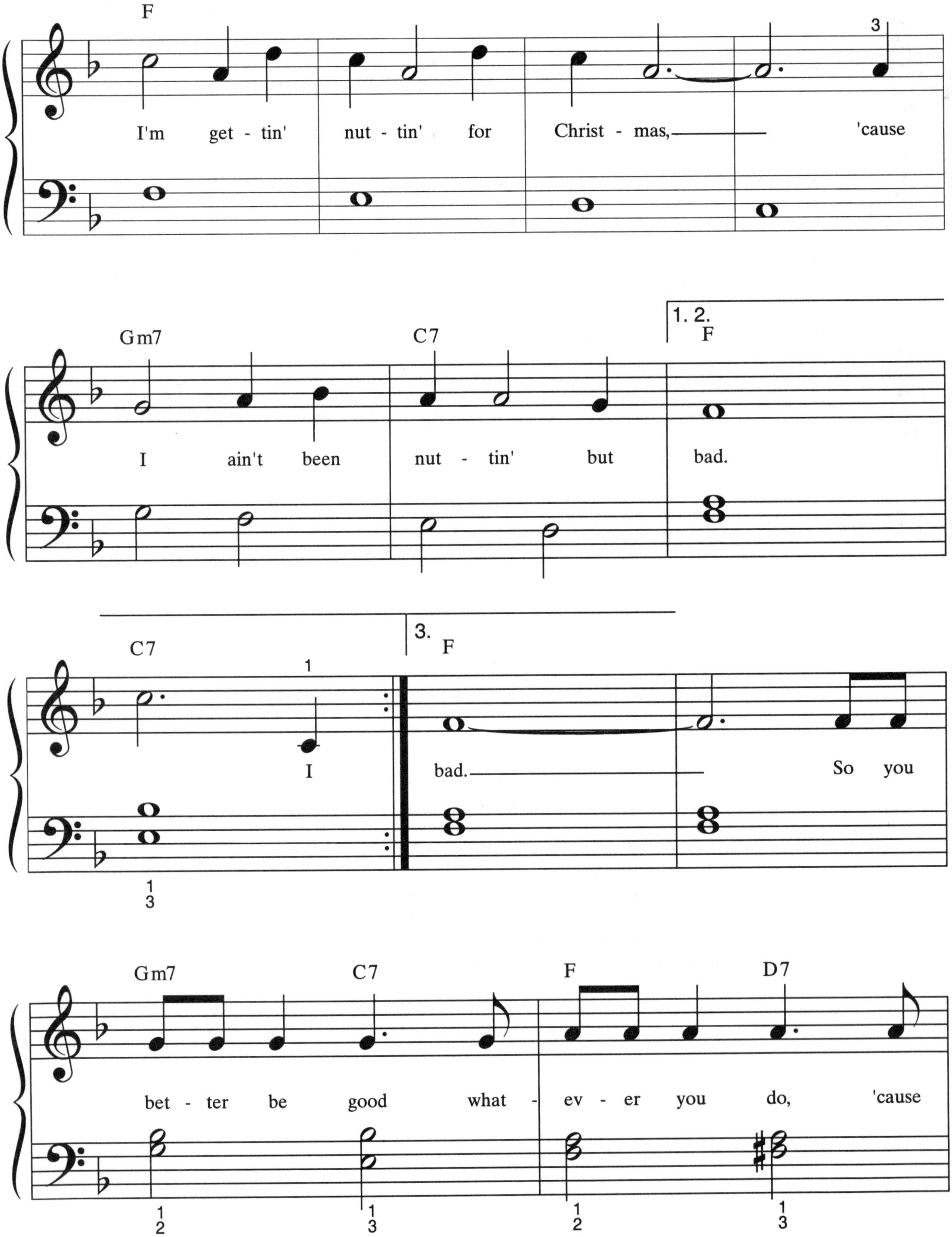
F
3
I'm get - tin' nut - tin' for Christ - mas, 'cause
Gm7
C7
1. 2.
F
I ain't been nut - tin' but bad.
C7
1
3.
F
I bad. So you
1
3
Gm7
C7
F
D7
bet - ter be good what - ev - er you do, 'cause
1
2
1
3
1
2
1
3

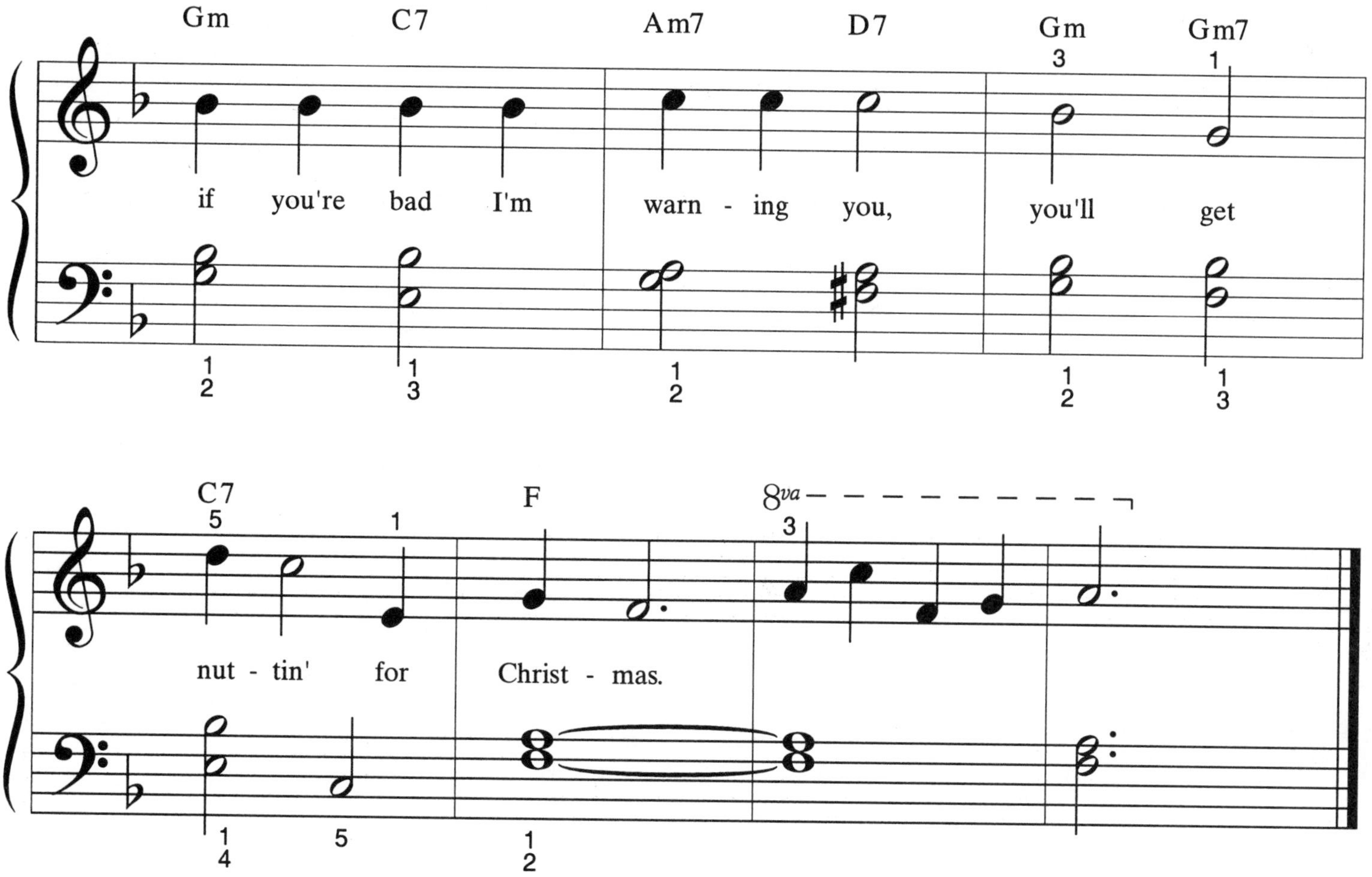
Gm C7 Am7 D7 Gm Gm7
if you're bad I'm warn - ing you, you'll get
C7 F 8va
nut - tin' for Christ - mas.

Verse 2:
I put a tack on teacher's chair; somebody snitched on me.
I tied a knot in Susie's hair; somebody snitched on me.
I did a dance on Mommy's plants; climbed a tree and tore my pants.
Filled the sugar bowl with ants; somebody snitched on me.So, . . .

Verse 3:
I won't be seeing Santa Claus; somebody snitched on me.
He won't come visit me because somebody snitched on me.
Next year I'll be going straight, next year I'll be good, just wait,
I'd start now but it's too late; somebody snitched on me. Oh, . . .

Deck the Halls

TRADITIONAL
Arranged by Richard Bradley

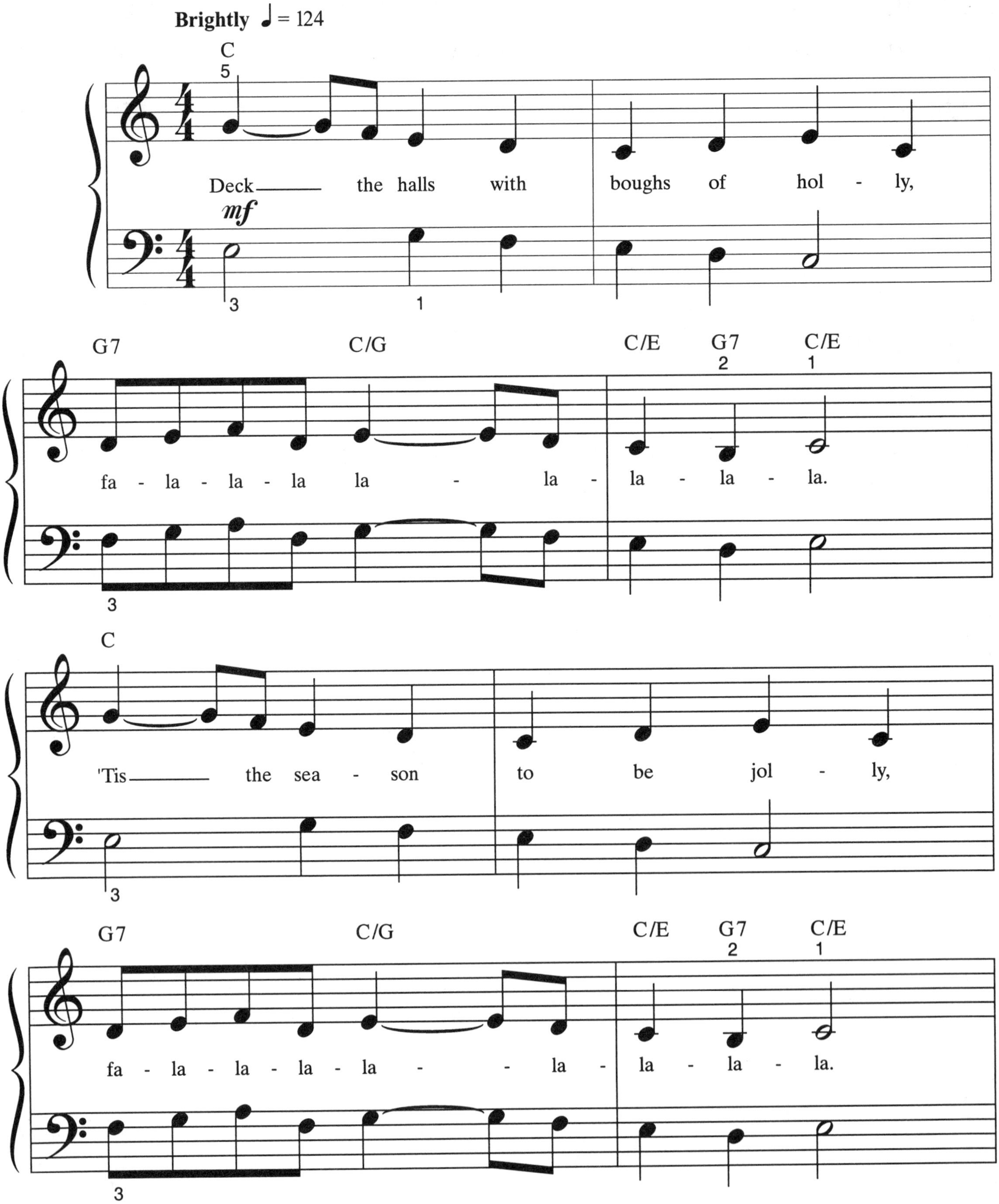
Brightly ♩ = 124
C
Deck the halls with boughs of hol - ly,
mf
G7 C/G C/E G7 C/E
fa - la - la - la la - la - la - la - la.
C
'Tis the sea - son to be jol - ly,
G7 C/G C/E G7 C/E
fa - la - la - la - la - la - la - la - la.

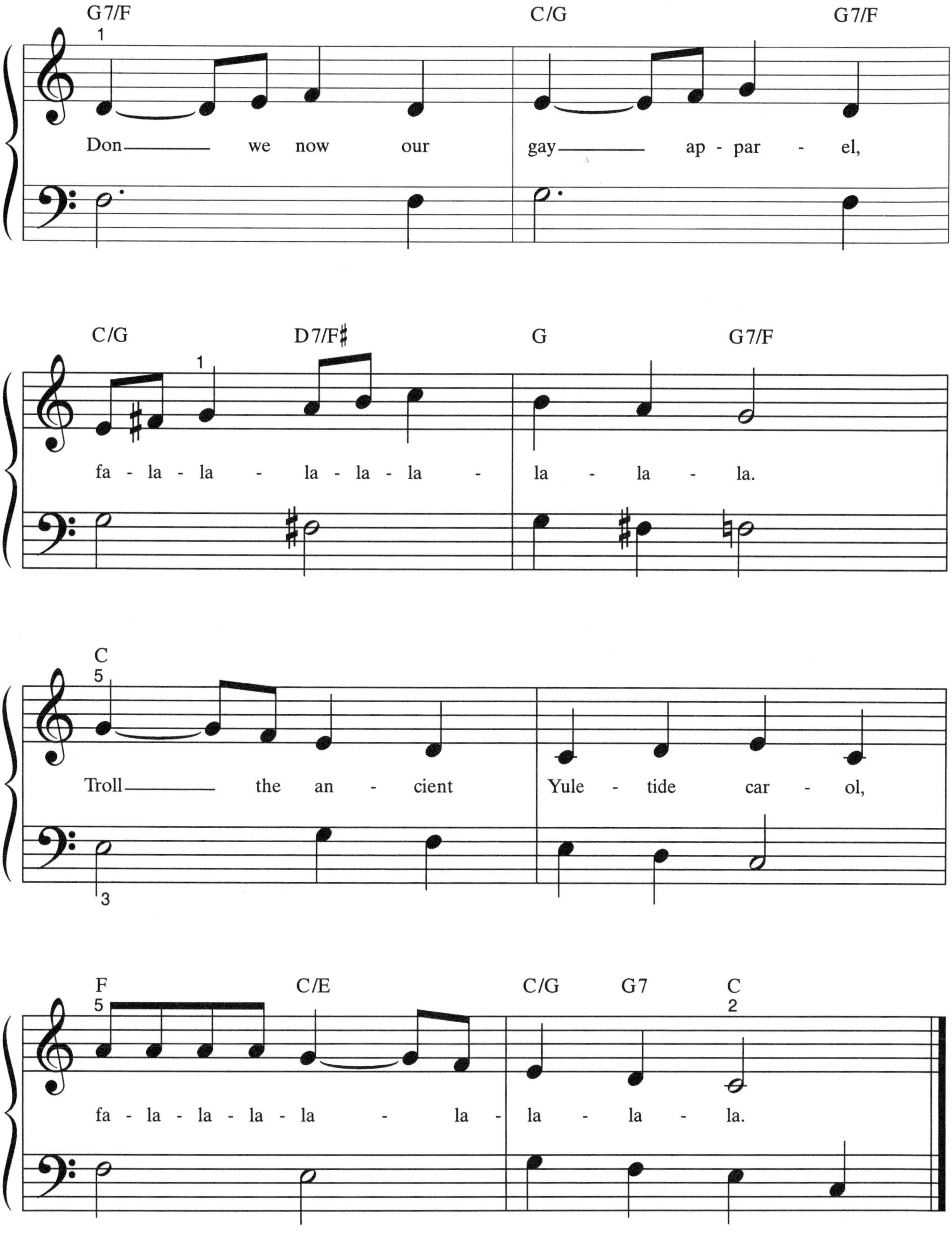
G7/F C/G G7/F
Don we now our gay ap - par - el,
C/G D7/F♯ G G7/F
fa - la - la - la - la - la - la - la - la.
C
Troll the an - cient Yule - tide car - ol,
F C/E C/G G7 C
fa - la - la - la - la - la - la - la - la.

O Little Town of Bethlehem

By
LEWIS H. REDNER
Arranged by Richard Bradley

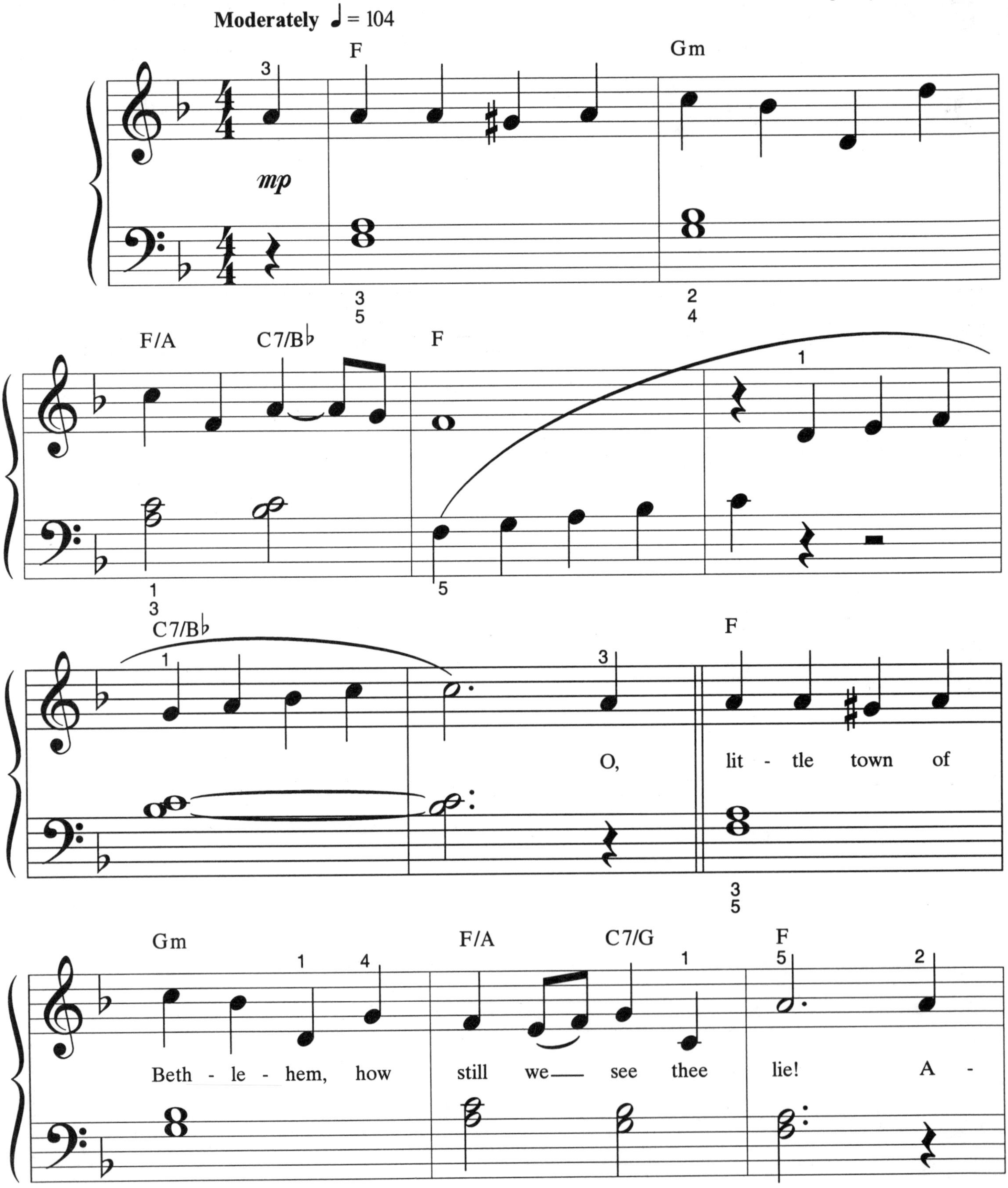

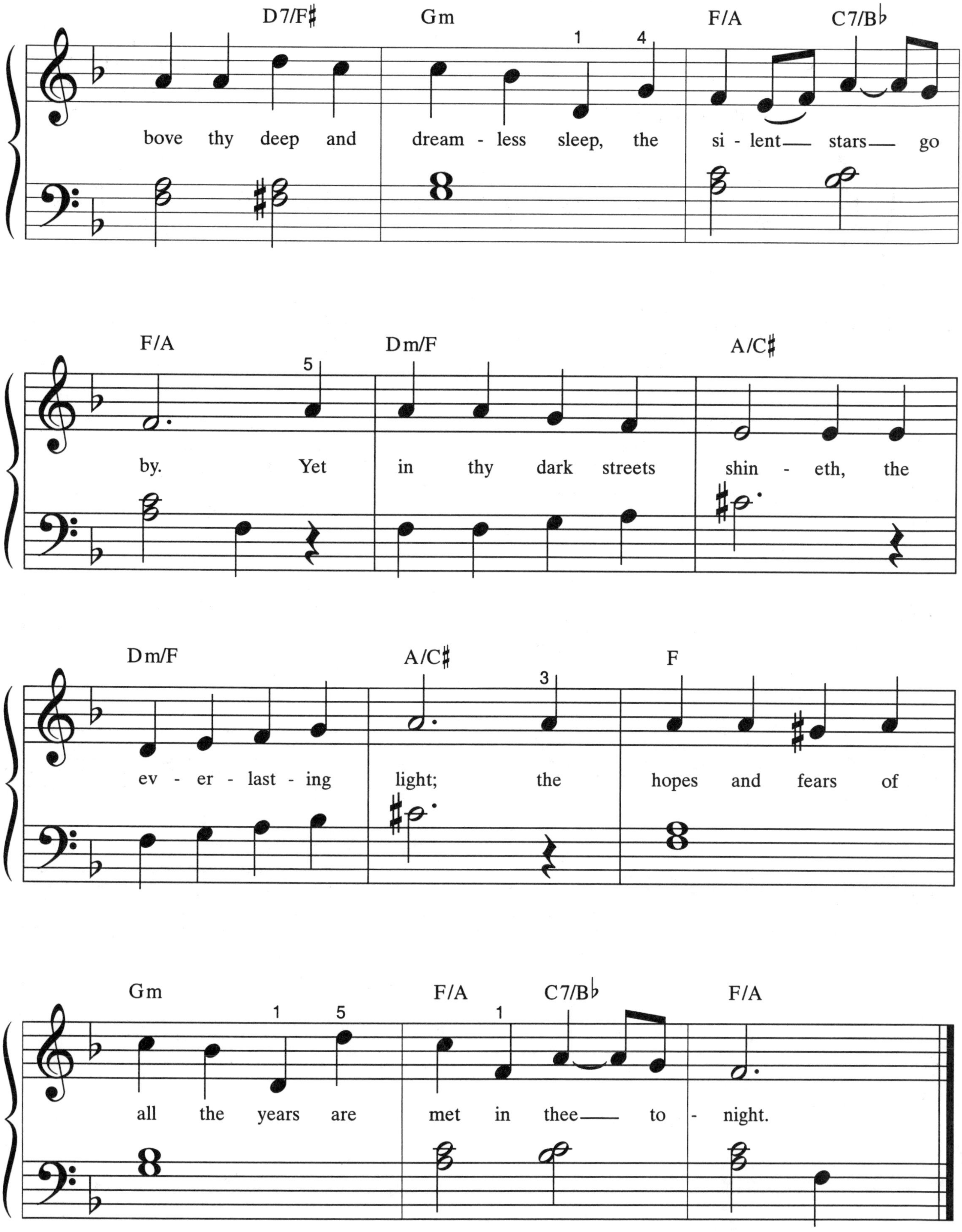
D7/F♯ Gm F/A C7/B♭
1 4
bove thy deep and dream - less sleep, the si - lent stars go
F/A Dm/F A/C♯
5
by. Yet in thy dark streets shin - eth, the
Dm/F A/C♯ F
3
ev - er - last - ing light; the hopes and fears of
Gm F/A C7/B♭ F/A
1 5 1
all the years are met in thee to - night.

The First Noel

TRADITIONAL
Arranged by Richard Bradley

Moderately slow ♩ = 92
C G
The first No - el, the
mp
F C F
an - gel did say, was to cer - tain poor
C G C
shep - herds in fields as they lay; in
G F
fields where they lay keep - ing their

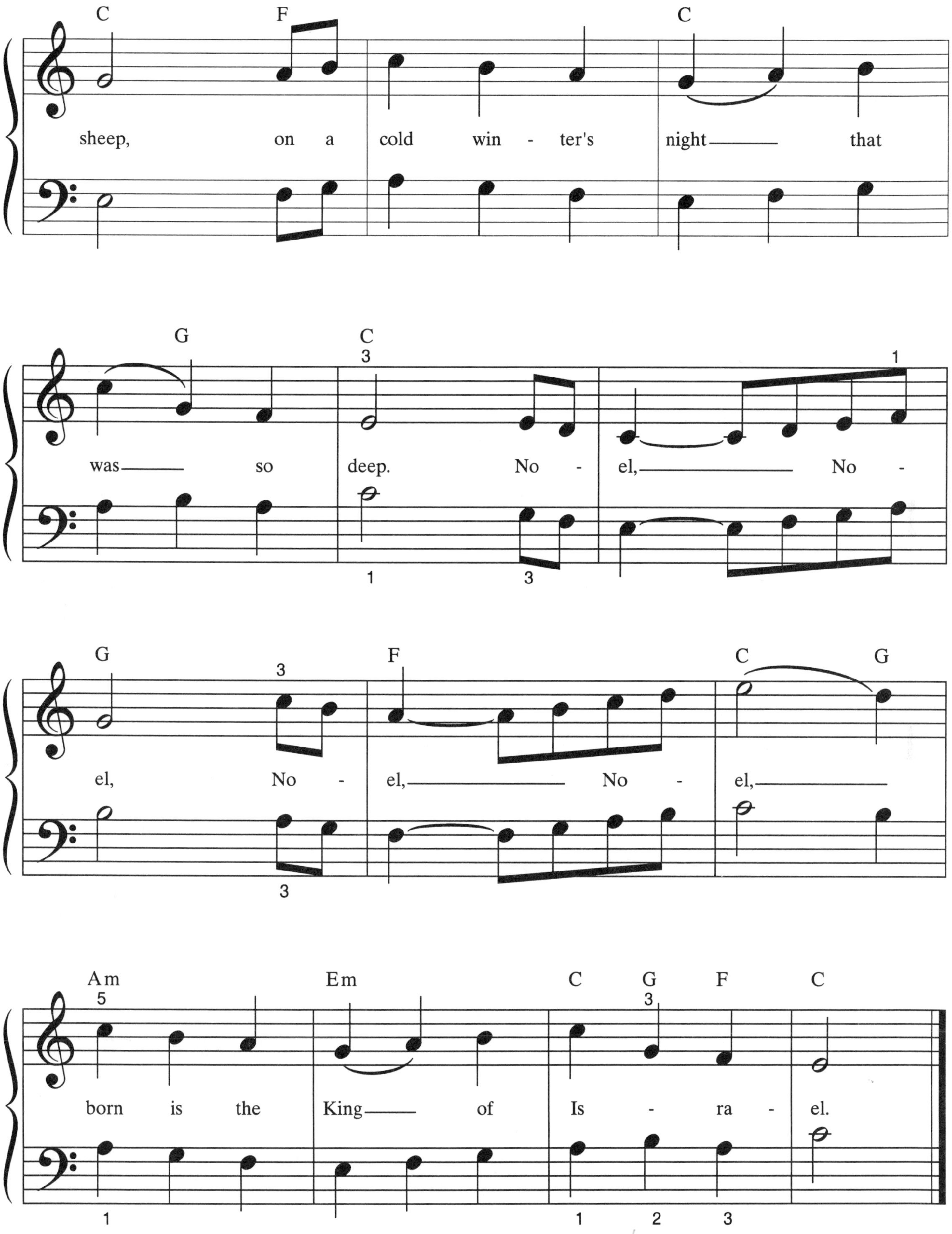
C F C
sheep, on a cold win - ter's night that
G C
was so deep. No - el, No -
G F C G
el, No - el, No - el,
Am Em C G F C
born is the King of Is - ra - el.

The Little Drummer Boy

Words and Music by
KATHERINE DAVIS, HENRY ONORATI
and HARRY SIMEONE
Arranged by Richard Bradley

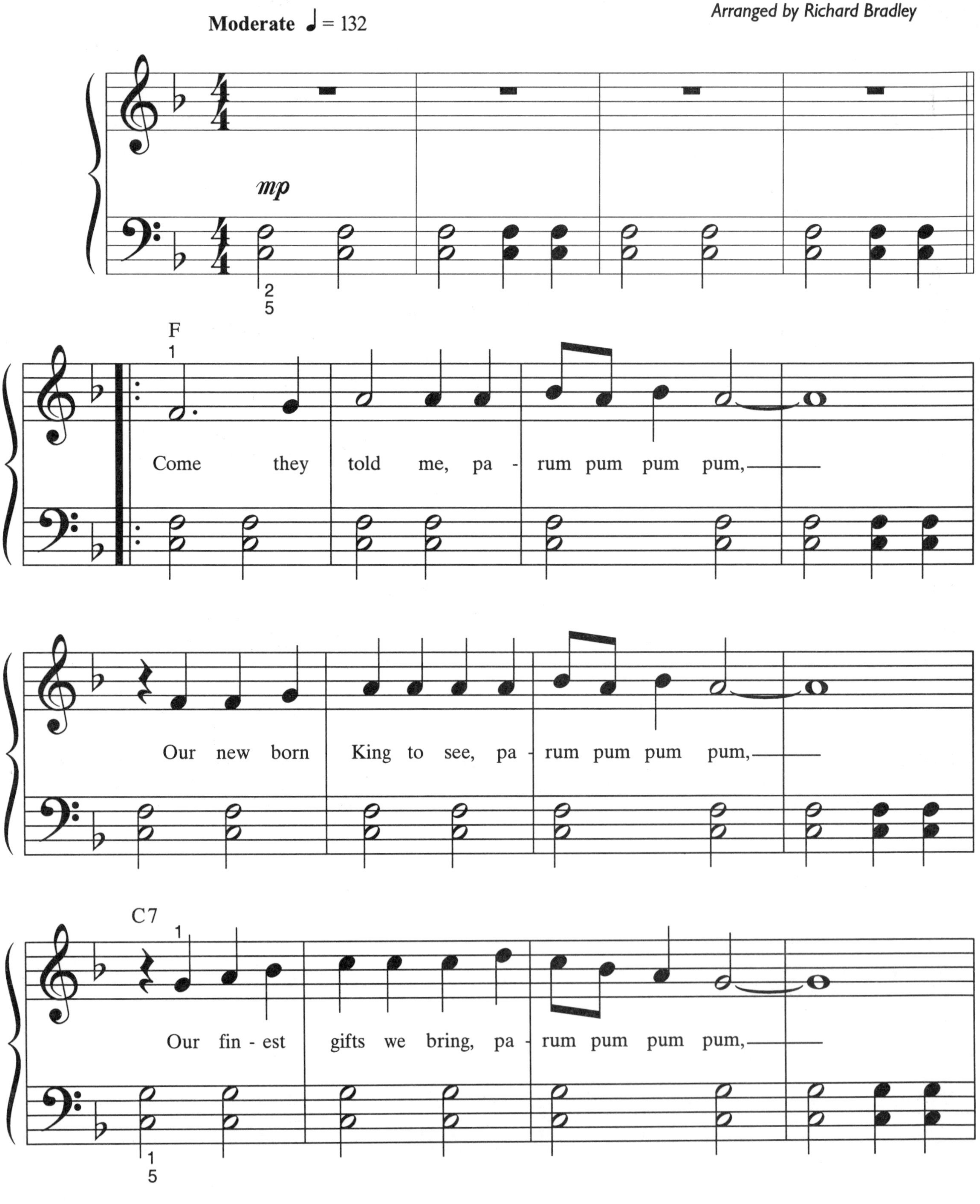
Moderate ♩ = 132
mp
F
Come they told me, pa - rum pum pum pum,
Our new born King to see, pa - rum pum pum pum,
C7
Our fin - est gifts we bring, pa - rum pum pum pum,

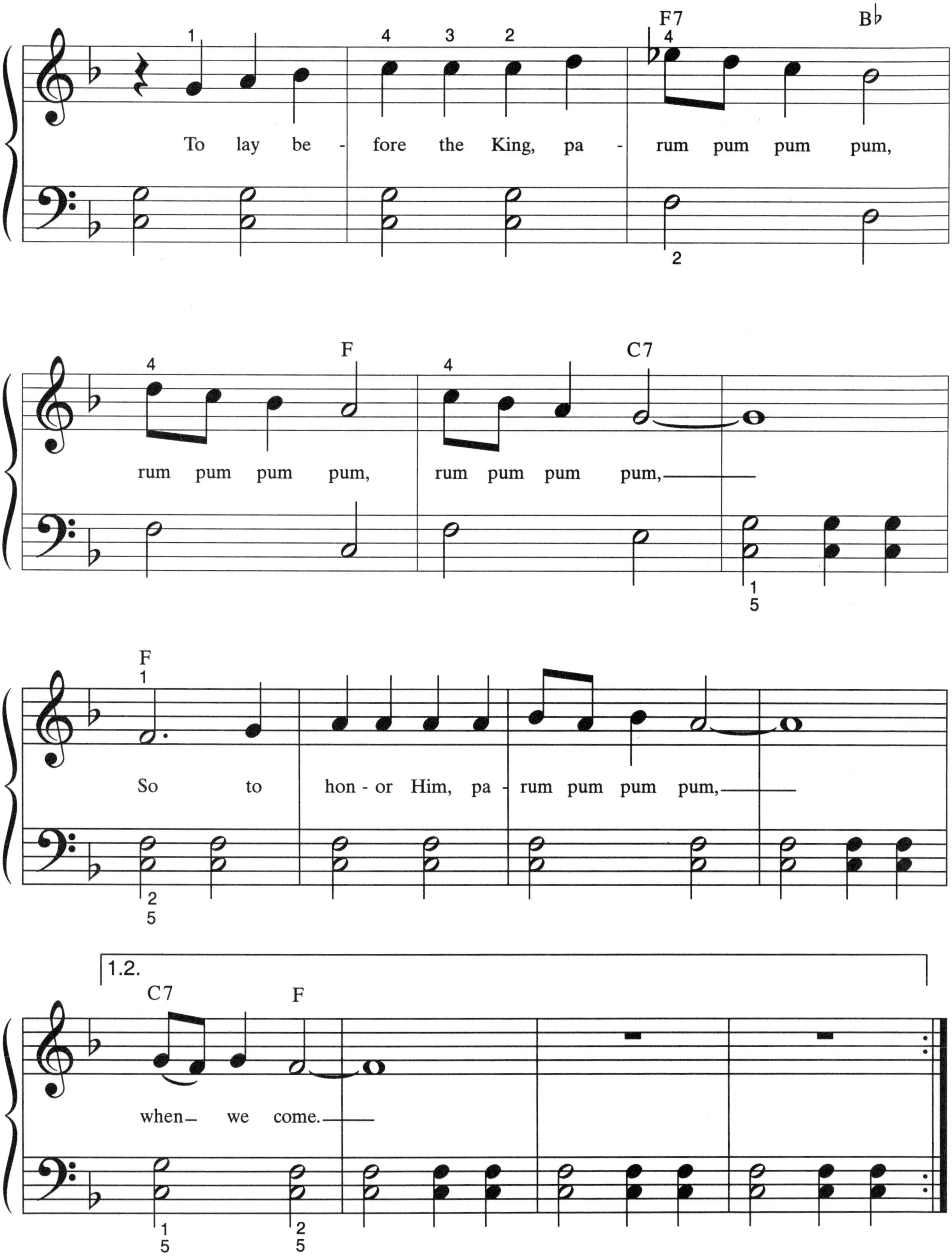
F7 B♭
To lay be - fore the King, pa - rum pum pum pum,
F C7
rum pum pum pum, rum pum pum pum,
F
So to hon - or Him, pa - rum pum pum pum,
1.2.
C7 F
when we come.

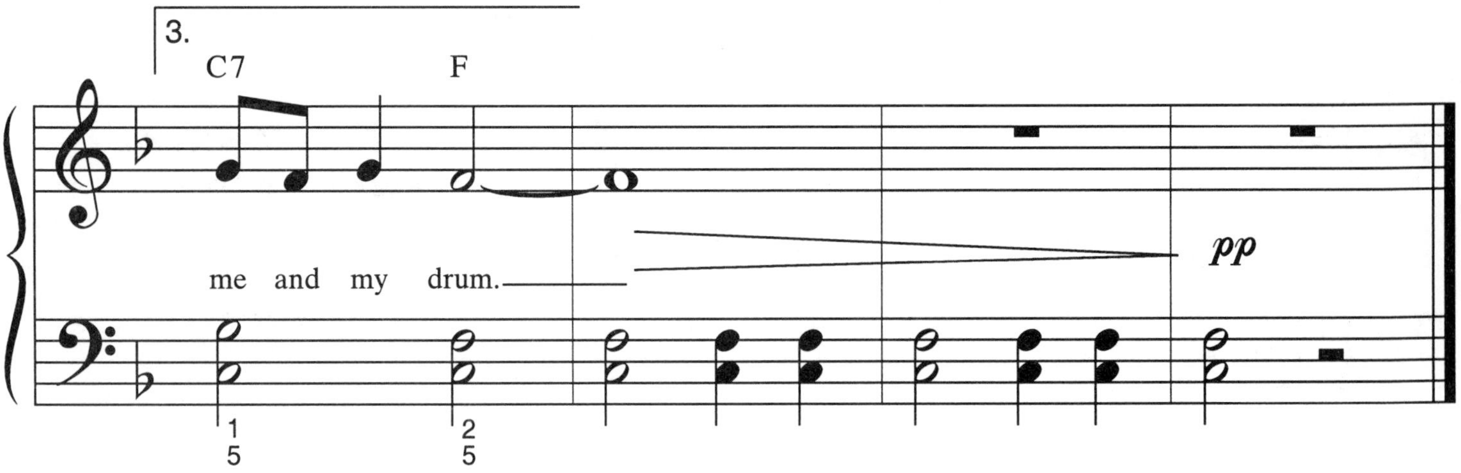

Verse 2:
Baby Jesu, pa-rum pum pum pum,
I am a poor boy too, pa-rum pum pum pum,
I have no gift to bring, pa-rum pum pum pum,
That's fit to give our King, pa-rum pum pum pum,
Rum pum pum pum, rum pum pum pum,
Shall I play for you, pa-rum pum pum pum,
On my drum?

Verse 3:
Mary nodded, pa-rum pum pum pum,
The Ox and Lamb kept time, pa-rum pum pum pum,
I played my drum for Him, pa-rum pum pum pum,
I played my best for Him, pa-rum pum pum pum,
Rum pum pum pum, rum pum pum pum.
Then He smiled at me, pa-rum pum pum pum,
Me and my drum.

Christmas Lullaby

Lyrics by
PEGGY LEE

Music by
CY COLEMAN
Arranged by Richard Bradley

Moderately slow ♩ = 86

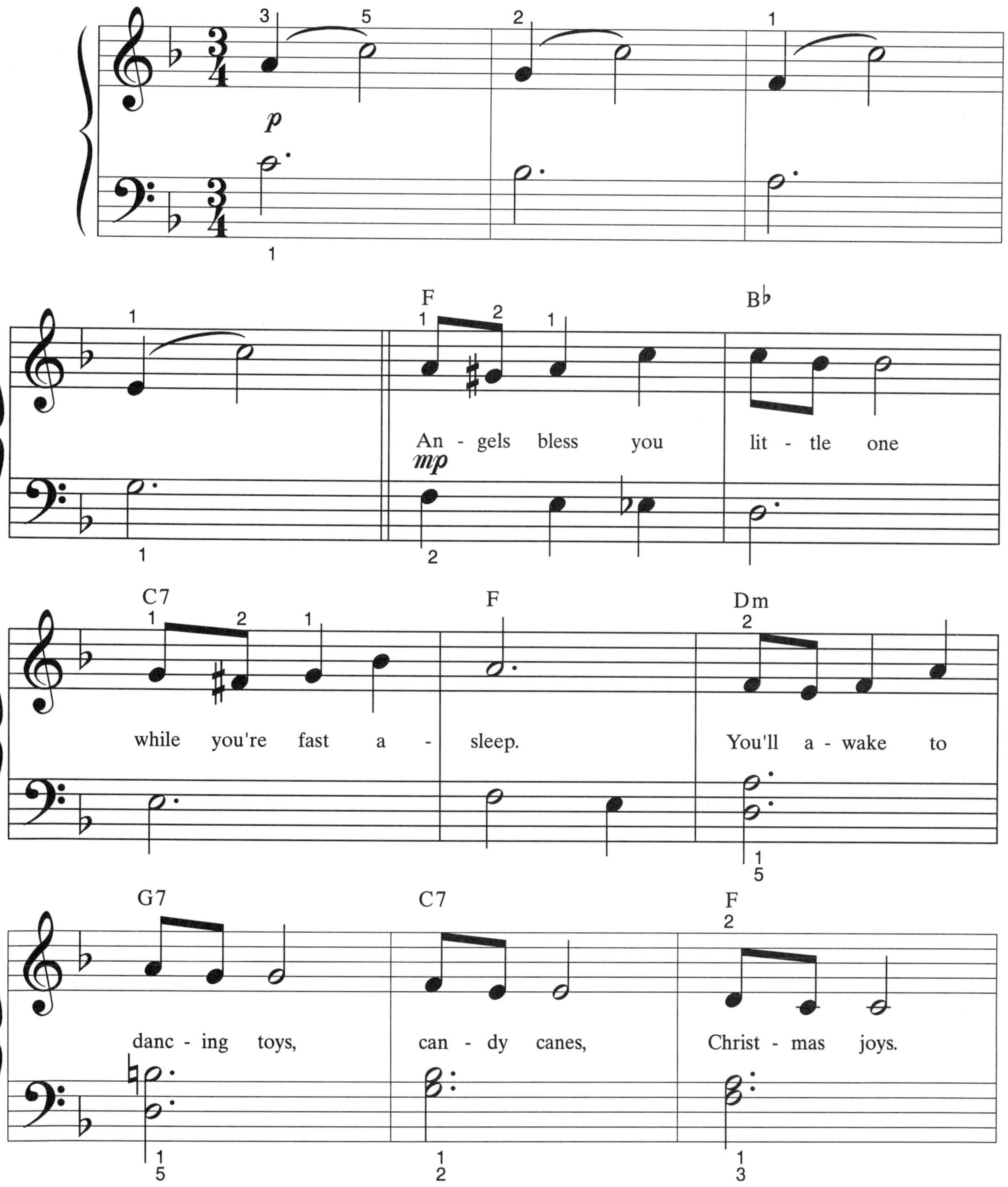
p
F
B♭
An - gels bless you lit - tle one
mp
C7
F
Dm
while you're fast a - sleep.
You'll a - wake to
G7
C7
F
danc - ing toys,
can - dy canes,
Christ - mas joys.

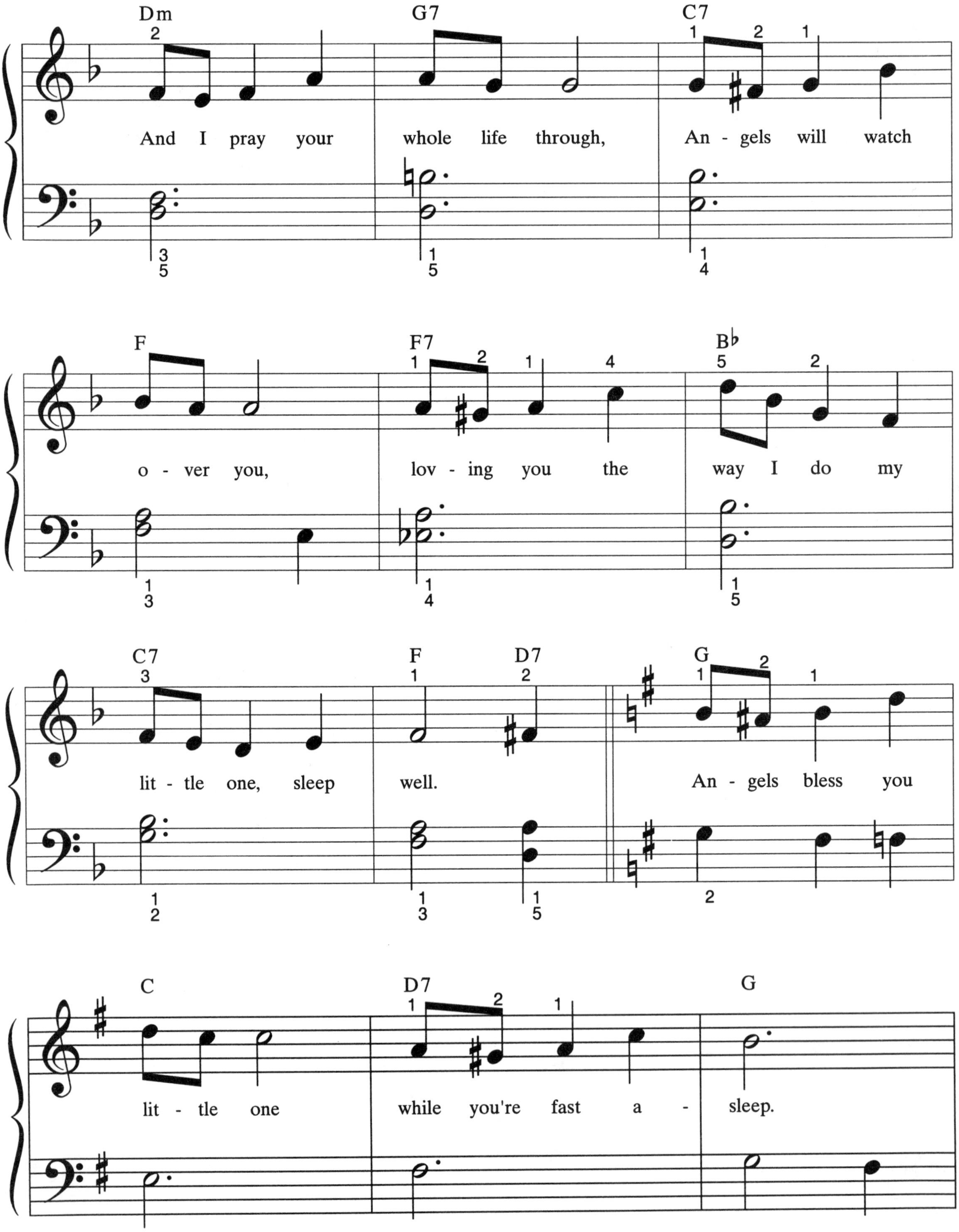
Dm G7 C7
And I pray your whole life through, An - gels will watch
F F7 B♭
o - ver you, lov - ing you the way I do my
C7 F D7 G
lit - tle one, sleep well. An - gels bless you
C D7 G
lit - tle one while you're fast a - sleep.

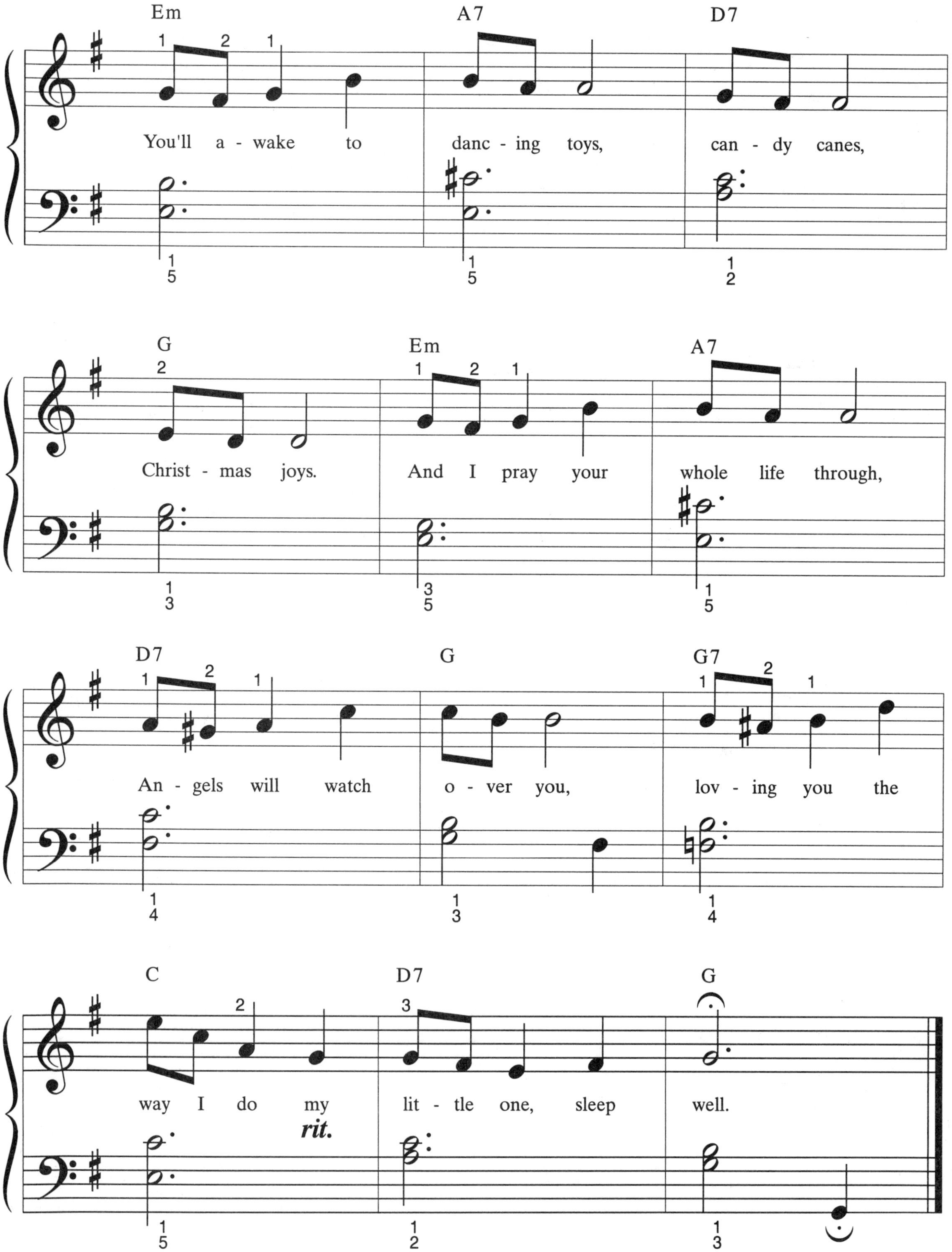
Em A7 D7
You'll a - wake to danc - ing toys, can - dy canes,
G Em A7
Christ - mas joys. And I pray your whole life through,
D7 G G7
An - gels will watch o - ver you, lov - ing you the
C D7 G
way I do my lit - tle one, sleep well.
rit.

O Holy Night

Words and Music by
ADOLPHE ADAM
Arranged by Richard Bradley

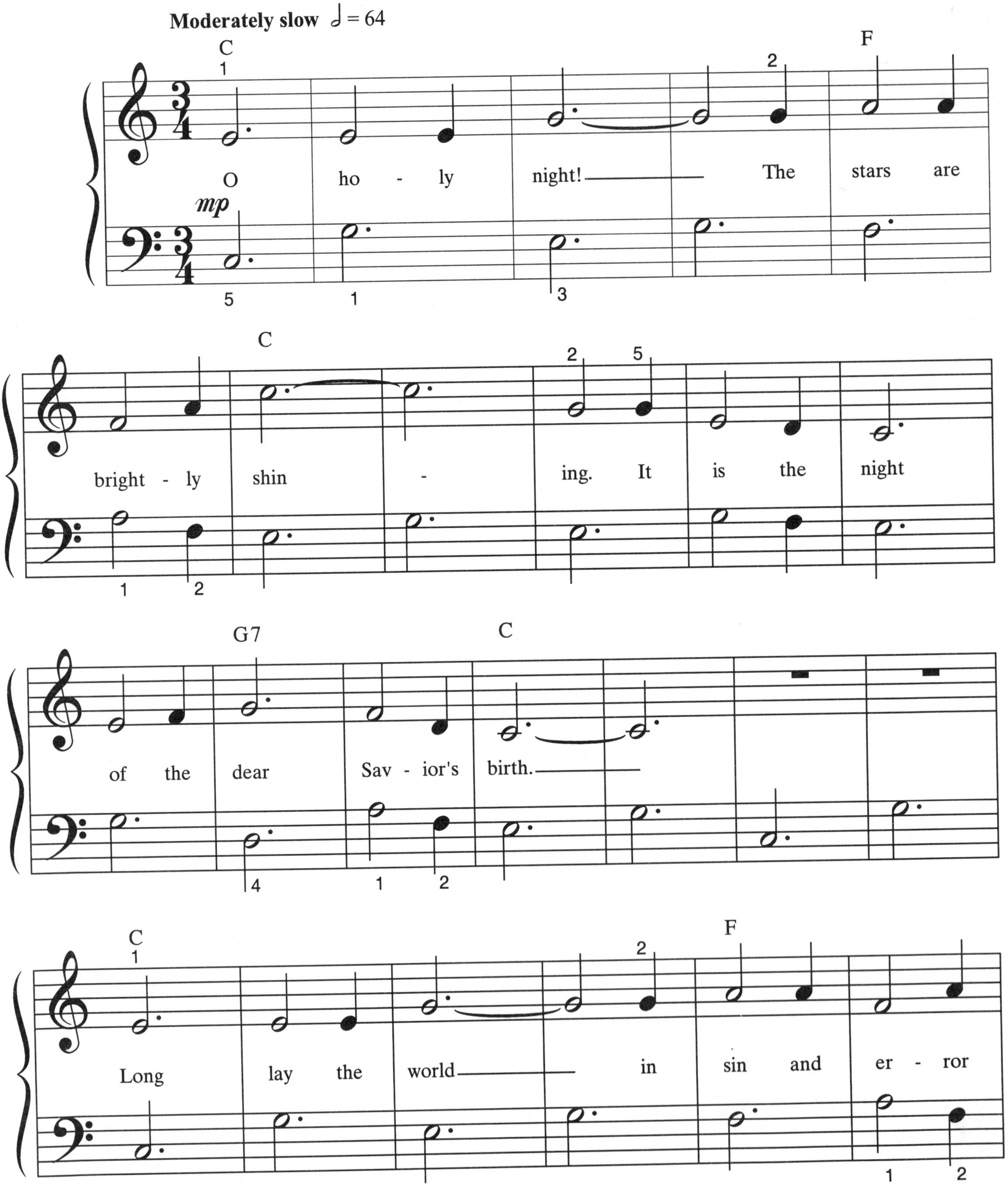
Moderately slow ♩ = 64
C F G7
mp
O ho - ly night! The stars are bright - ly shin - ing. It is the night
of the dear Sav - ior's birth.
Long lay the world in sin and er - ror

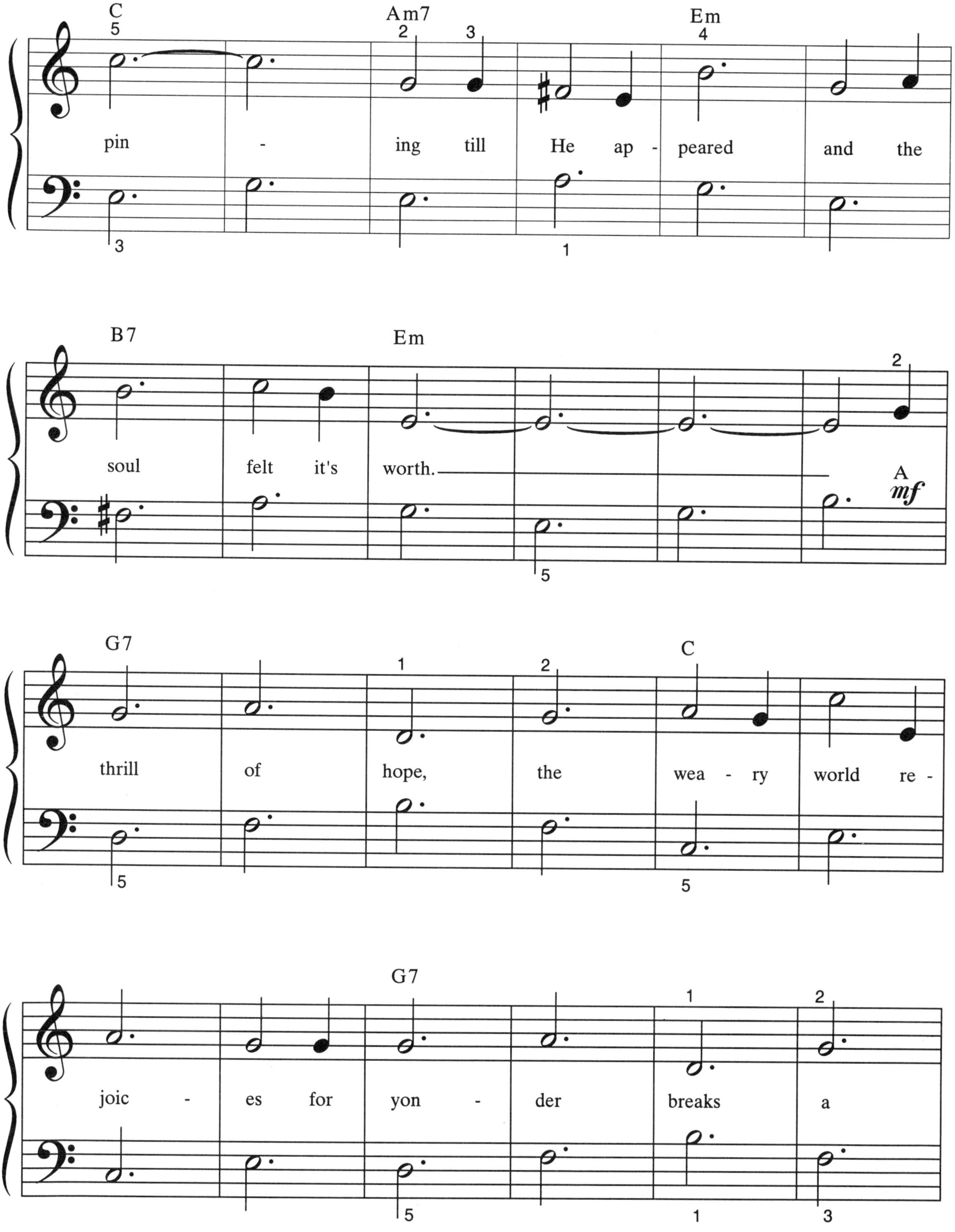
C Am7 Em
pin - ing till He ap - peared and the
B7 Em
soul felt it's worth.
A
mf
G7 C
thrill of hope, the wea - ry world re -
G7
joic - es for yon - der breaks a

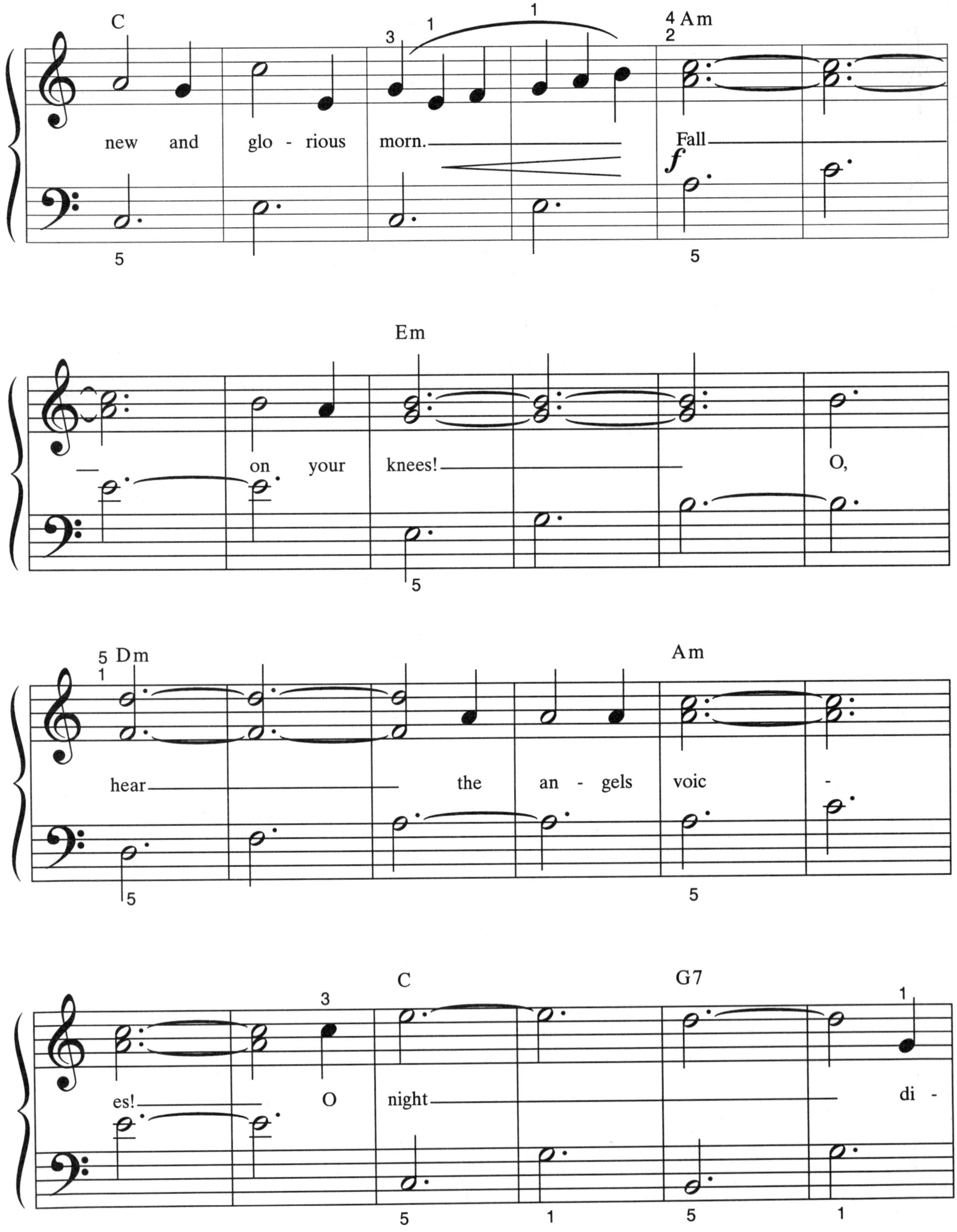
C
Am
new and glo - rious morn.
Fall
f
Em
— on your knees!
O,
Dm
Am
hear the an - gels voic -
C
G7
es! O night di -

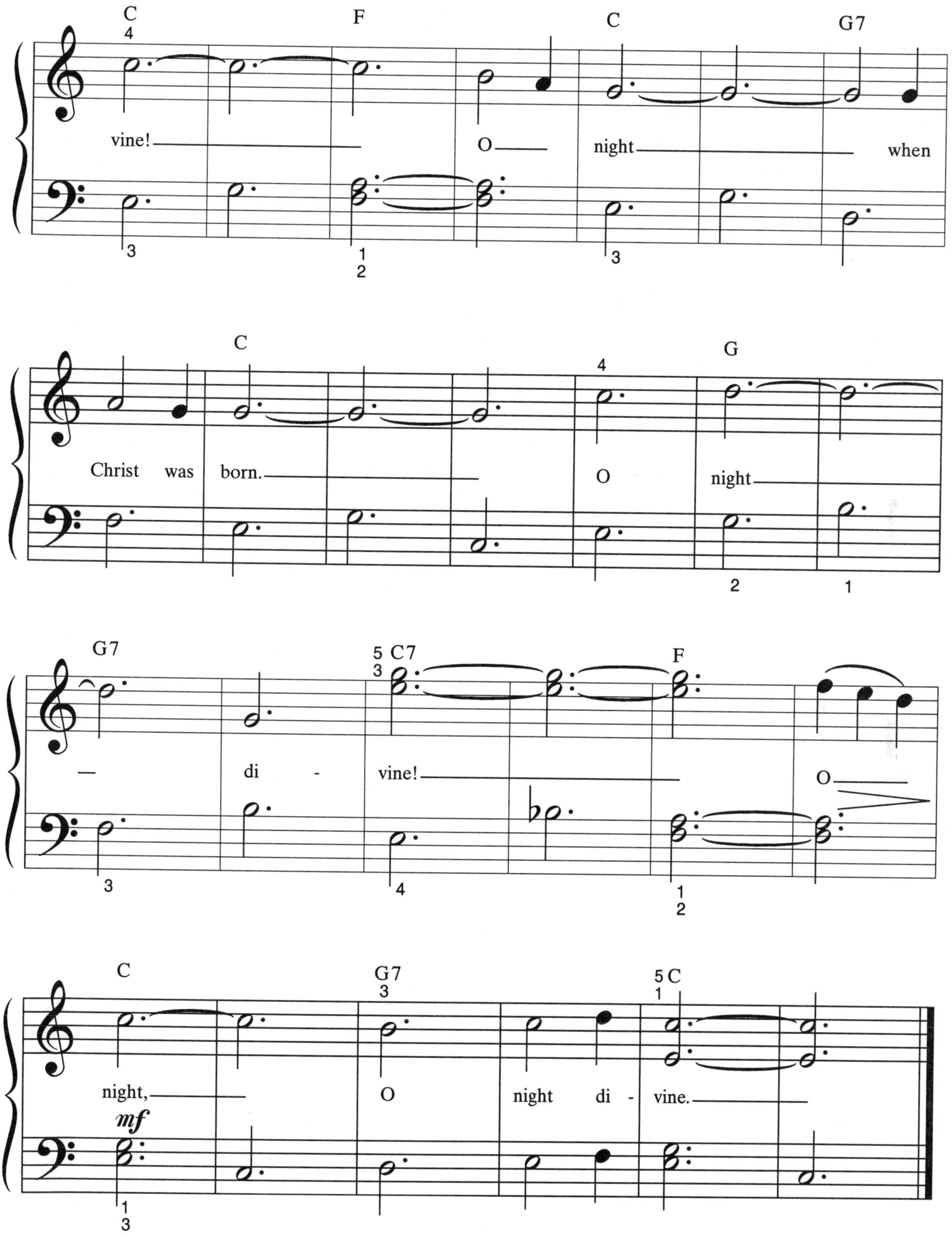
C F C G7
vine! O night when
C G
Christ was born. O night
G7 C7 F
di - vine! O
C G7 C
night, O night di - vine.
mf

Angels We Have Heard on High

TRADITIONAL
Arranged by Richard Bradley

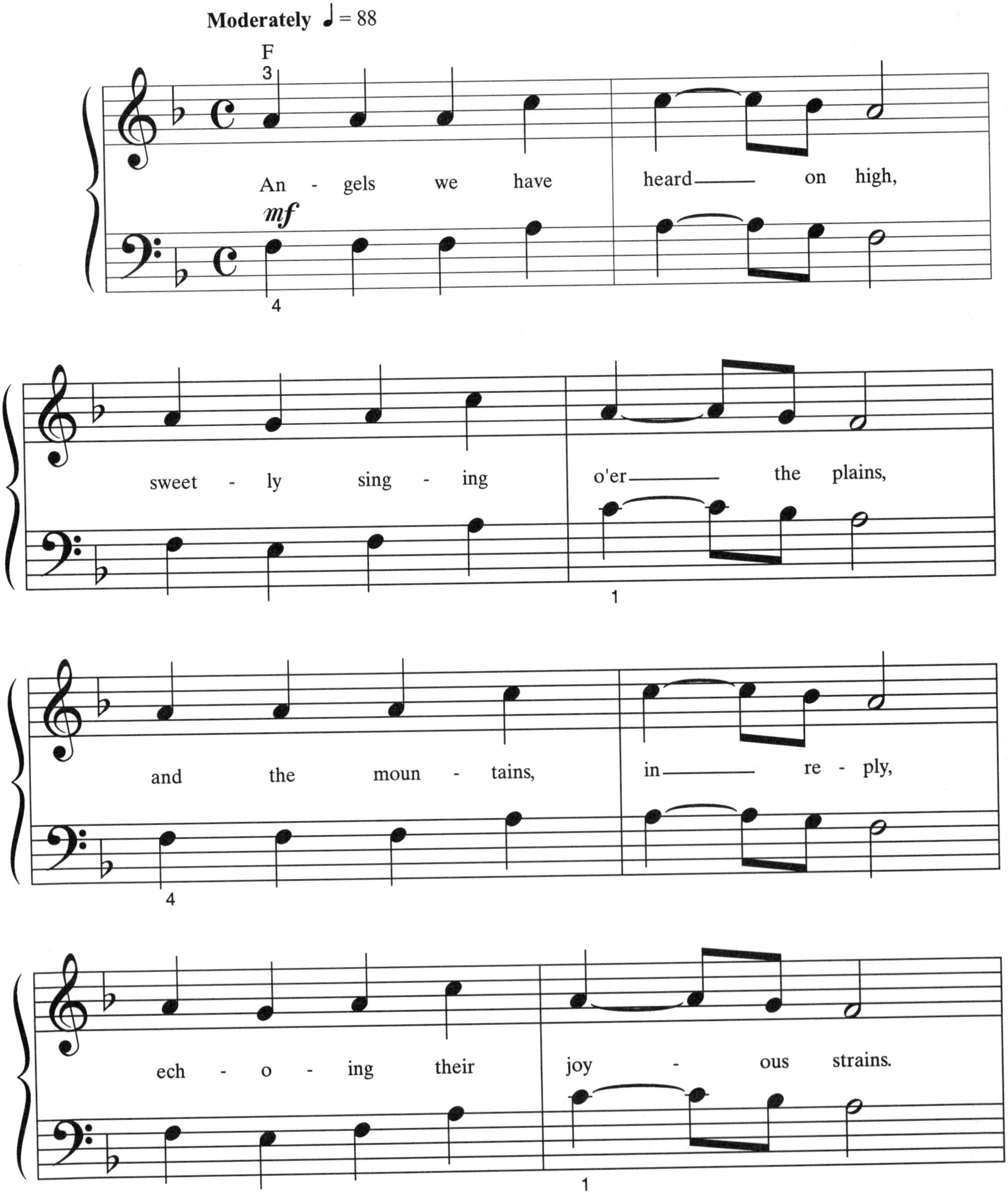
Moderately ♩ = 88
F
mf
An - gels we have heard on high,
sweet - ly sing - ing o'er the plains,
and the moun - tains, in re - ply,
ech - o - ing their joy - ous strains.

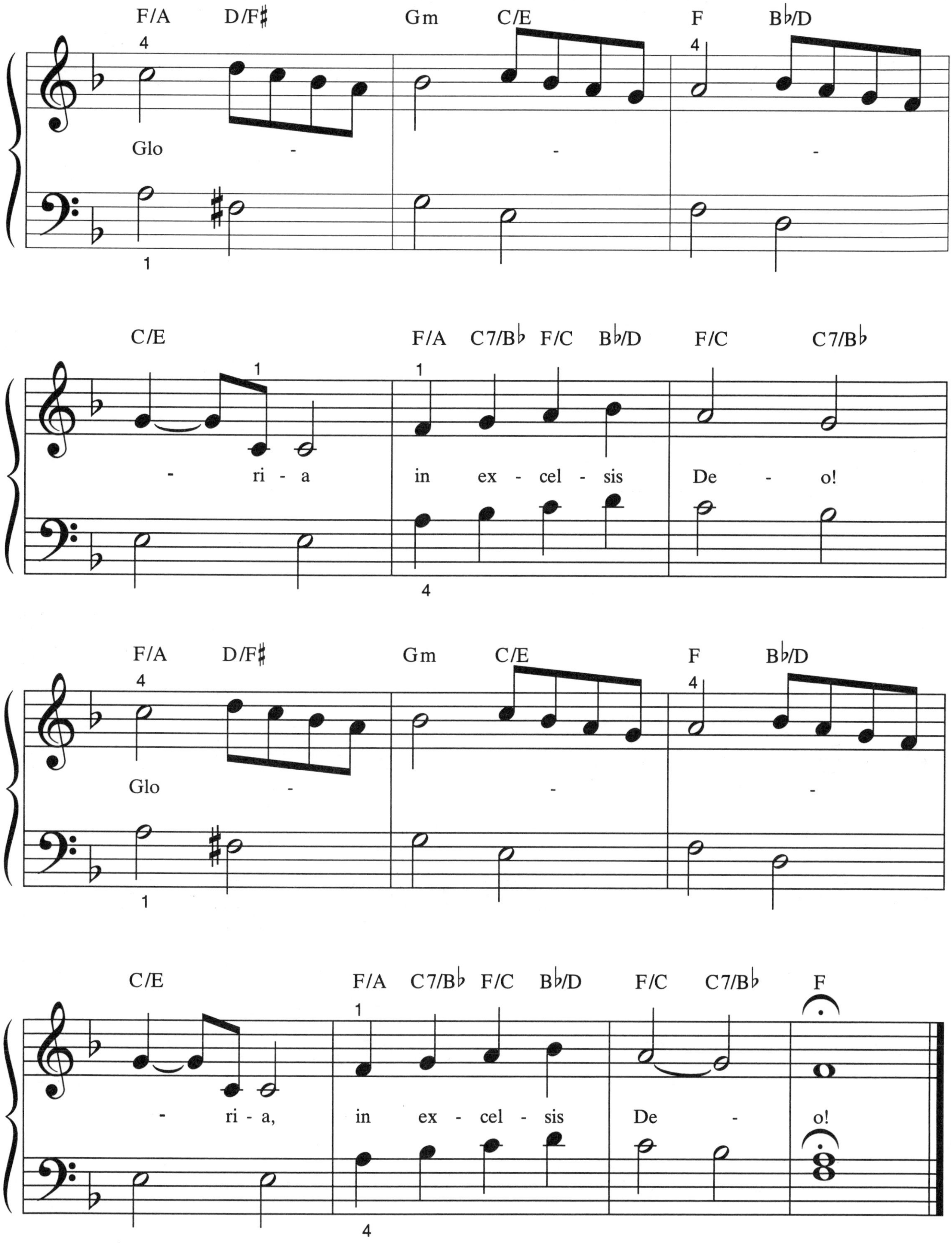
F/A D/F♯ Gm C/E F B♭/D
Glo - - -
C/E F/A C7/B♭ F/C B♭/D F/C C7/B♭
- ri - a in ex - cel - sis De - o!
F/A D/F♯ Gm C/E F B♭/D
Glo - - -
C/E F/A C7/B♭ F/C B♭/D F/C C7/B♭ F
- ri - a, in ex - cel - sis De - o!

Sleigh Ride

Words by
MITCHELL PARISH

Music by
LEROY ANDERSON
Arranged by Richard Bradley

Moderately bright 𝅗𝅥 = 82

G
Am7
D7
Just hear those sleigh bells jin - gle - ing, ring - ting - tin - gle - ing,
mf
too. Come on, it's love - ly weath - er for a
Bb
sleigh ride to - geth - er with you. Out - side the
snow is fall - ing and friends are call - ing, "Yoo hoo."

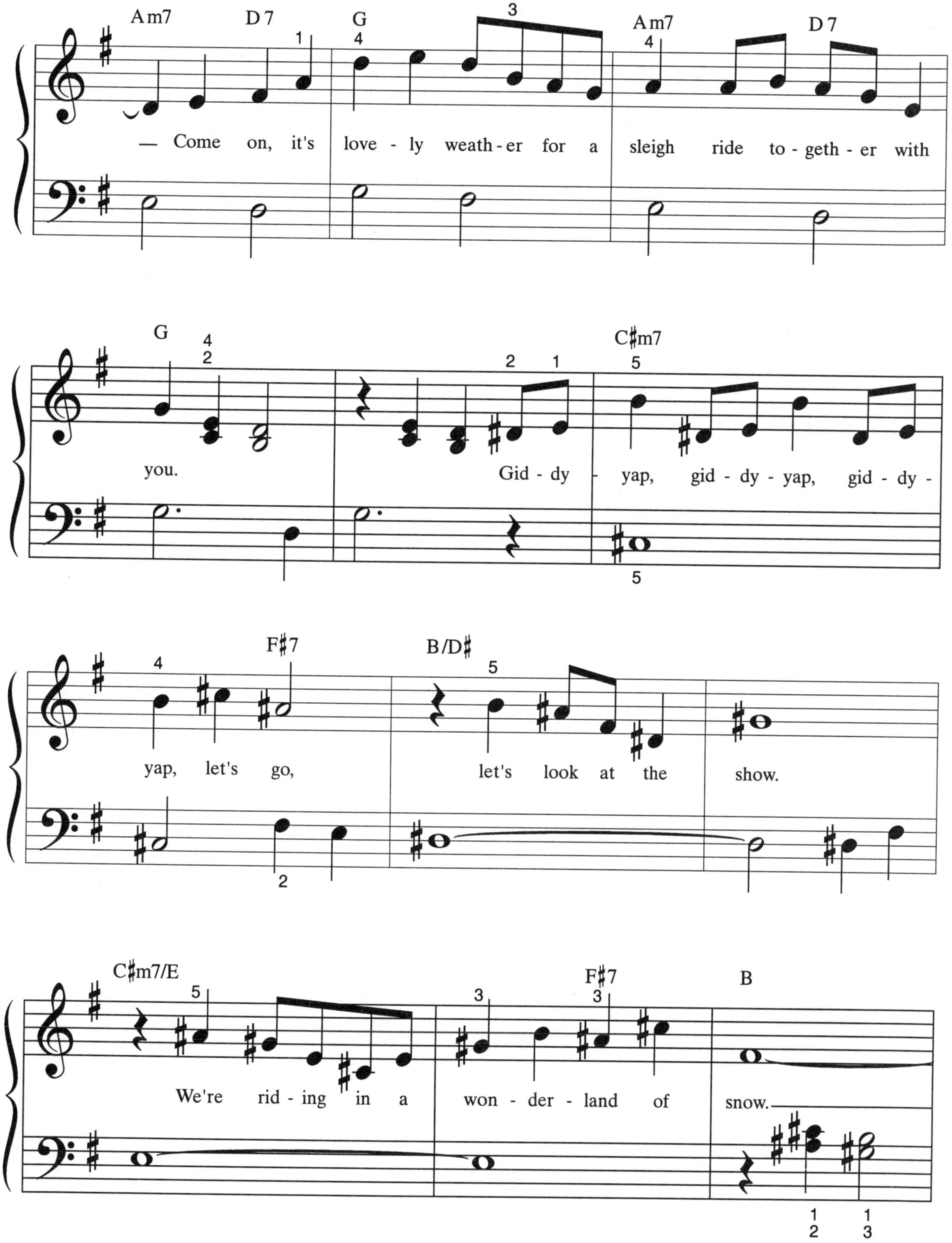
Am7 D7 G Am7 D7
— Come on, it's love - ly weath - er for a sleigh ride to - geth - er with
G C♯m7
you. Gid - dy - yap, gid - dy - yap, gid - dy -
F♯7 B/D♯
yap, let's go, let's look at the show.
C♯m7/E F♯7 B
We're rid - ing in a won - der - land of snow.

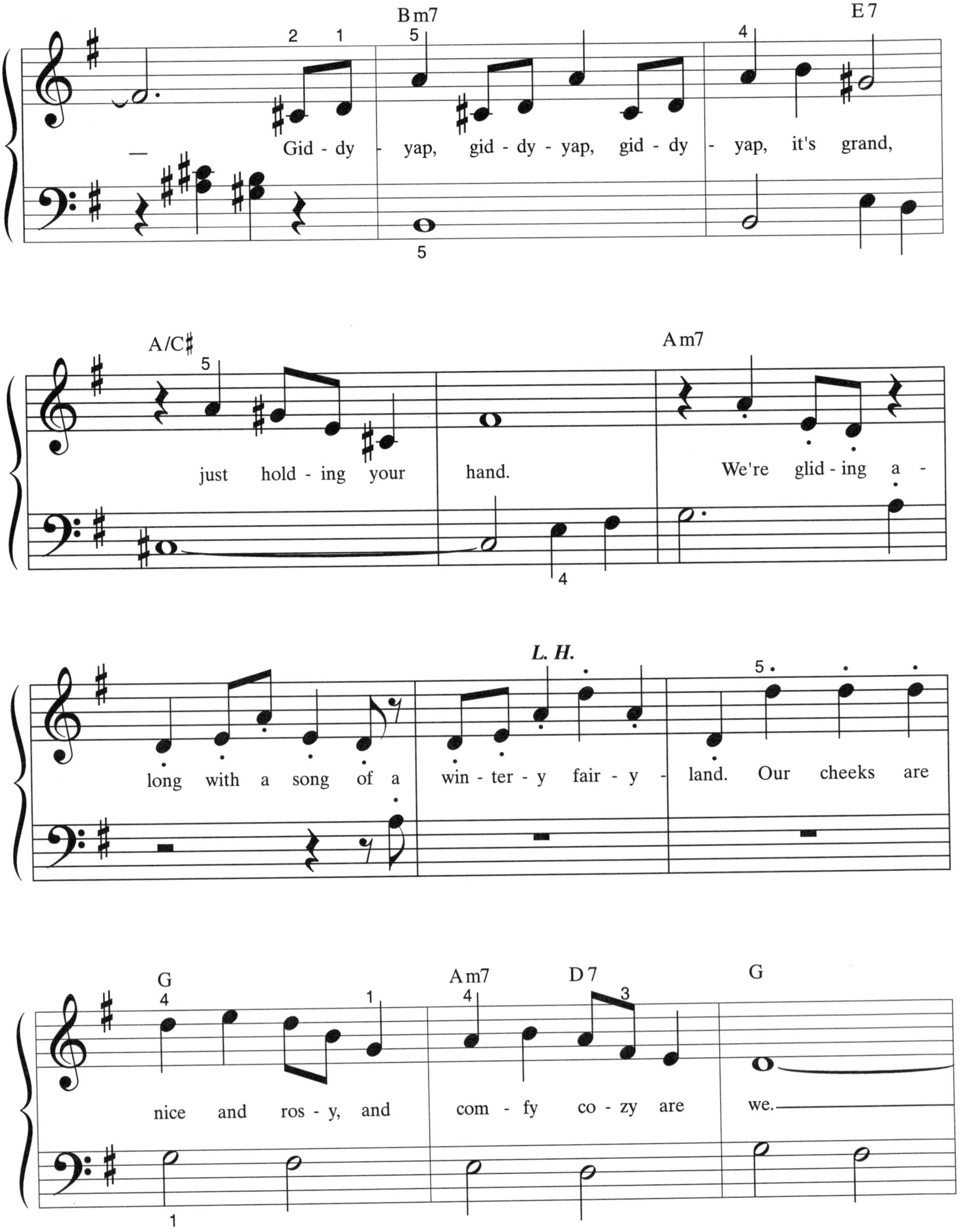
Bm7
E7
— Gid - dy - yap, gid - dy - yap, gid - dy - yap, it's grand,
A/C♯
Am7
just hold - ing your hand. We're glid - ing a -
L. H.
long with a song of a win - ter - y fair - y - land. Our cheeks are
G
Am7
D7
G
nice and ros - y, and com - fy co - zy are we.

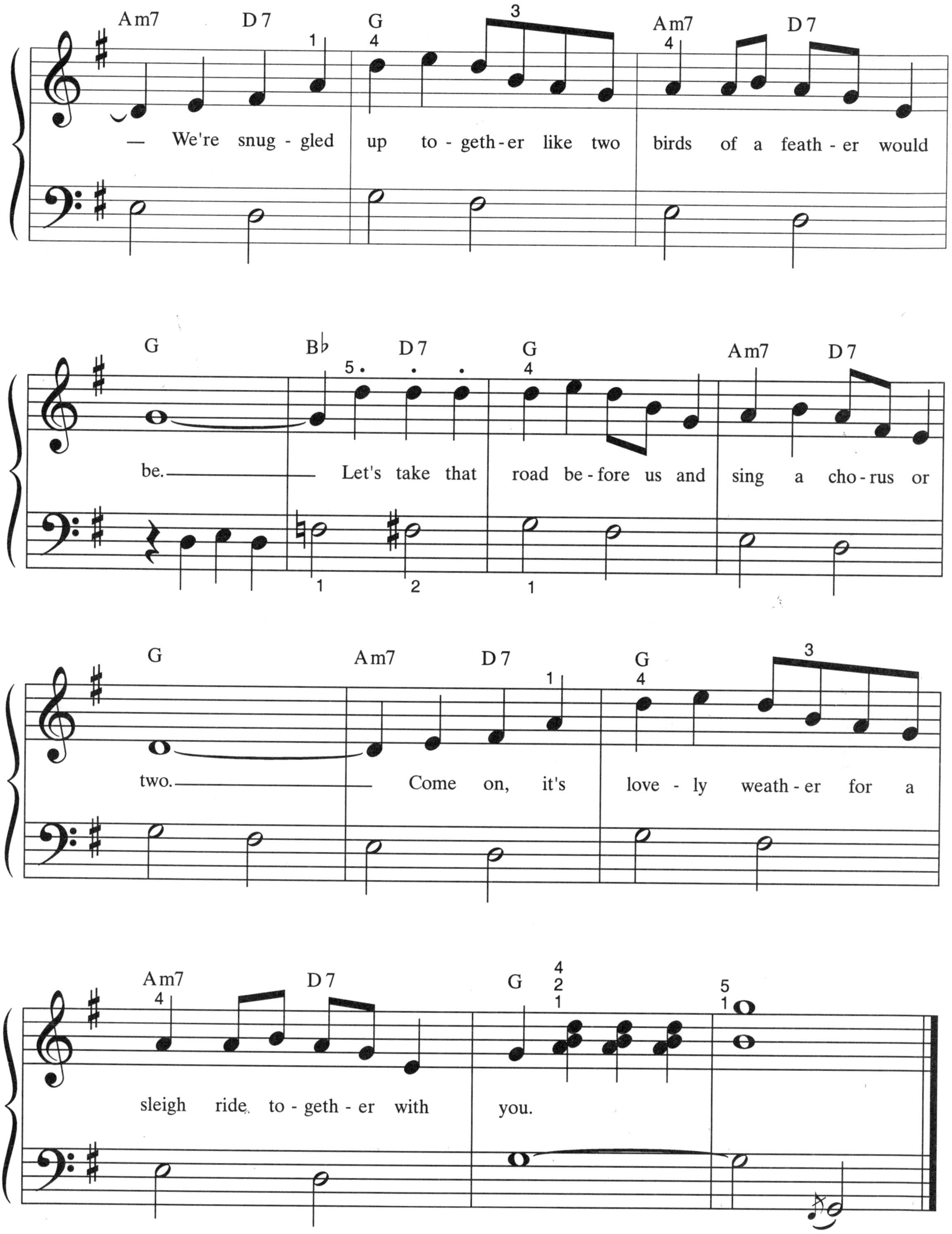
Am7 D7 G Am7 D7
— We're snug - gled up to - geth - er like two birds of a feath - er would
G B♭ D7 G Am7 D7
be. Let's take that road be - fore us and sing a cho - rus or
G Am7 D7 G
two. Come on, it's love - ly weath - er for a
Am7 D7 G
sleigh ride to - geth - er with you.

Jingle Bells

By
J. PIERPONT
Arranged by Richard Bradley

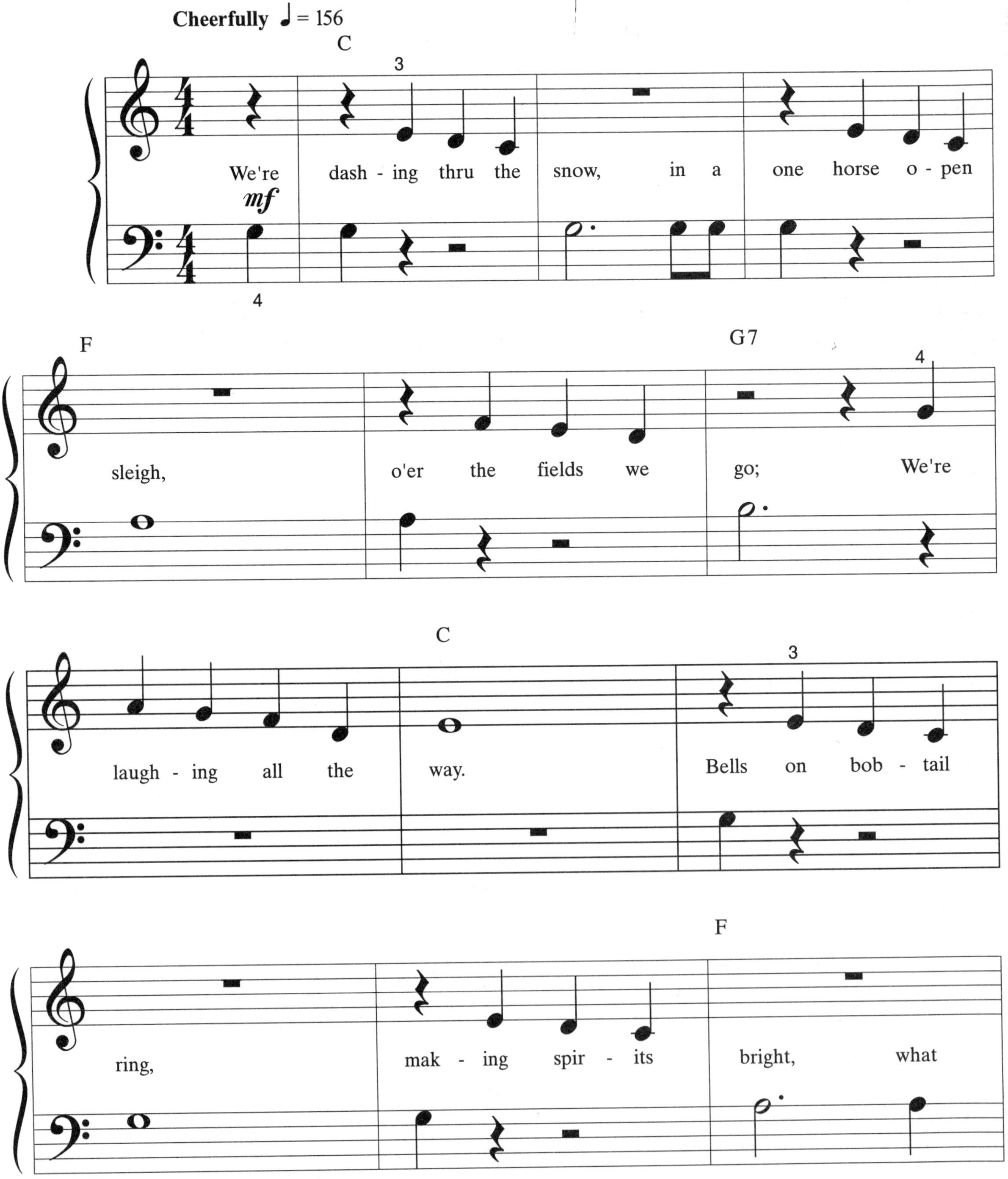
Cheerfully ♩ = 156
C
G7
F
mf
We're dash - ing thru the snow, in a one horse o - pen
sleigh, o'er the fields we go; We're
laugh - ing all the way. Bells on bob - tail
ring, mak - ing spir - its bright, what

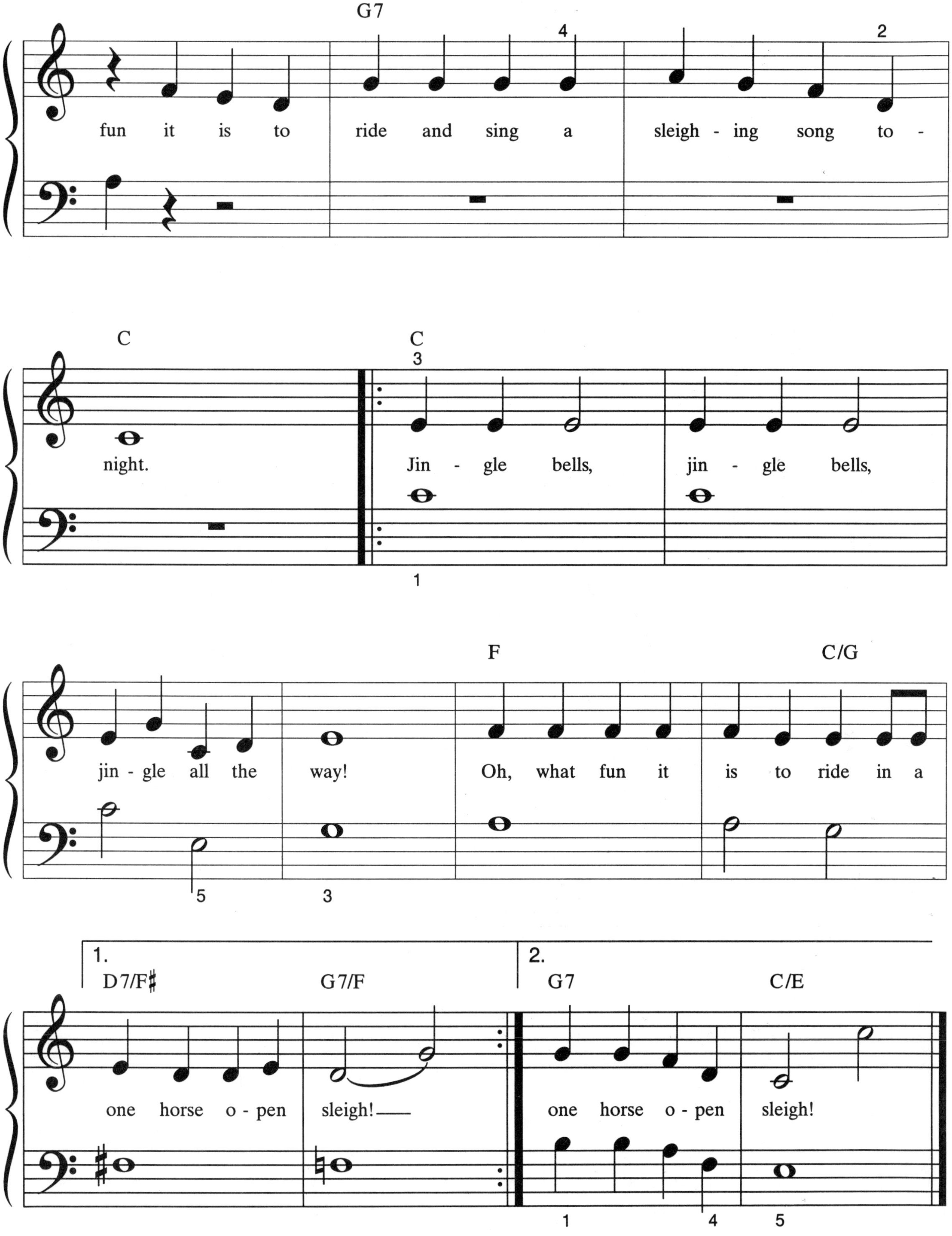
G7
4
2
fun it is to ride and sing a sleigh - ing song to -
C
C
3
night.
Jin - gle bells, jin - gle bells,
1
F
C/G
jin - gle all the way! Oh, what fun it is to ride in a
5
3
1.
D7/F♯
G7/F
2.
G7
C/E
one horse o - pen sleigh!
one horse o - pen sleigh!
1
4
5

Jingle-Bell Rock

Words and Music by
JOE BEAL and JIM BOOTHE
Arranged by Richard Bradley

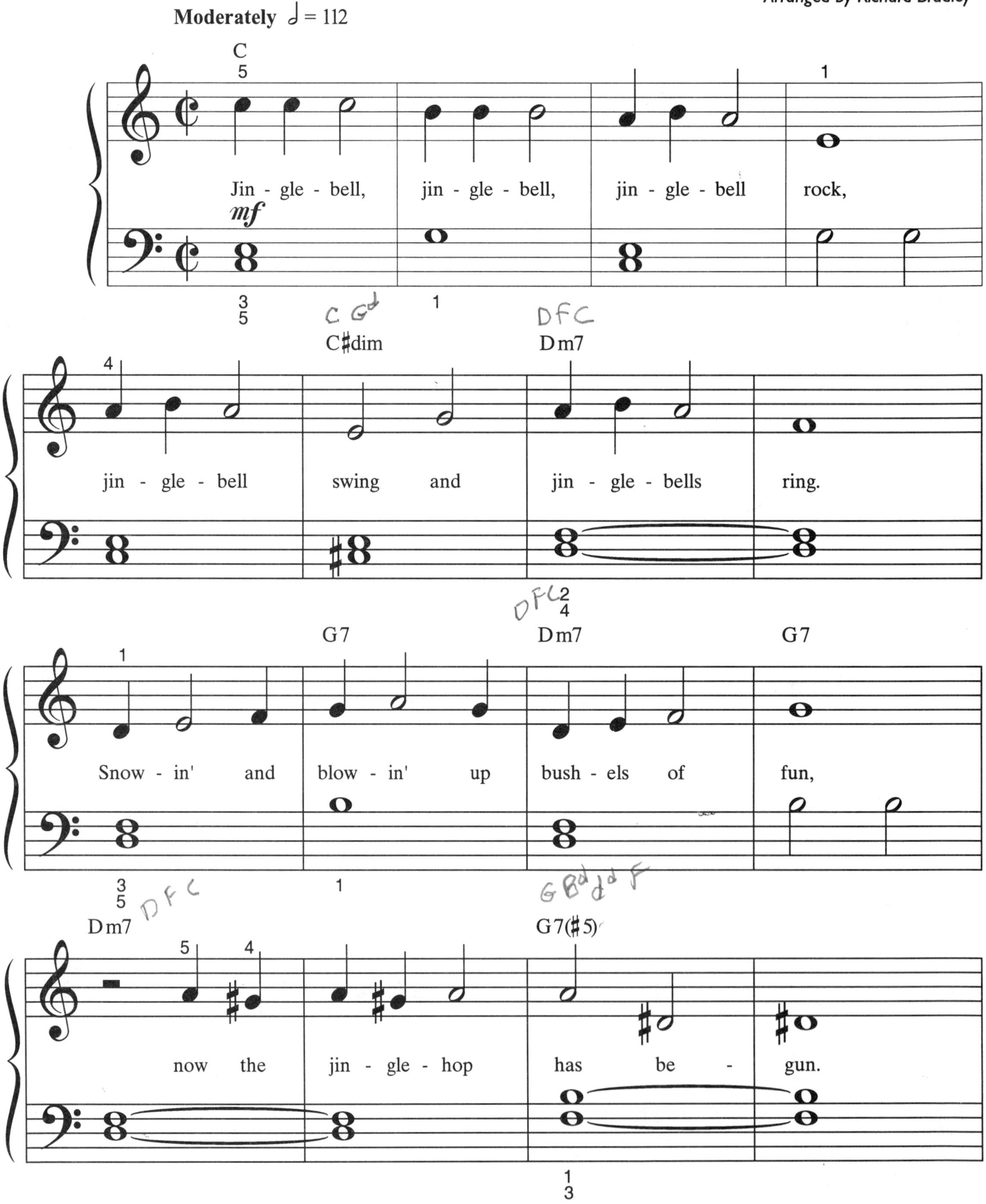
Moderately 𝅗𝅥 = 112
C
Jin - gle - bell, jin - gle - bell, jin - gle - bell rock,
mf
C♯dim
Dm7
jin - gle - bell swing and jin - gle - bells ring.
G7
Dm7
G7
Snow - in' and blow - in' up bush - els of fun,
Dm7
G7(♯5)
now the jin - gle - hop has be - gun.

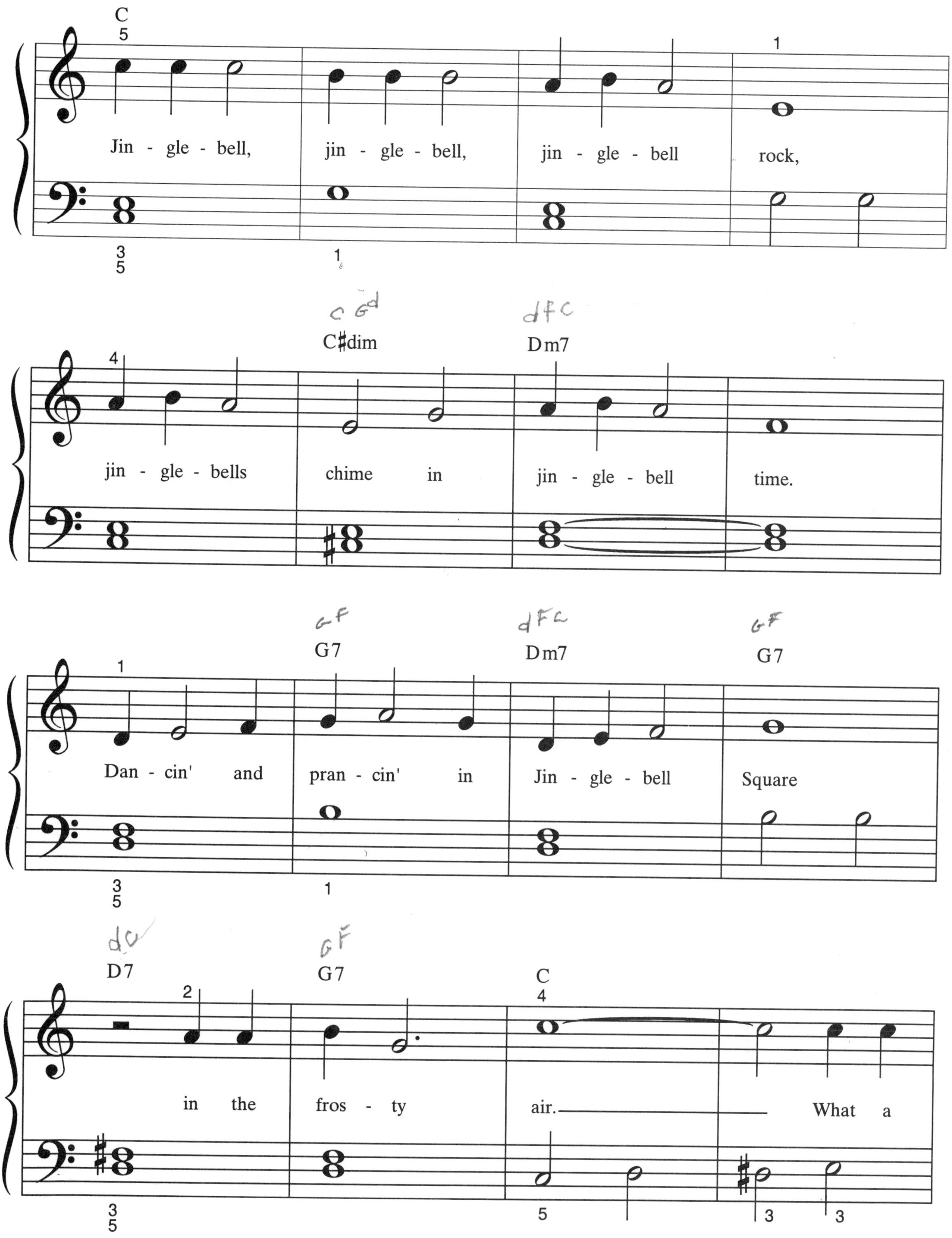
C
Jin - gle - bell, jin - gle - bell, jin - gle - bell rock,
C♯dim
Dm7
jin - gle - bells chime in jin - gle - bell time.
G7
Dm7
G7
Dan - cin' and pran - cin' in Jin - gle - bell Square
D7
G7
C
in the fros - ty air. What a

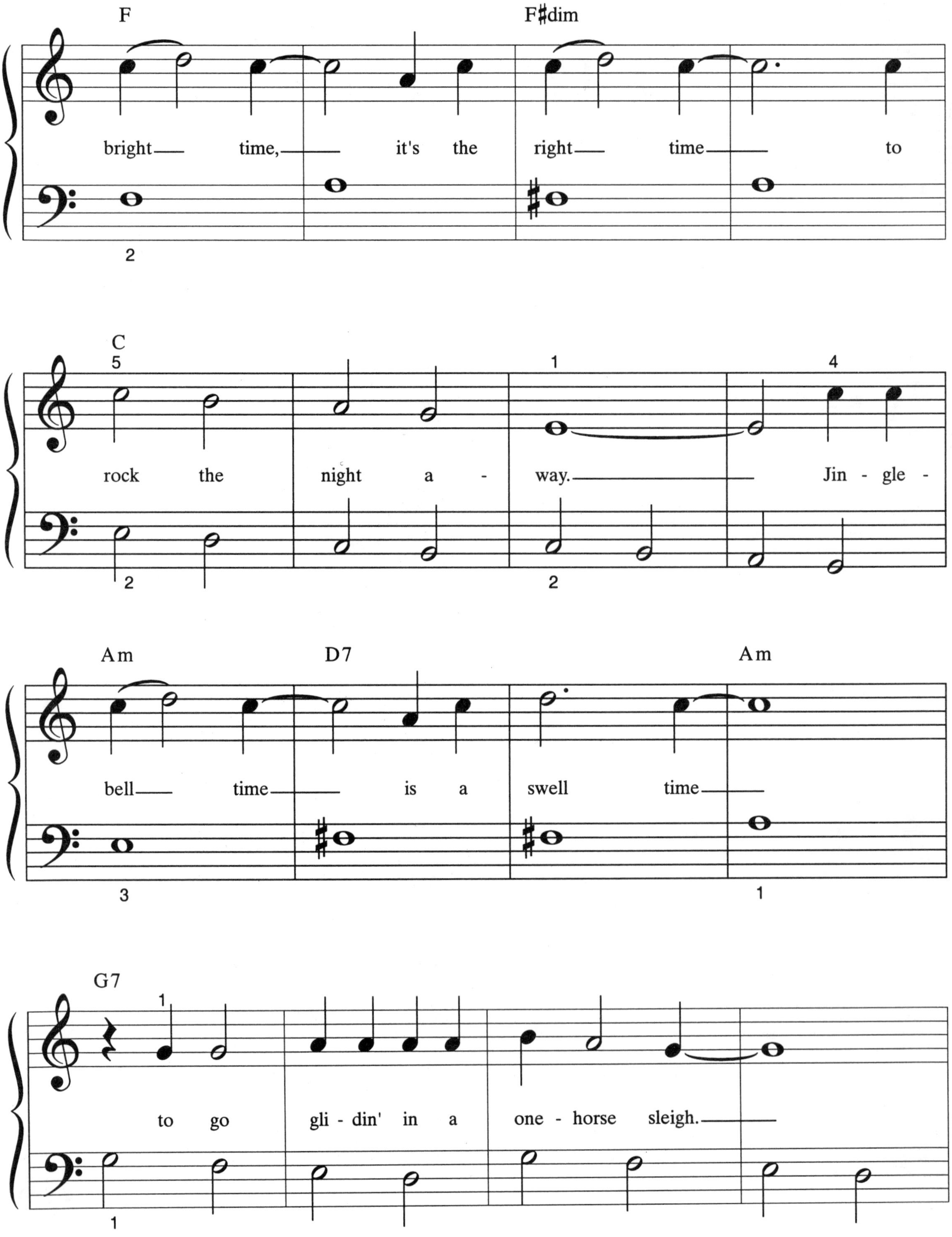
F
F♯dim
bright time, it's the right time to
C
rock the night a - way. Jin - gle -
Am
D7
Am
bell time is a swell time
G7
to go gli - din' in a one - horse sleigh.

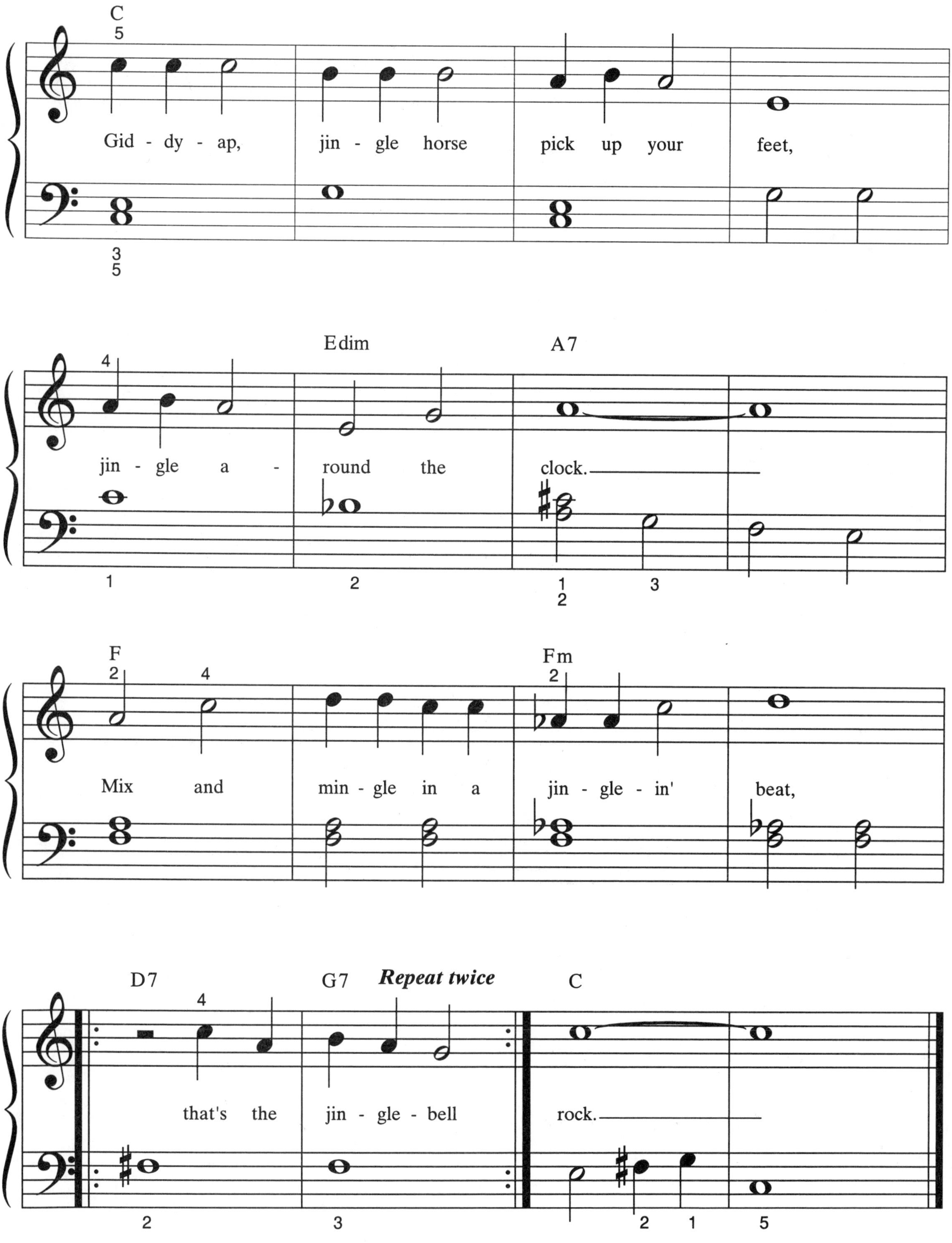
C
Gid - dy - ap, jin - gle horse pick up your feet,
Edim A7
jin - gle a - round the clock.
F Fm
Mix and min - gle in a jin - gle - in' beat,
D7 G7 Repeat twice C
that's the jin - gle - bell rock.

Where Are You Christmas?

From the Universal Motion Picture
Dr. Seuss' How the Grinch Stole Christmas

Words and Music by
JAMES HORNER, WILL JENNINGS
and MARIAH CAREY
Arranged by Richard Bradley

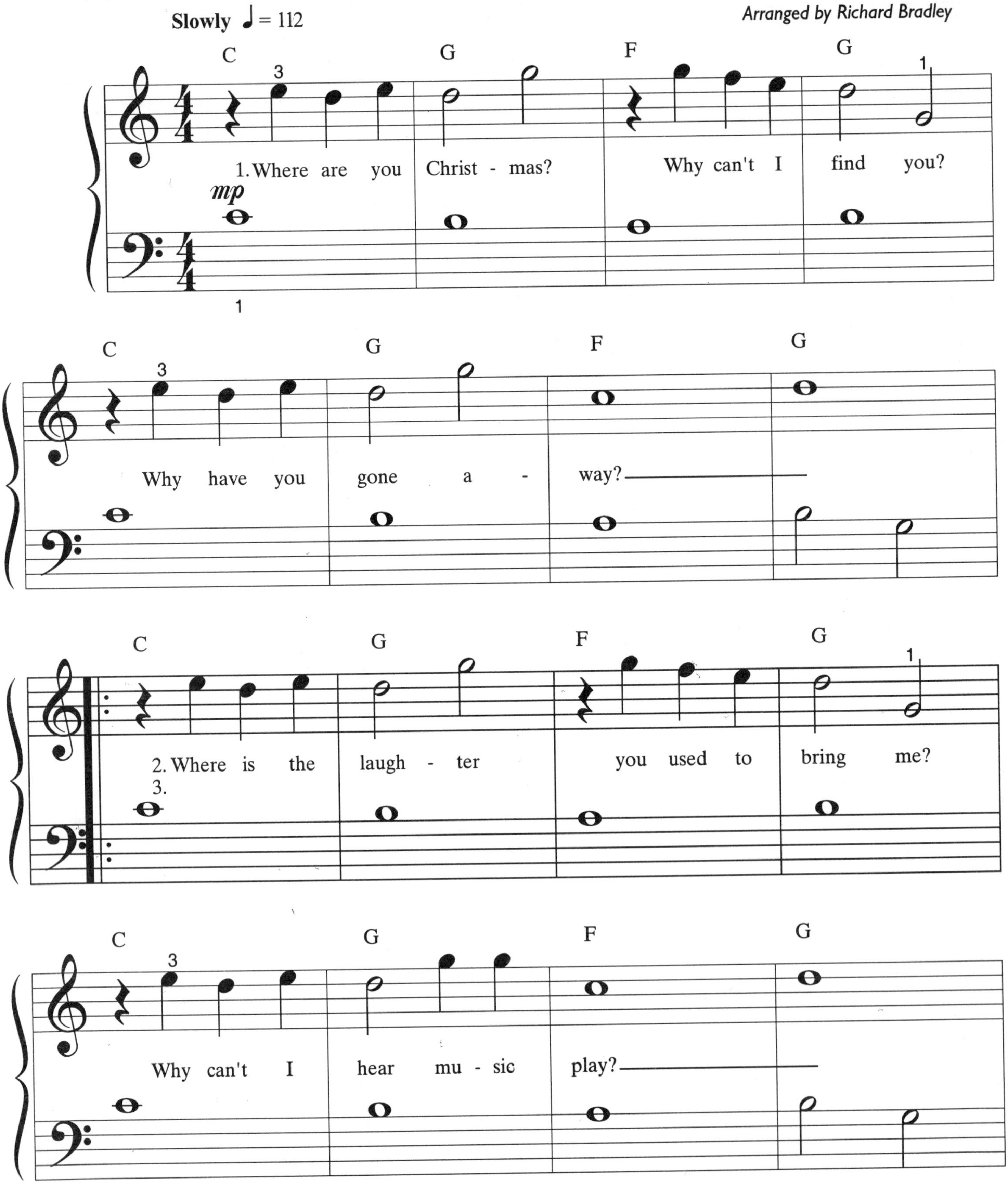
Slowly ♩ = 112
C G F G
mp
1. Where are you Christ - mas? Why can't I find you?
Why have you gone a - way?
2. Where is the laugh - ter you used to bring me?
3.
Why can't I hear mu - sic play?

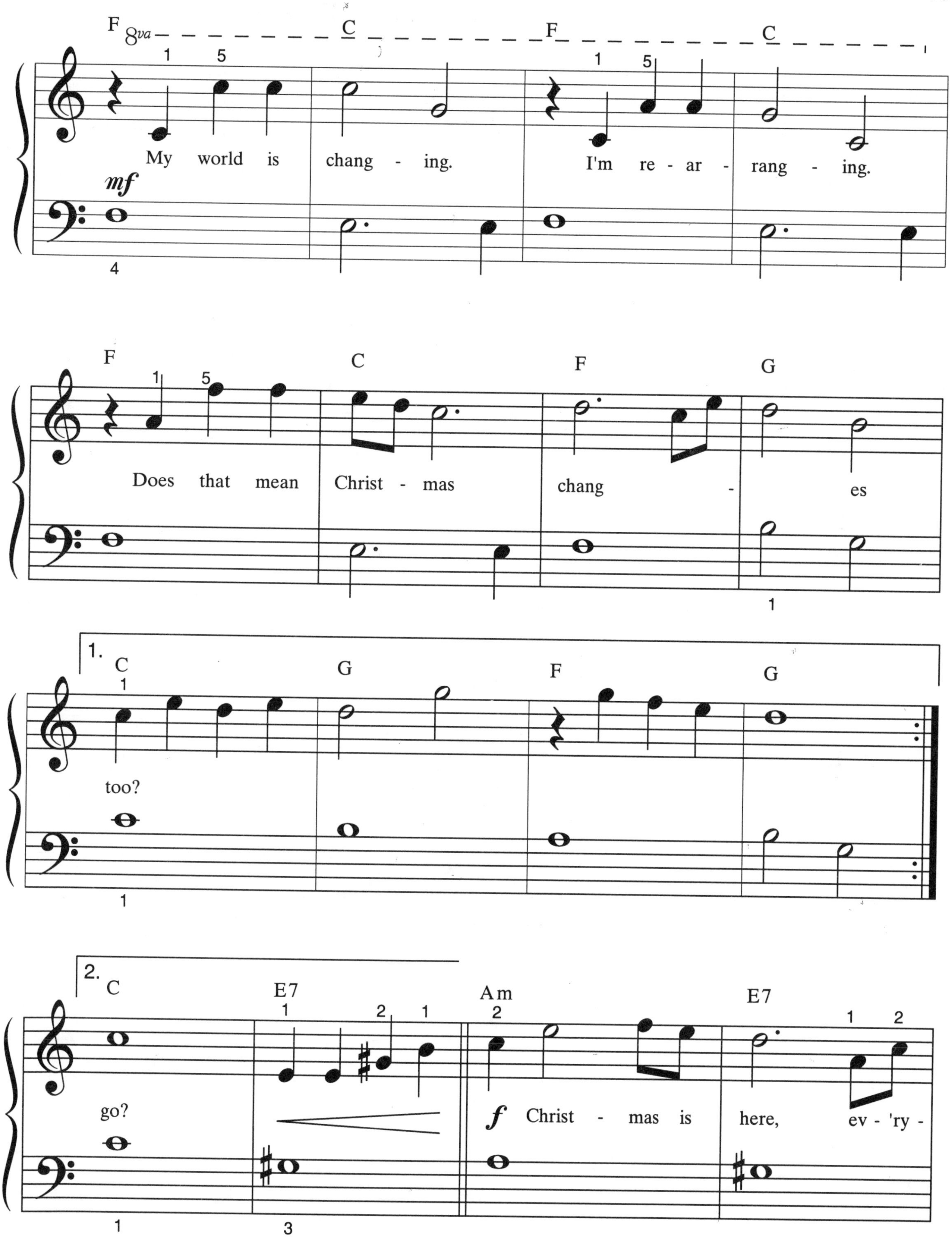
F 8va C F C
My world is chang - ing. I'm re - ar - rang - ing.
mf
F C F G
Does that mean Christ - mas chang - es
1.
C G F G
too?
2.
C E7 Am E7
go?
f Christ - mas is here, ev - 'ry -

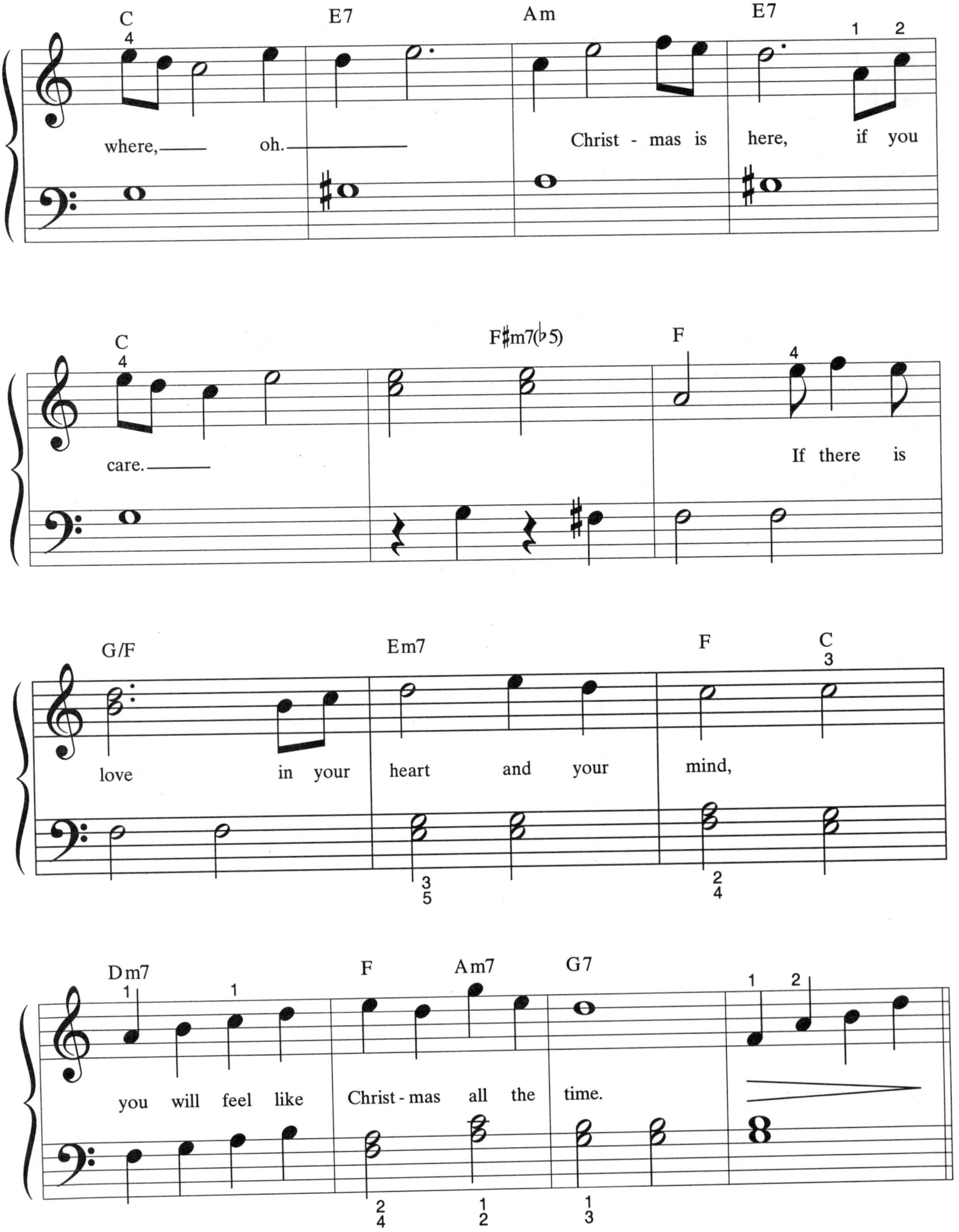
C E7 Am E7
where, oh. Christ - mas is here, if you
C F♯m7(♭5) F
care. If there is
G/F Em7 F C
love in your heart and your mind,
Dm7 F Am7 G7
you will feel like Christ - mas all the time.

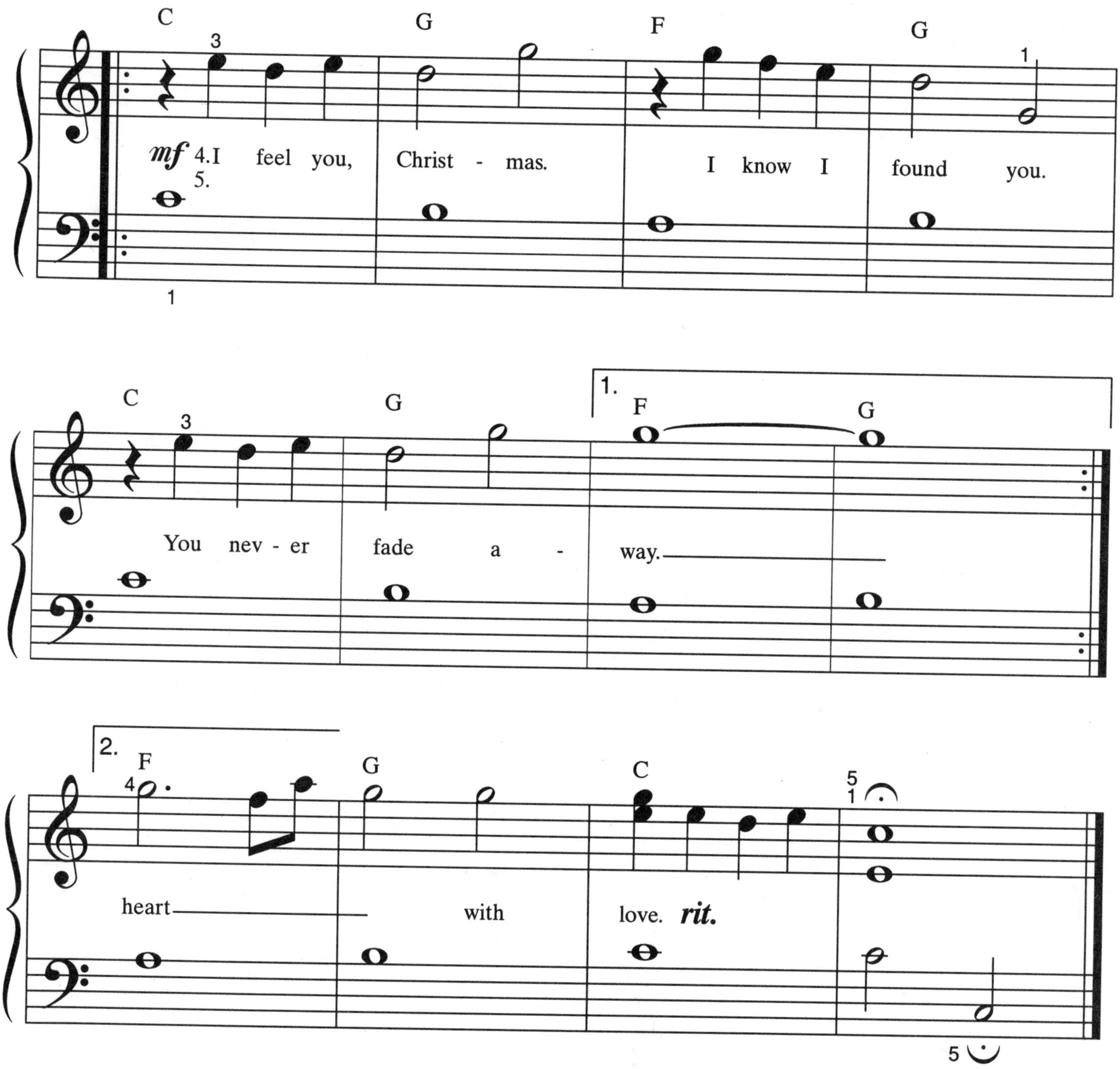
C G F G
mf 4.I feel you, Christ - mas. I know I found you.
5.
C G
You nev - er fade a - way.
1. F G
2. F G C
heart with love. rit.

Verse 3:
Where are you Christmas?
Do you remember
The one you used to know?
I'm not the same one.
See what the time's done.
Is that why you have let me go?
Oh,

Verse 5:
The joy of Christmas
Stays here inside us,
Fills each and every heart with love.

You're a Mean One, Mr. Grinch

From the Universal Motion Picture
Dr. Seuss' How the Grinch Stole Christmas

Lyrics by DR. SEUSS
Music by ALBERT HAGUE
Arranged by Richard Bradley

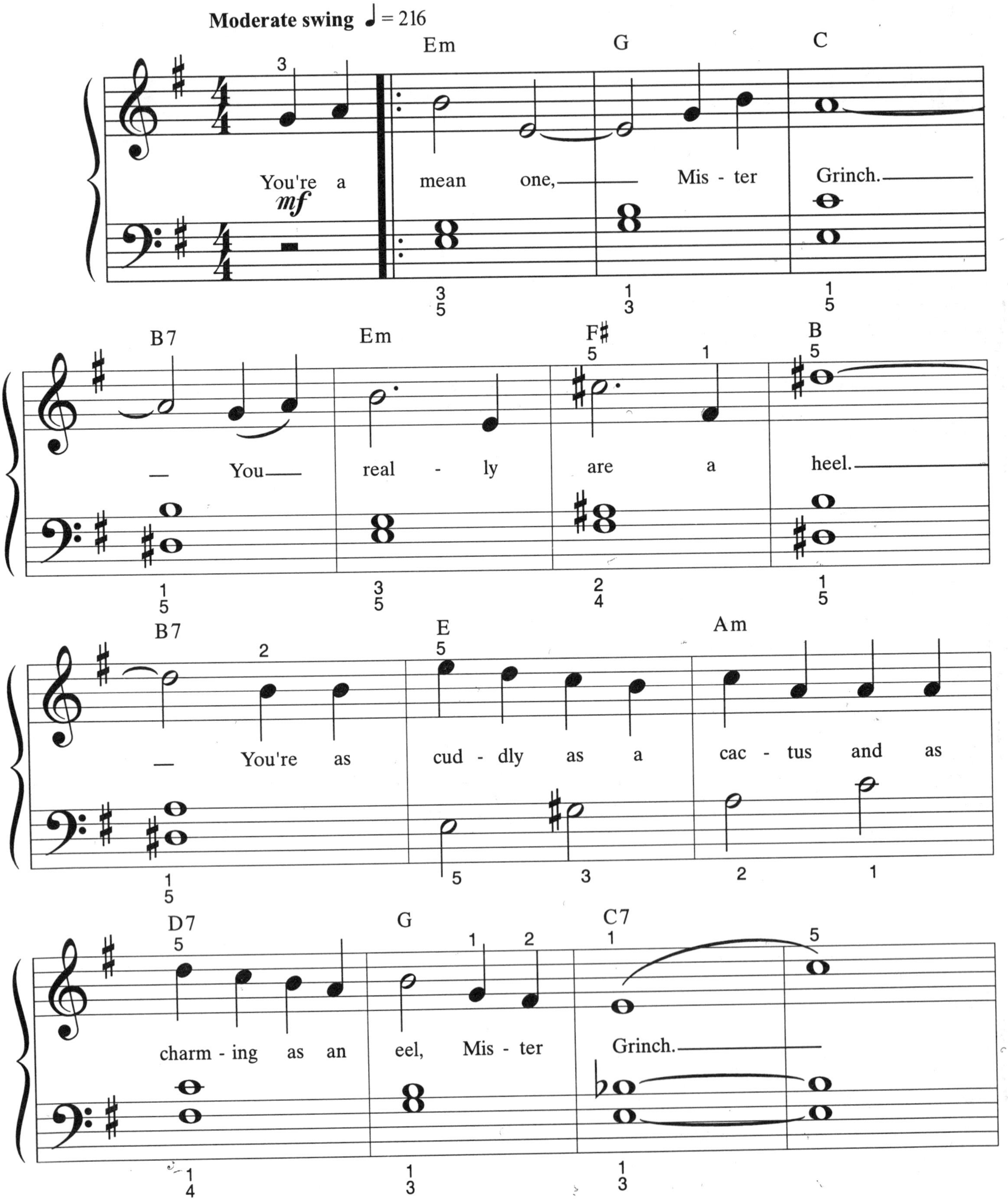
Moderate swing ♩ = 216
Em G C
You're a mean one, Mis - ter Grinch.
mf
B7 Em F♯ B
You real - ly are a heel.
B7 E Am
You're as cud - dly as a cac - tus and as
D7 G C7
charm - ing as an eel, Mis - ter Grinch.

F♯
You're a bad ba - na - na with a
1. 2.
B7
greas - y black
Em
peel.
You're a
3.
B7
sea - sick croc - o - dile.
Em

Verse 2:
Just face the music.
You're a monster, Mr. Grinch.
Yes you are.
Your heart's an empty hole.
Your brain is full of spiders,
You got garlic in your soul, Mr. Grinch.
I wouldn't touch you with a
Thirty-nine-and -a- half-foot pole.

Verse 3:
You're a vile one, Mr. Grinch.
You have termites in your smile.
You have all the tender sweetness
Of a seasick crocodile, Mr. Grinch.
Given the choice between you,
I'd take the seasick crocodile.

Pat-a-Pan

TRADITIONAL
Arranged by Richard Bradley

Cheerfully ♩ = 142
Am
mf
Wil - lie, take your lit - tle drum, Rob - in, bring your fife and come. When we play the fife and drum, Tu - re - lu - re - lu, pat - a - pat - a - pan. When we hear the fife and drum, Christ - mas should be

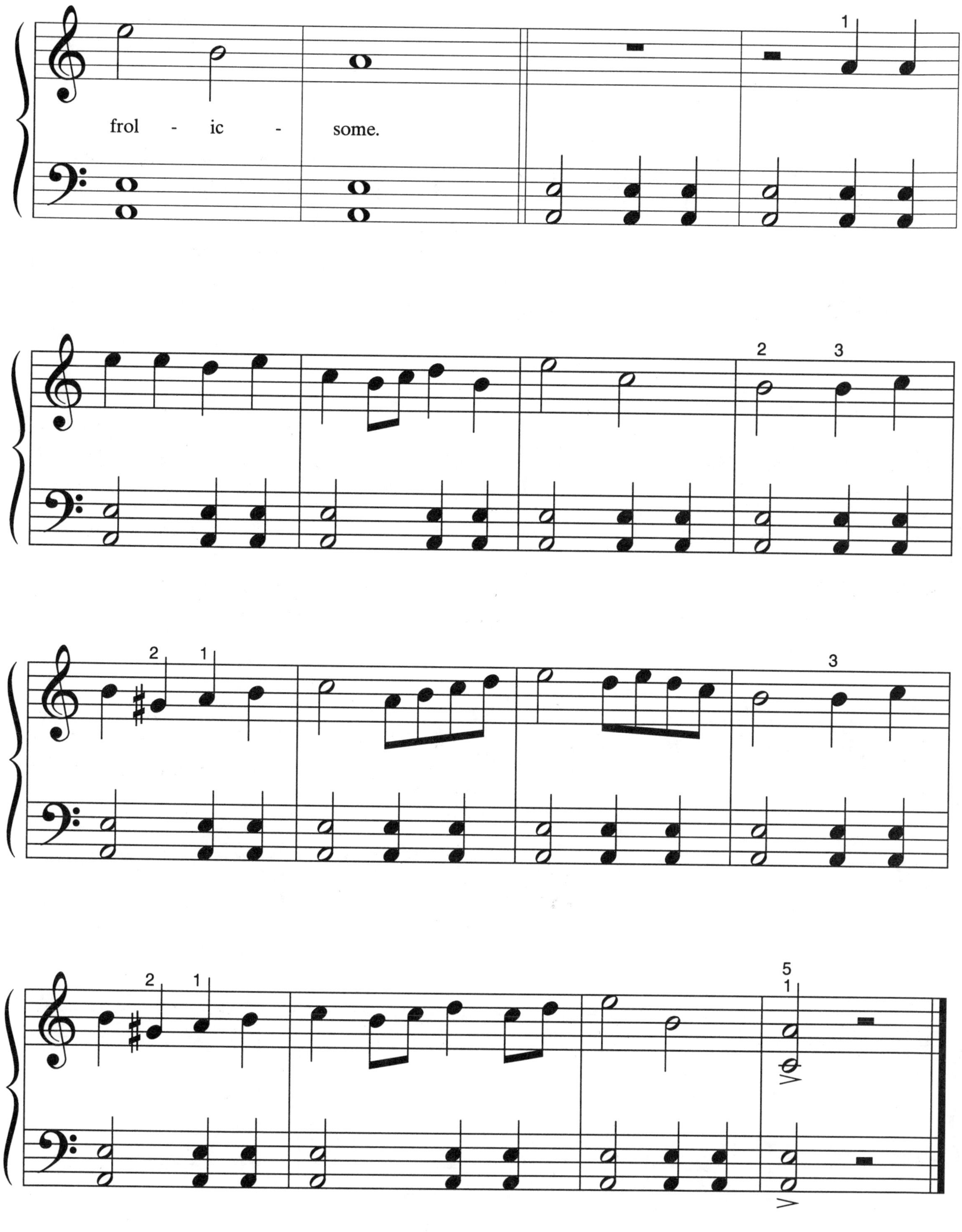
frol - ic - some.

Fum, Fum, Fum

TRADITIONAL
Arranged by Richard Bradley

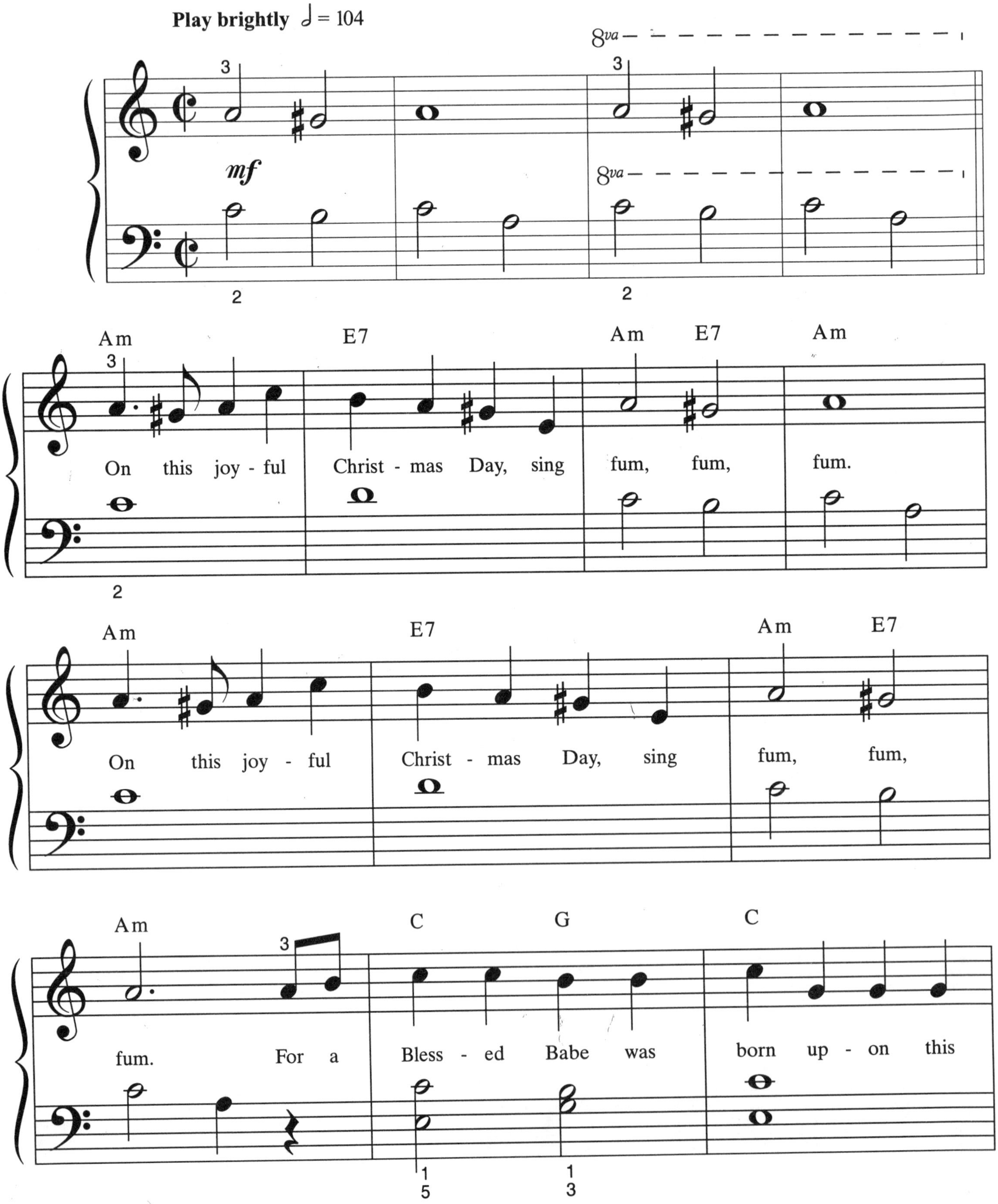

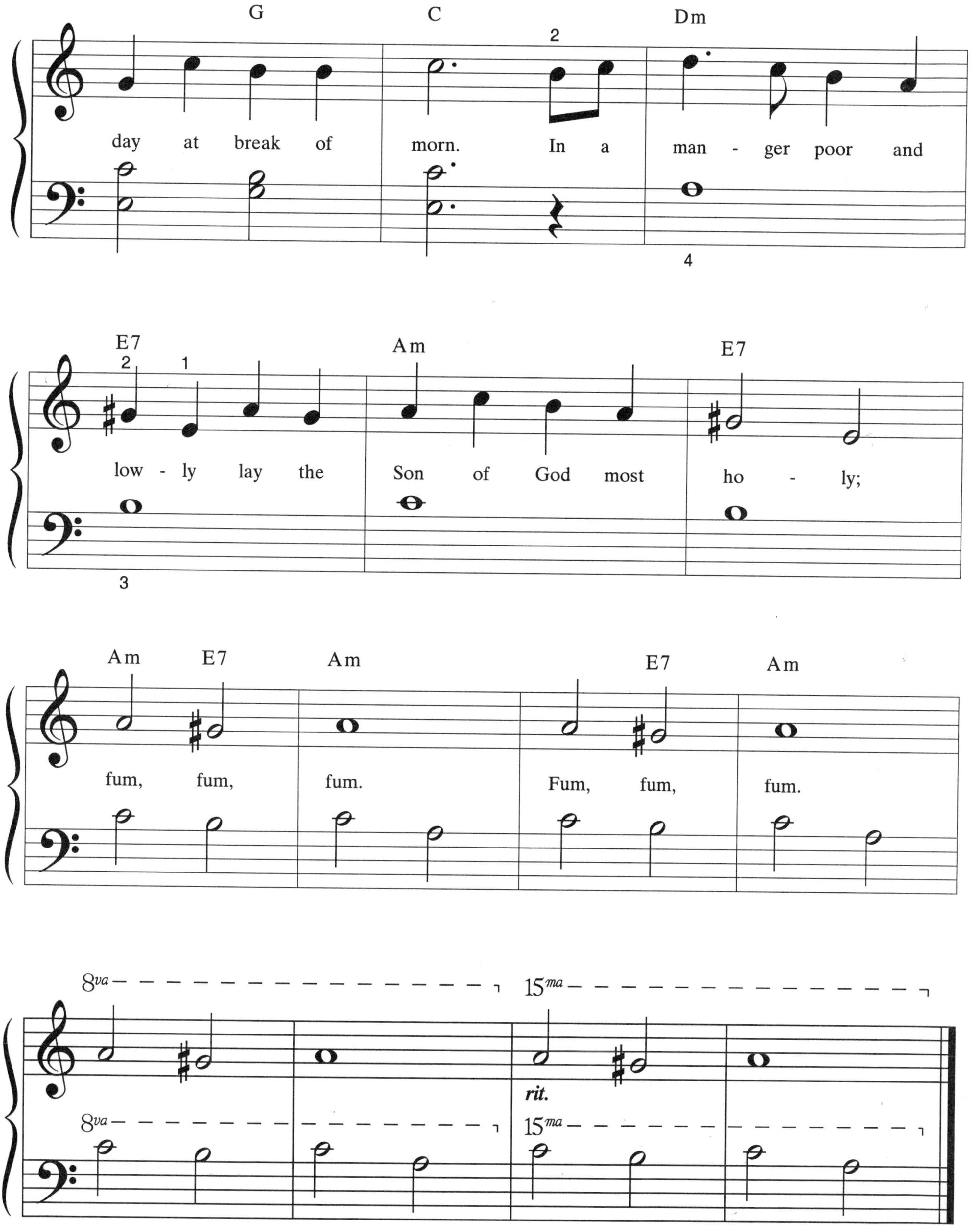
G C Dm
day at break of morn. In a man - ger poor and
E7 Am E7
low - ly lay the Son of God most ho - ly;
Am E7 Am E7 Am
fum, fum, fum. Fum, fum, fum.
8va
15ma
rit.

Go Tell It on the Mountain

TRADITIONAL SPIRITUAL
Arranged by Richard Bradley

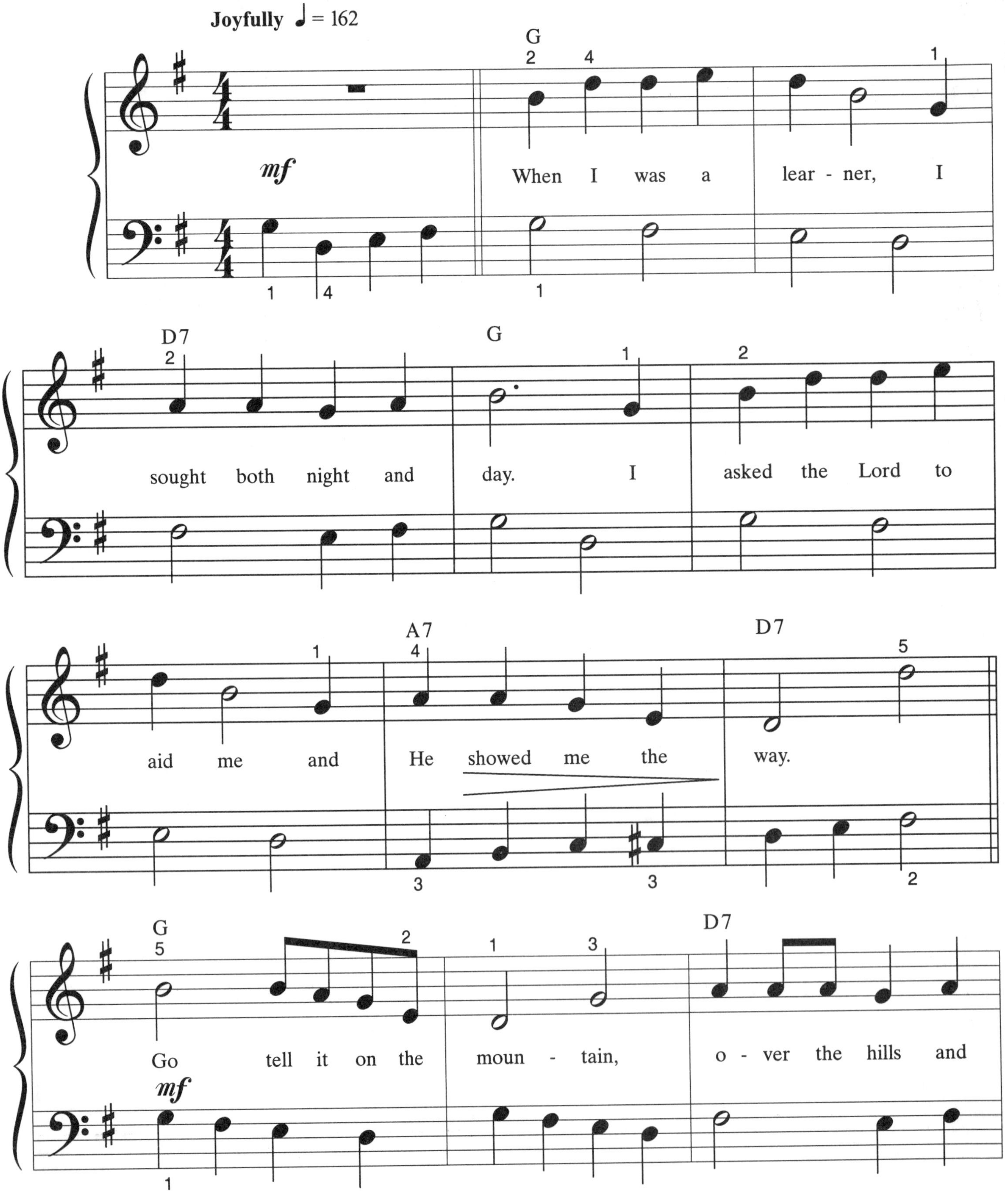

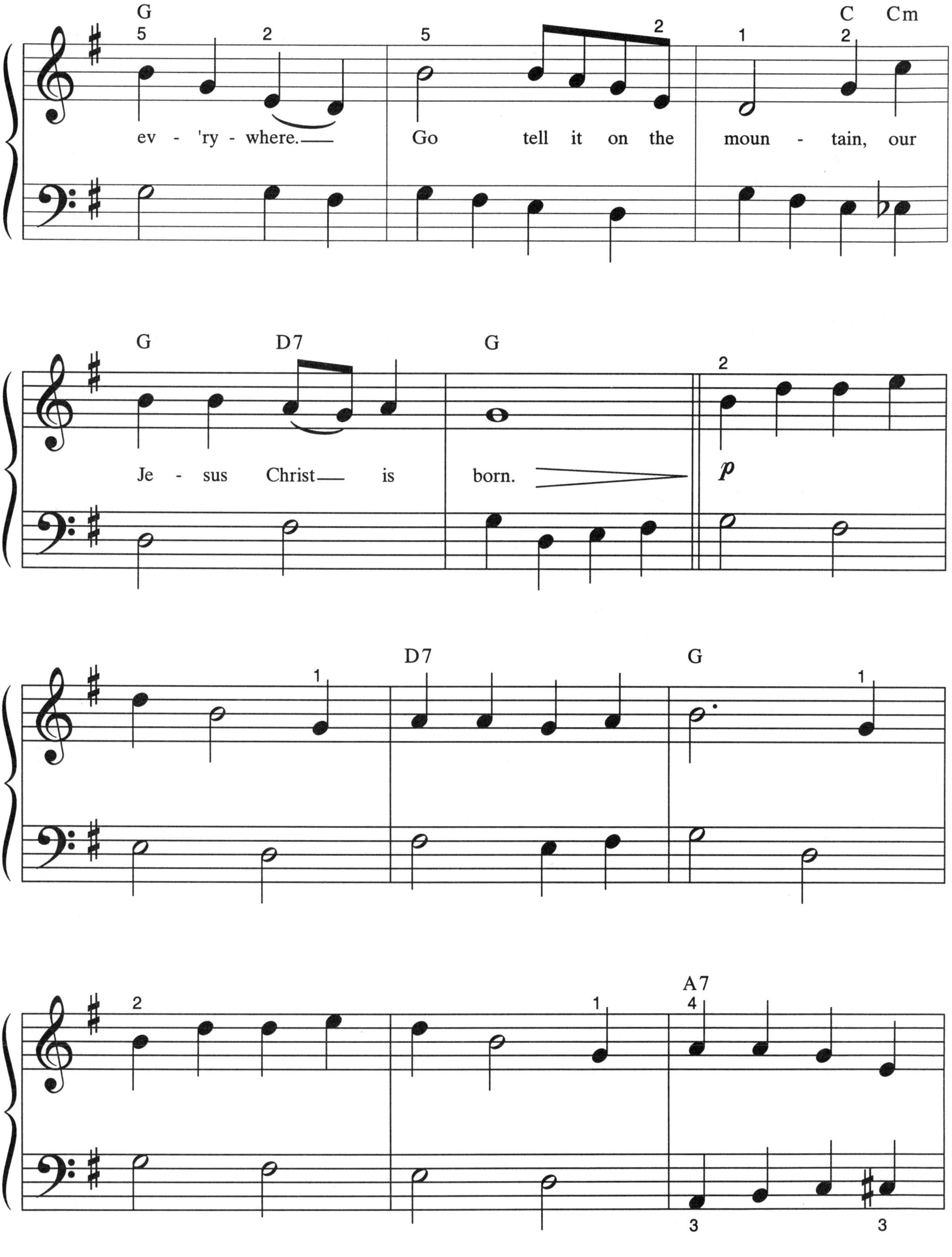
G
ev - 'ry - where.
Go tell it on the
C Cm
moun - tain, our
G D7
Je - sus Christ is
G
born.
p
D7
G
A7

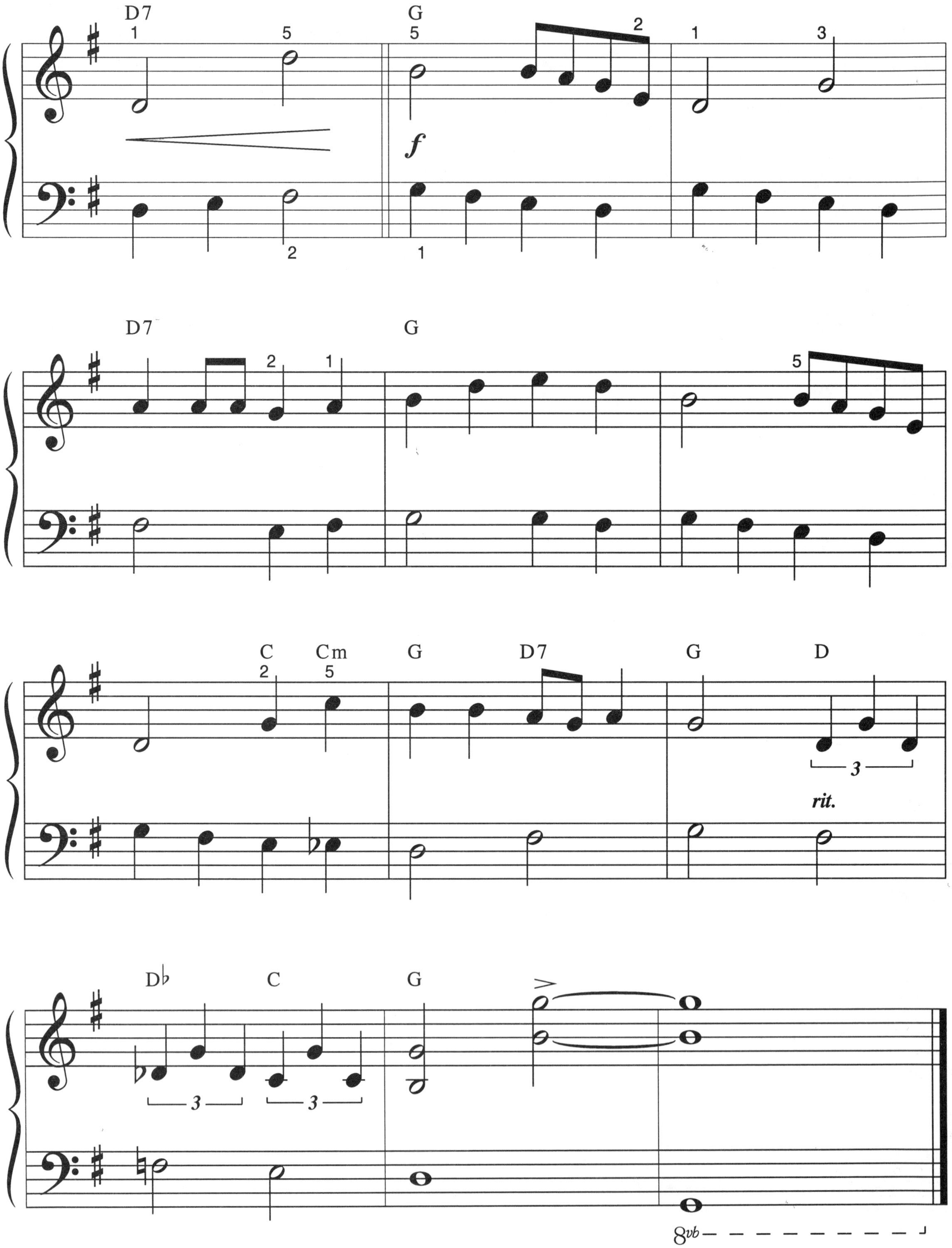
D7
G
f
D7
G
C
Cm
G
D7
G
D
rit.
D♭
C
G
8vb

Jolly Old Saint Nicholas

TRADITIONAL
Arranged by Richard Bradley

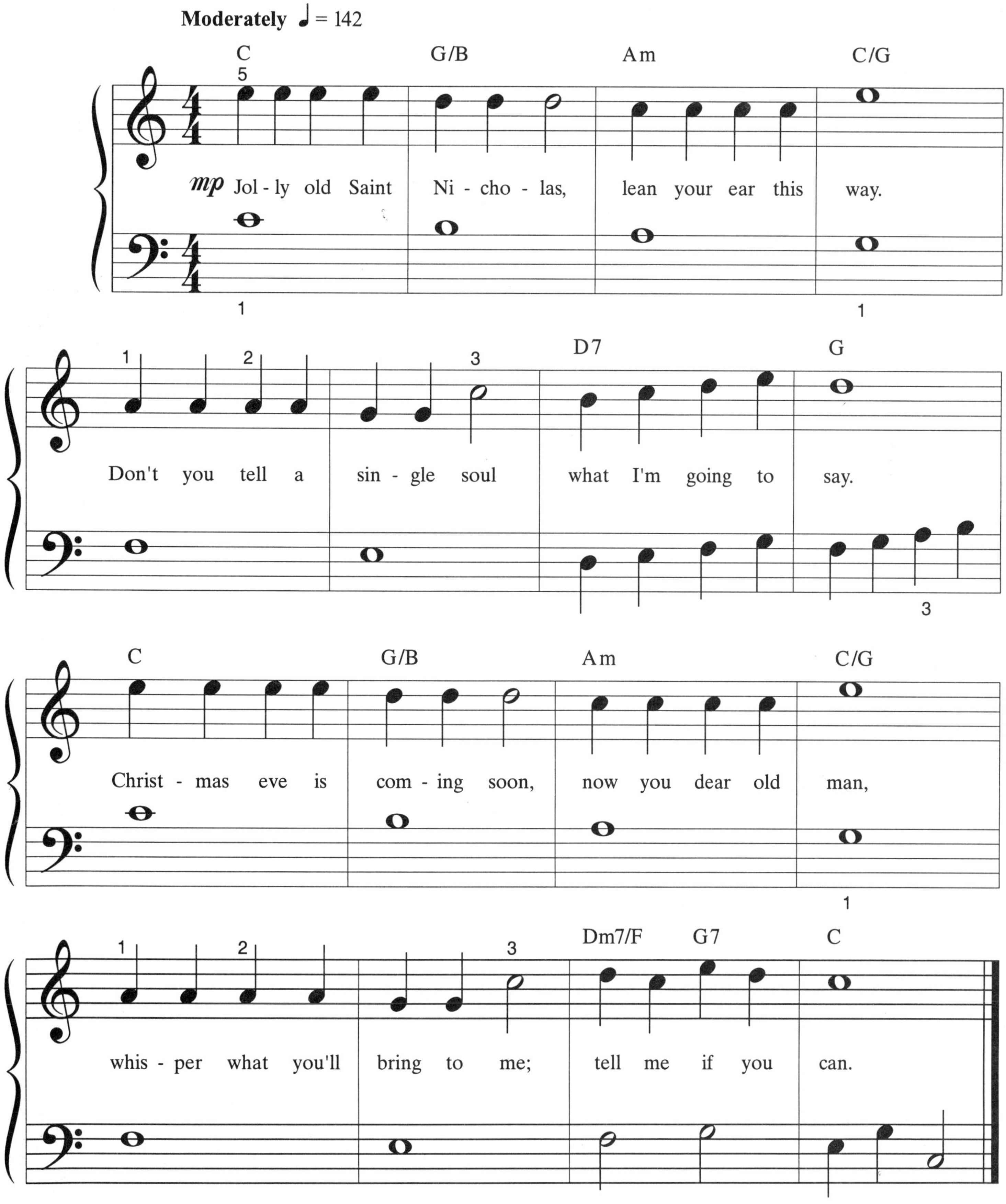
Moderately ♩ = 142
C G/B Am C/G
mp
Jol - ly old Saint Ni - cho - las, lean your ear this way.
D7 G
Don't you tell a sin - gle soul what I'm going to say.
C G/B Am C/G
Christ - mas eve is com - ing soon, now you dear old man,
Dm7/F G7 C
whis - per what you'll bring to me; tell me if you can.

Winter Wonderland

Words by
DICK SMITH

Music by
FELIX BERNARD
Arranged by Richard Bradley

Moderately ♩ = 124
C
Sleigh bells ring, are you lis - t'nin'? In the
G7
lane, snow is glis - t'nin', a beau - ti - ful sight, we're hap - py to - night,
D7 G7 C
walk - in' in a win - ter won - der - land! Gone a - way is the
G7
blue - bird. Here to stay is a new bird. He sings a love song as
He's sing - ing a song as

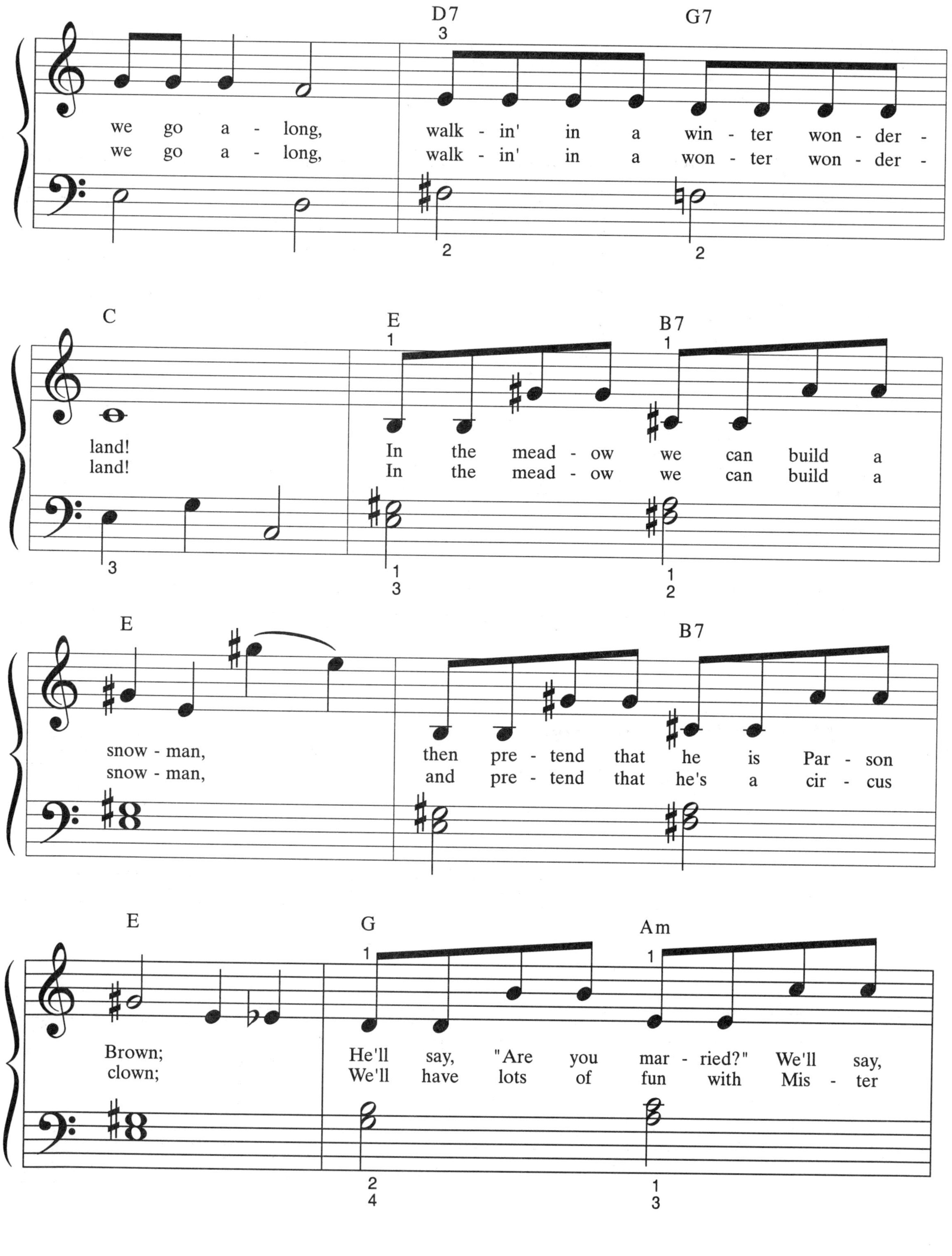
D7 G7
3
we go a - long,
we go a - long,
walk - in' in a win - ter won - der -
walk - in' in a won - ter won - der -
2 2
C E B7
1 1
land!
land!
In the mead - ow we can build a
In the mead - ow we can build a
3 1 1
3 2
E B7
snow - man,
snow - man,
then pre - tend that he is Par - son
and pre - tend that he's a cir - cus
E G Am
1 1
Brown;
clown;
He'll say, "Are you mar - ried?" We'll say,
We'll have lots of fun with Mis - ter
2 1
4 3

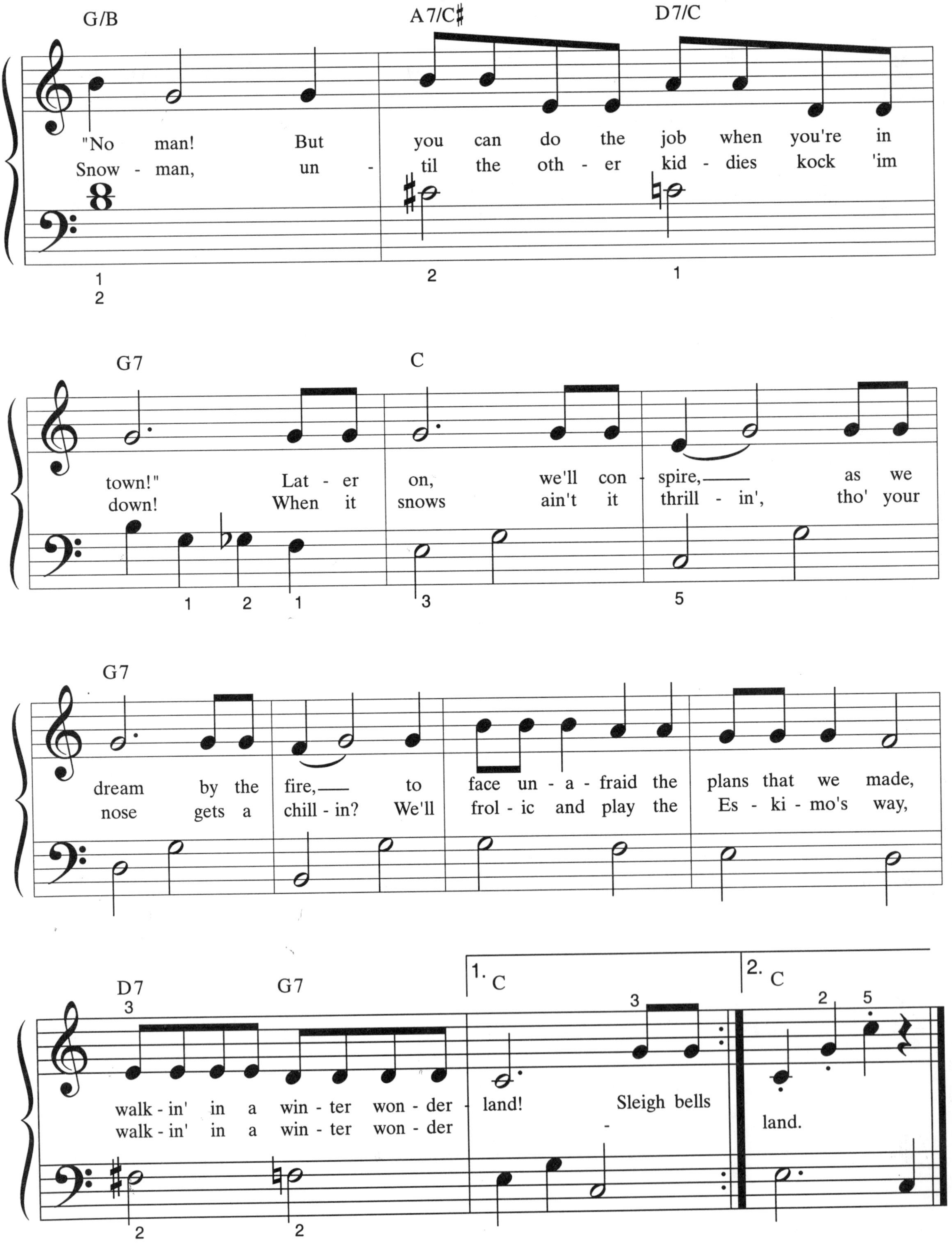
G/B A7/C♯ D7/C
"No man! But you can do the job when you're in
Snow - man, un - til the oth - er kid - dies kock 'im
G7 C
town!" Lat - er on, we'll con - spire, as we
down! When it snows ain't it thrill - in', tho' your
G7
dream by the fire, to face un - a - fraid the plans that we made,
nose gets a chill - in? We'll frol - ic and play the Es - ki - mo's way,
D7 G7 1. C 2. C
walk - in' in a win - ter won - der - land! Sleigh bells
walk - in' in a win - ter won - der - land.

Let It Snow! Let It Snow! Let It Snow!

Words by
SAMMY CAHN

Music by
JULE STYNE
Arranged by Richard Bradley

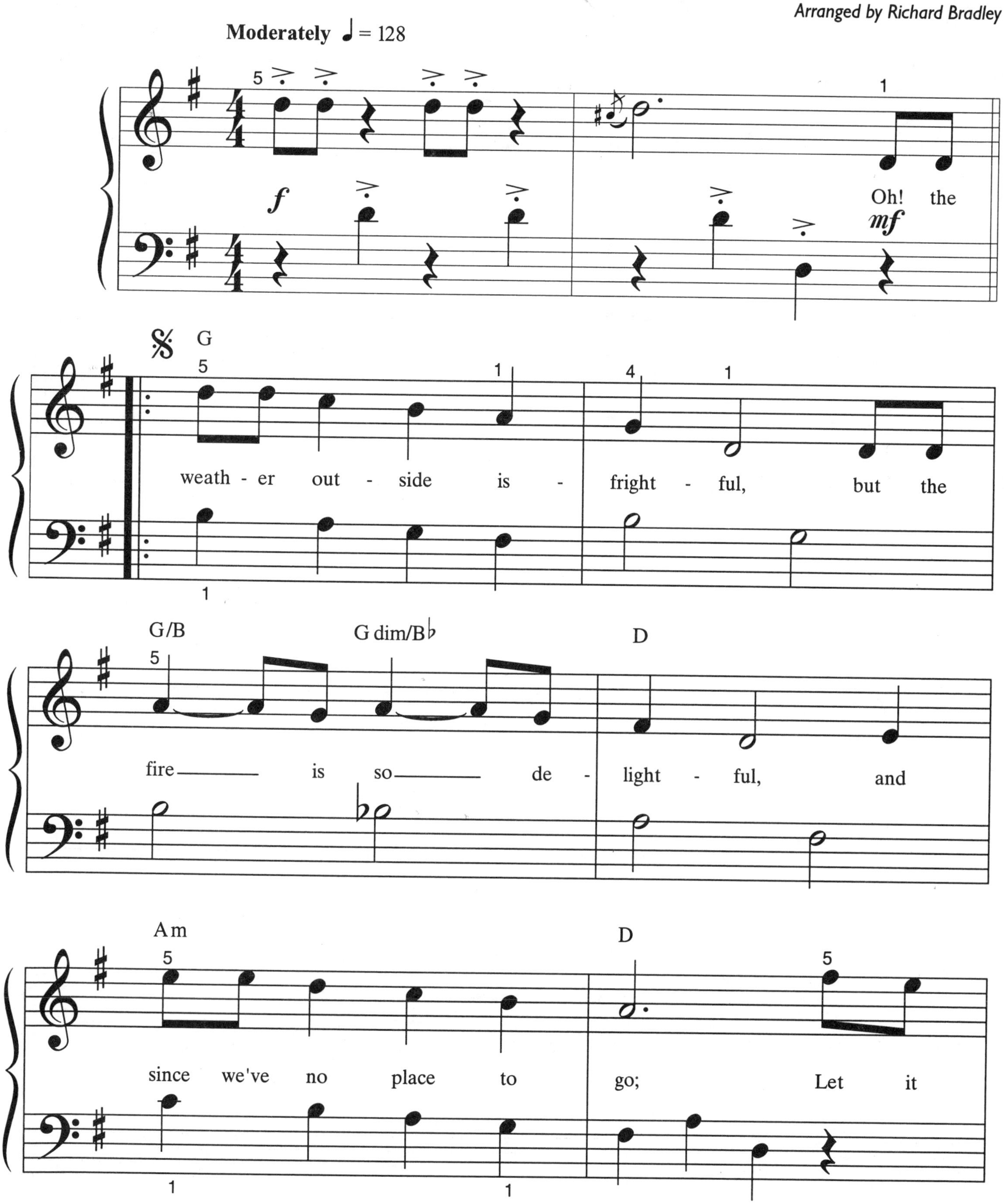
Moderately ♩ = 128
Oh! the
G
weath - er out - side is - fright - ful, but the
G/B
G dim/B♭
D
fire is so de - light - ful, and
Am
D
since we've no place to go; Let it

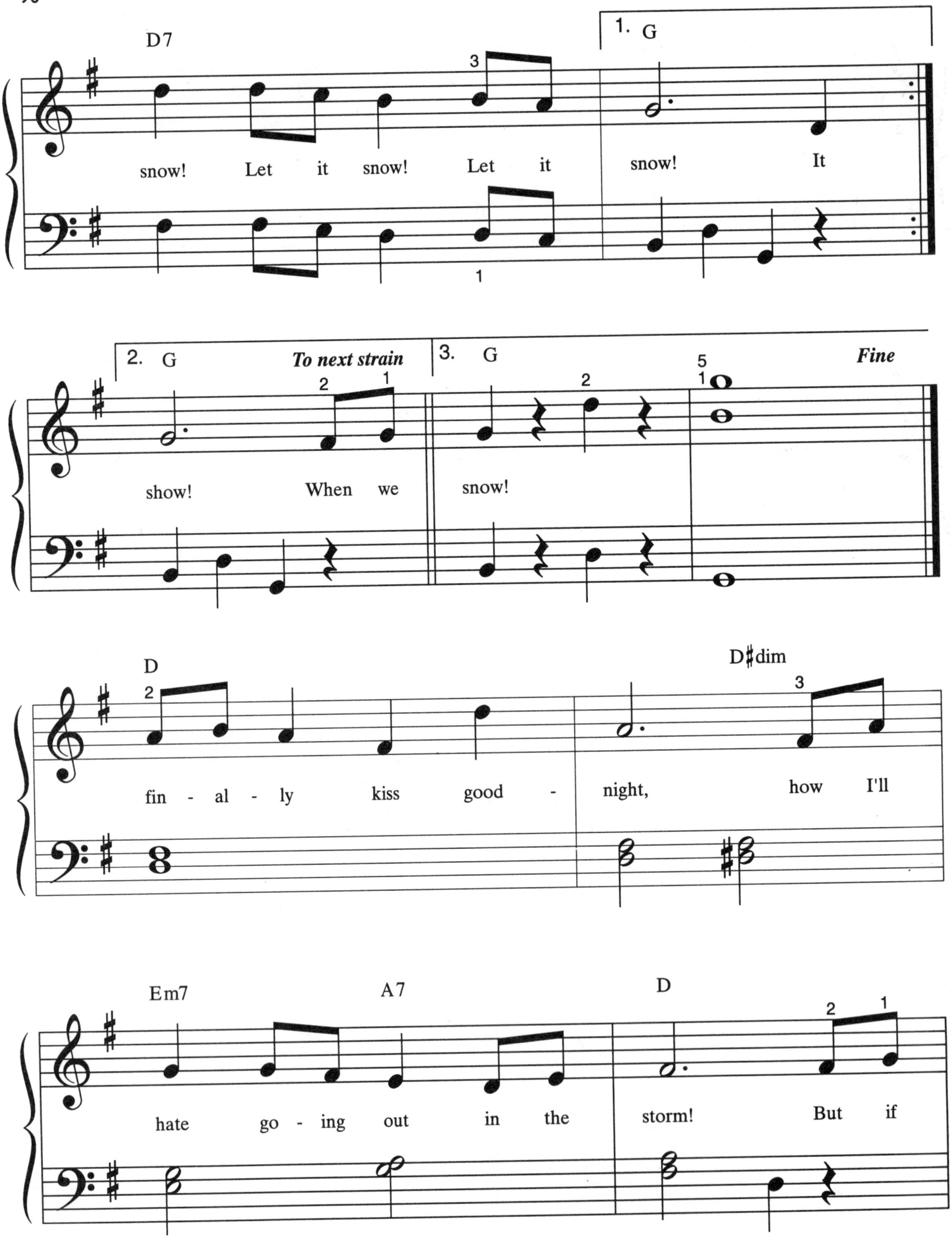
D7
1. G
3
snow! Let it snow! Let it snow! It
1
2. G
To next strain
3. G
Fine
2 1
2
5
1
show! When we
snow!
D
D♯dim
2
3
fin - al - ly kiss good - night, how I'll
Em7
A7
D
2 1
hate go - ing out in the storm! But if

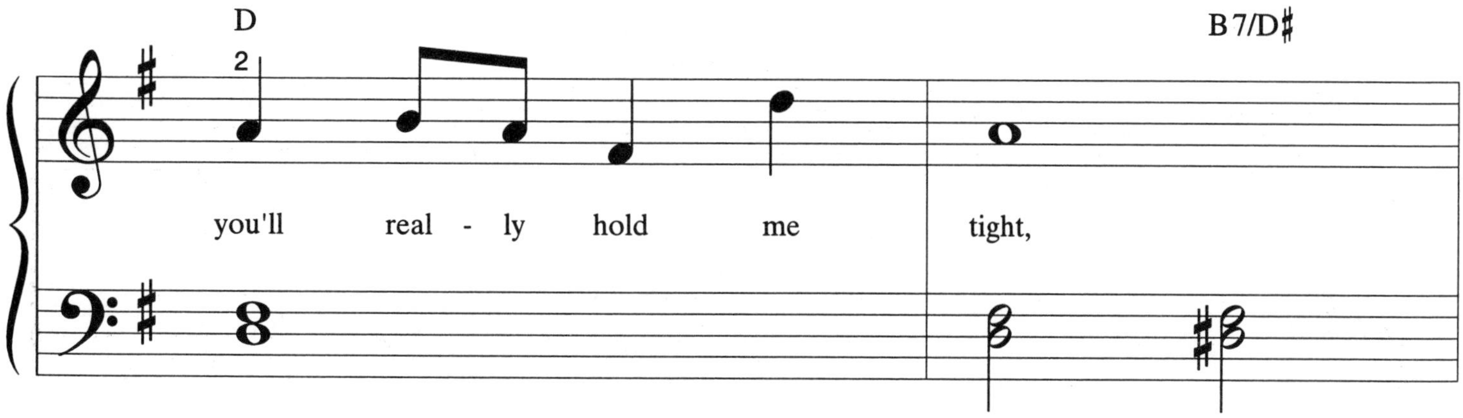
D
B7/D♯
2
you'll real - ly hold me
tight,

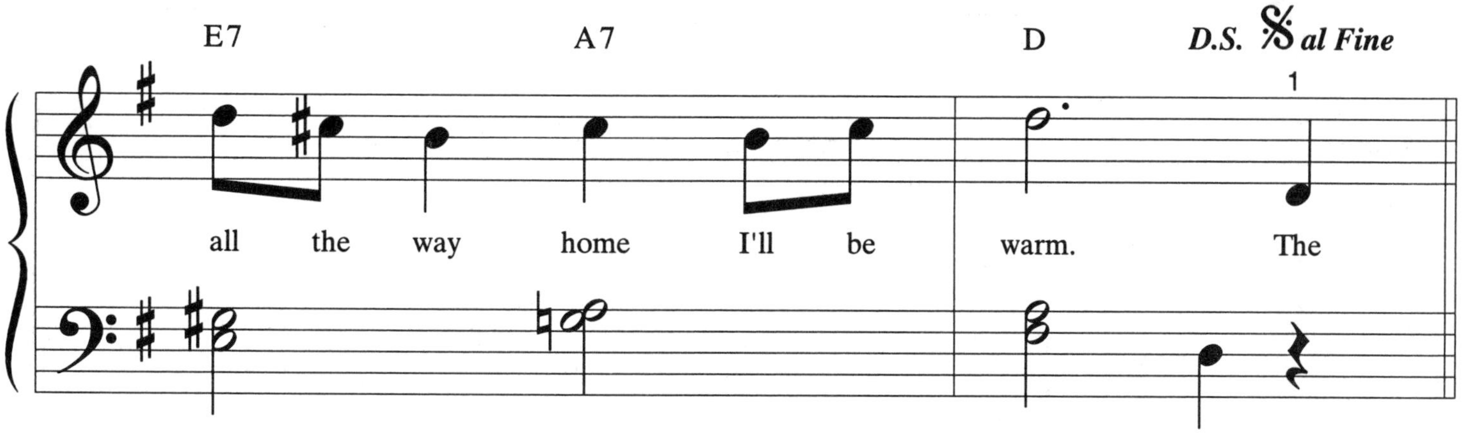
E7
A7
D
D.S. 𝄋 al Fine
1
all the way home I'll be
warm. The

Verse 2:
It doesn't show signs of stopping
And I brought some corn for popping;
The lights are turned way down low,
Let it snow! Let it snow! Let it snow!

Verse 3:
The fire is slowly dying,
And my dear, we're still goodbyeing.
But as long as you love me so,
Let it snow! Let it snow! Let it snow!

I'll Be Home for Christmas

Words by
KIM GANNON

Music by
WALTER KENT
Arranged by Richard Bradley

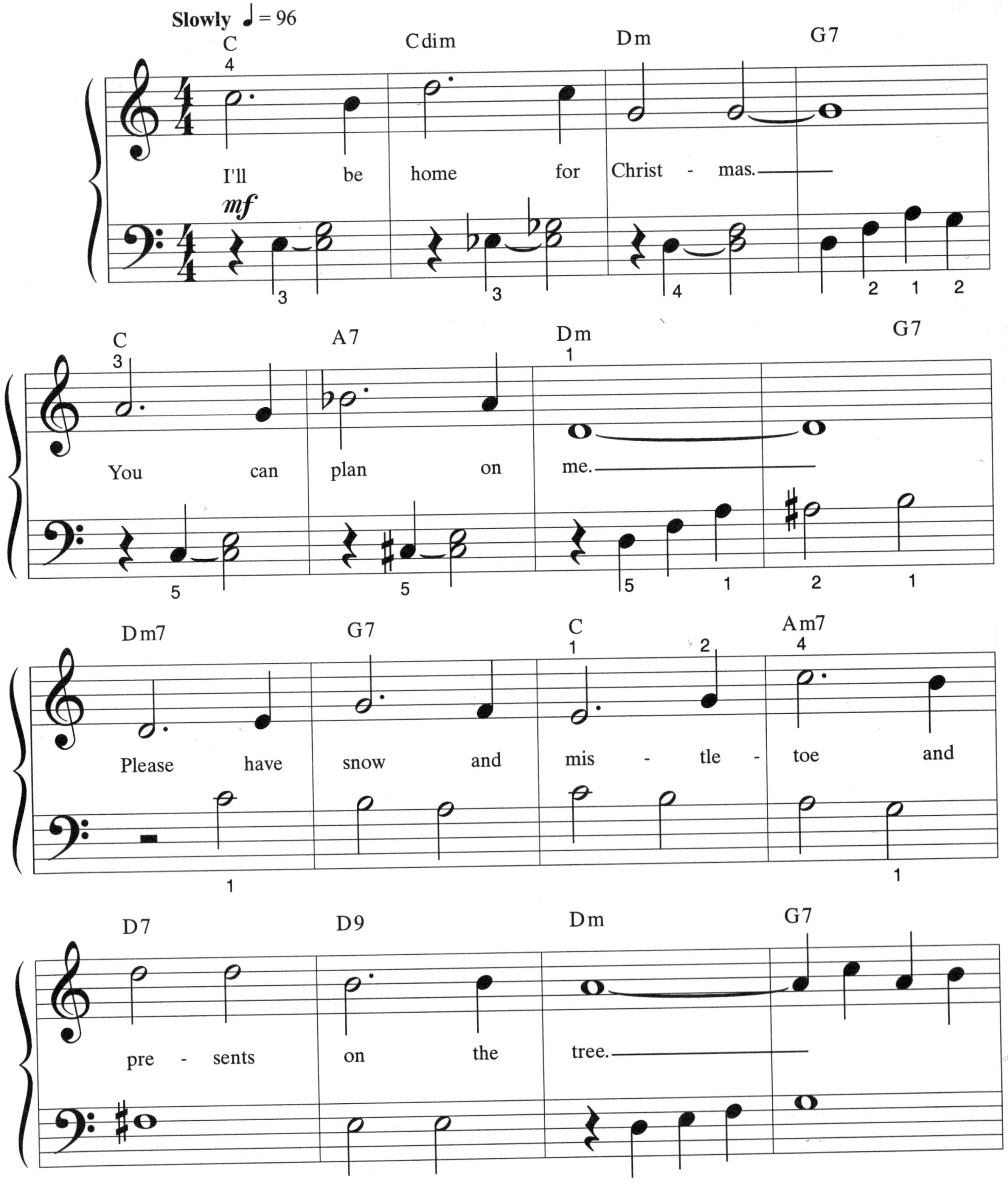
Slowly ♩ = 96
C
Cdim
Dm
G7
I'll be home for Christ - mas.
mf
A7
You can plan on me.
Dm7
C
Am7
Please have snow and mis - tle - toe and
D7
D9
pre - sents on the tree.

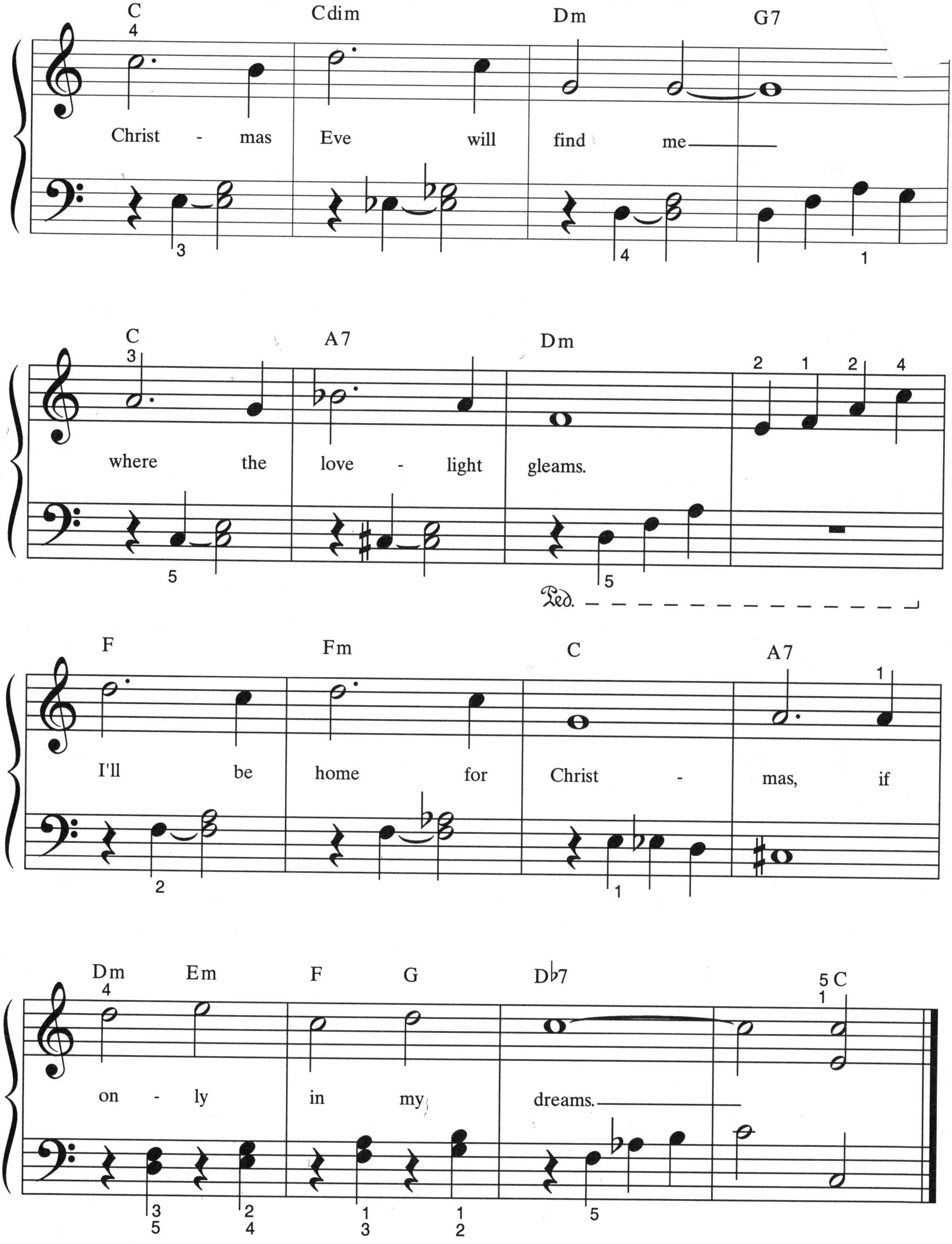
C
Cdim
Dm
G7
Christ - mas Eve will find me
C
A7
Dm
where the love - light gleams.
Ped.
F
Fm
C
A7
I'll be home for Christ - mas, if
Dm
Em
F
G
D♭7
C
on - ly in my dreams.

Star of the East

Words by
GEORGE COOPER

Music by
AMANDA KENNEDY
Arranged by Richard Bradley

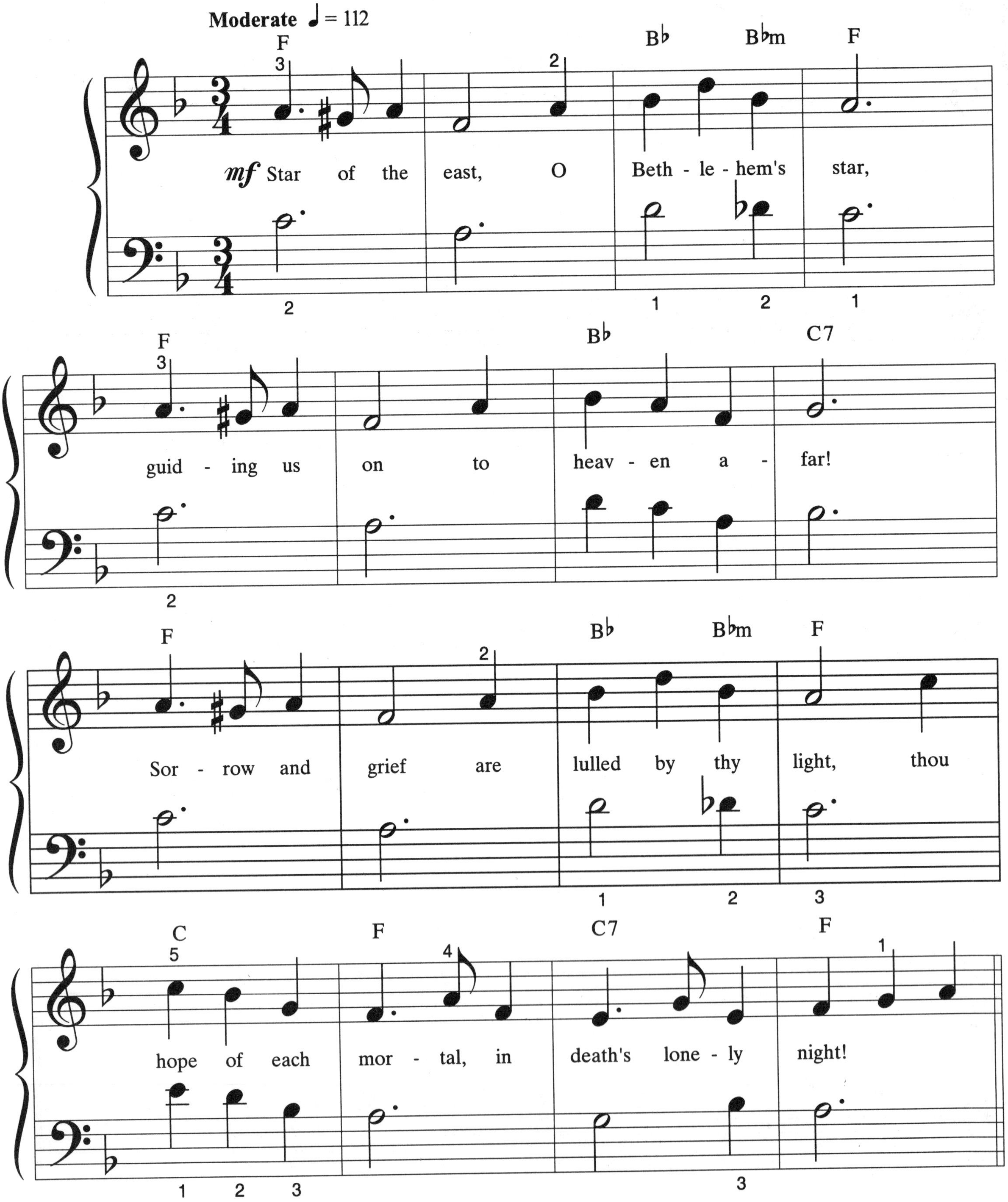

Moderate ♩ = 112
F
Bb
Bbm
F
mf Star of the east, O Beth - le - hem's star,
F
Bb
C7
guid - ing us on to heav - en a - far!
F
Bb
Bbm
F
Sor - row and grief are lulled by thy light, thou
C
F
C7
F
hope of each mor - tal, in death's lone - ly night!

Star of the East - 2 - 1

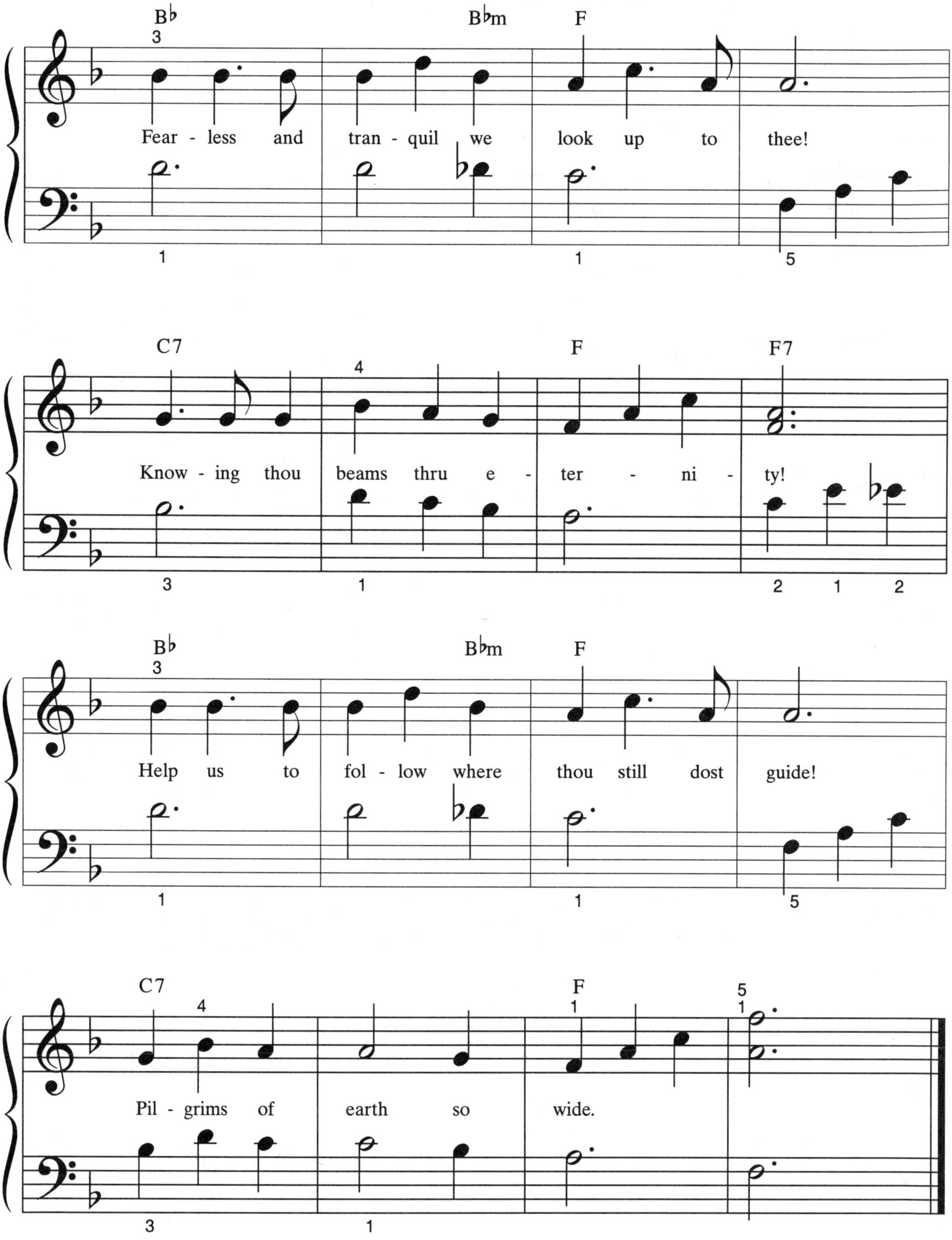
B♭ B♭m F
Fear - less and tran - quil we look up to thee!
C7 F F7
Know - ing thou beams thru e - ter - ni - ty!
B♭ B♭m F
Help us to fol - low where thou still dost guide!
C7 F
Pil - grims of earth so wide.

We Three Kings of Orient Are

By
JOHN HENRY HOPKINS, JR.
Arranged by Richard Bradley

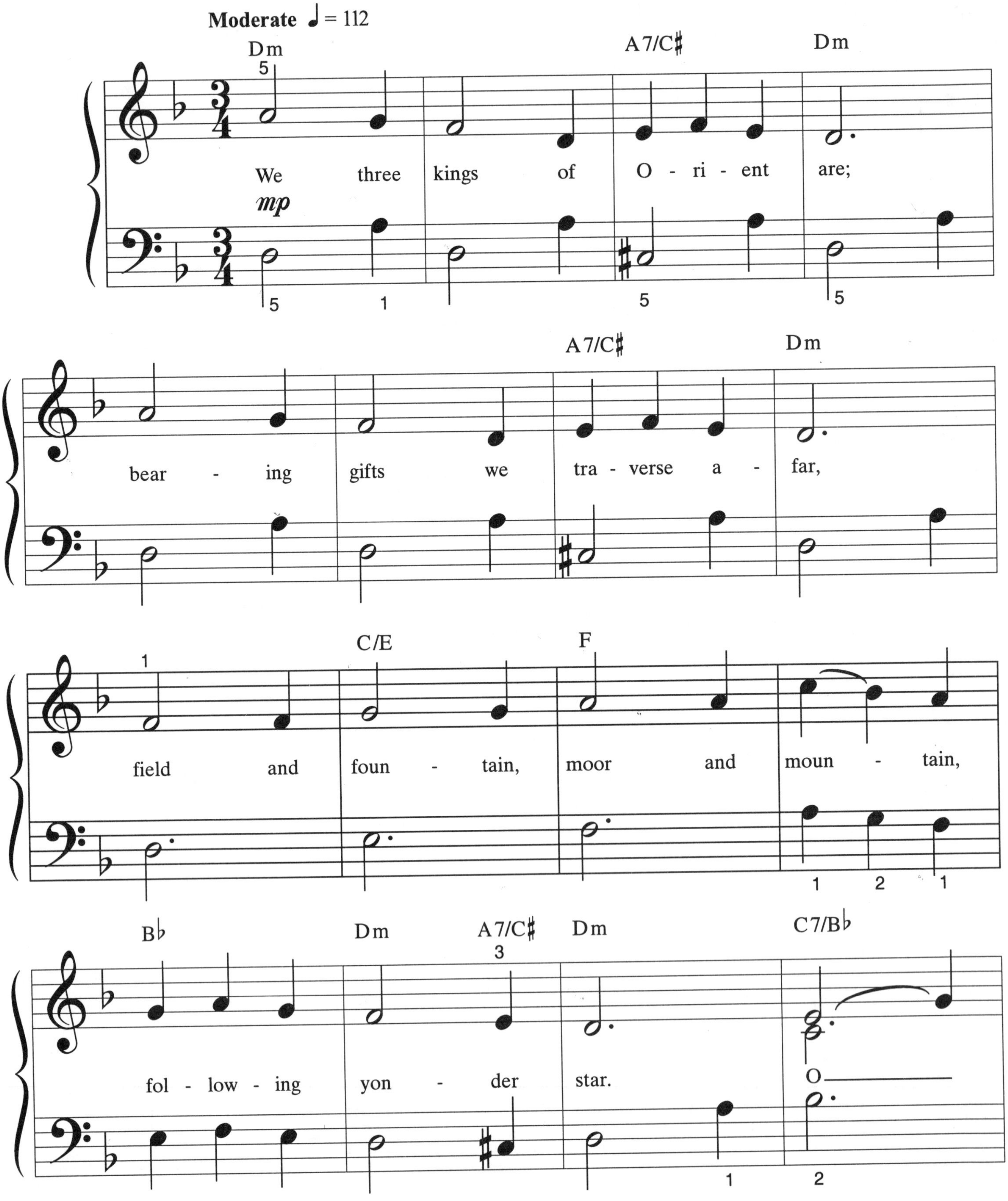
Moderate ♩ = 112
Dm
A7/C♯
Dm
We three kings of O - ri - ent are;
mp
bear - ing gifts we tra - verse a - far,
C/E
F
field and foun - tain, moor and moun - tain,
B♭
Dm
A7/C♯
Dm
C7/B♭
fol - low - ing yon - der star.
O

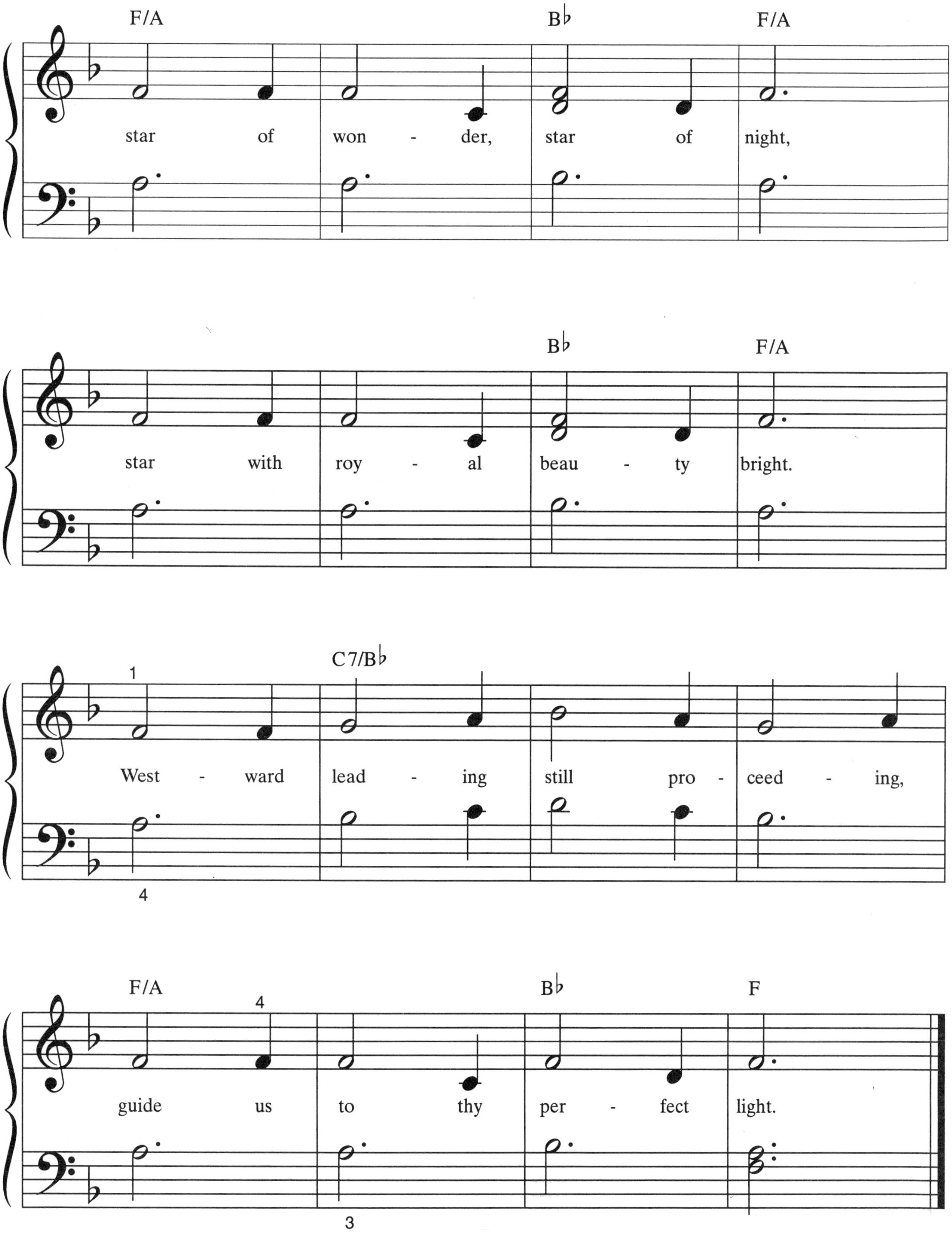
F/A
B♭
F/A
star of won - der, star of night,
B♭
F/A
star with roy - al beau - ty bright.
1
C7/B♭
West - ward lead - ing still pro - ceed - ing,
4
F/A
4
B♭
F
guide us to thy per - fect light.
3

O Come, All Ye Faithful

TRADITIONAL
Arranged by Richard Bradley

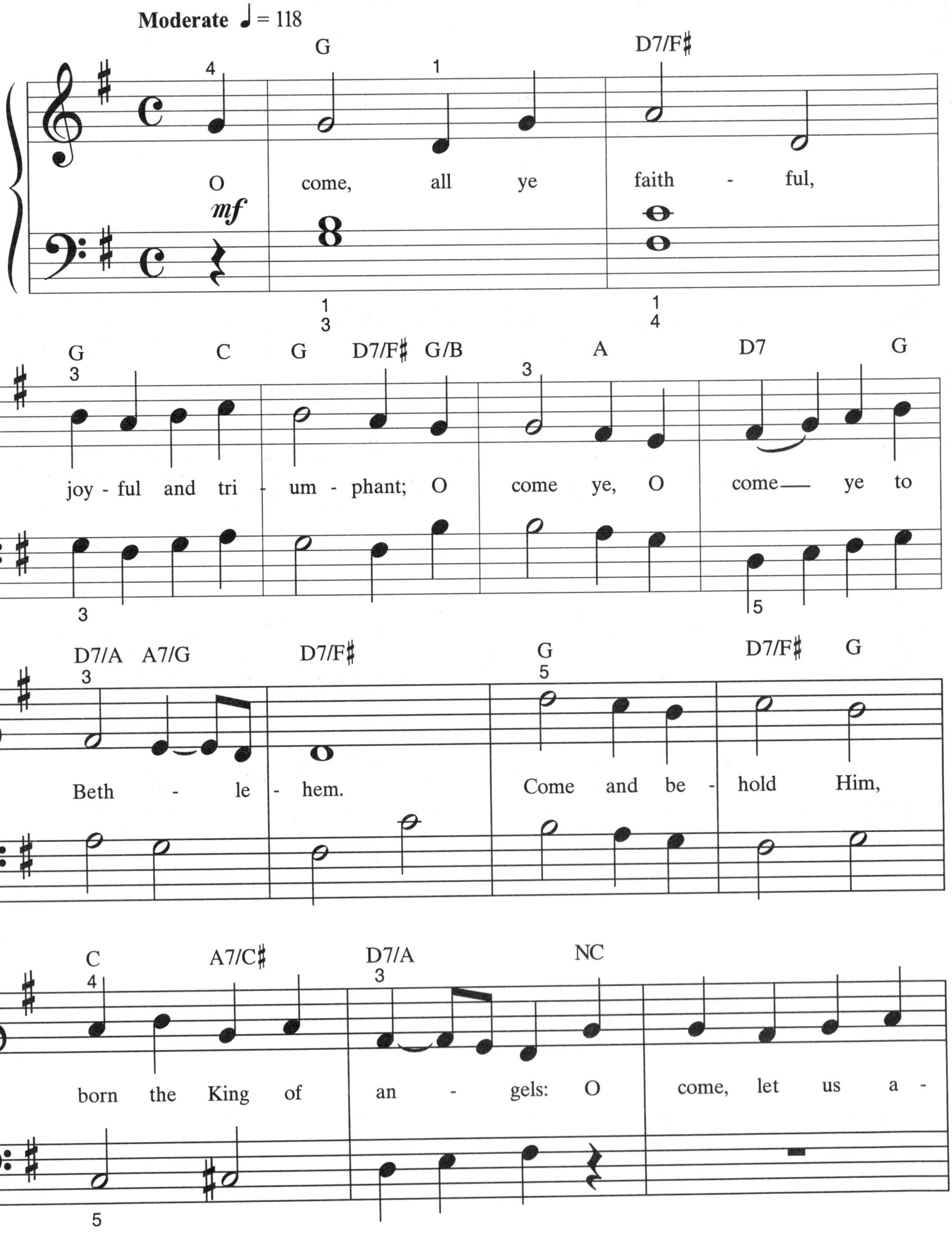
Moderate ♩ = 118
G D7/F♯
O come, all ye faithful,
mf
G C G D7/F♯ G/B A D7 G
joy - ful and tri - um - phant; O come ye, O come ye to
D7/A A7/G D7/F♯ G D7/F♯ G
Beth - le - hem. Come and be - hold Him,
C A7/C♯ D7/A NC
born the King of an - gels: O come, let us a -

O Come, All Ye Faithful - 2 - 1

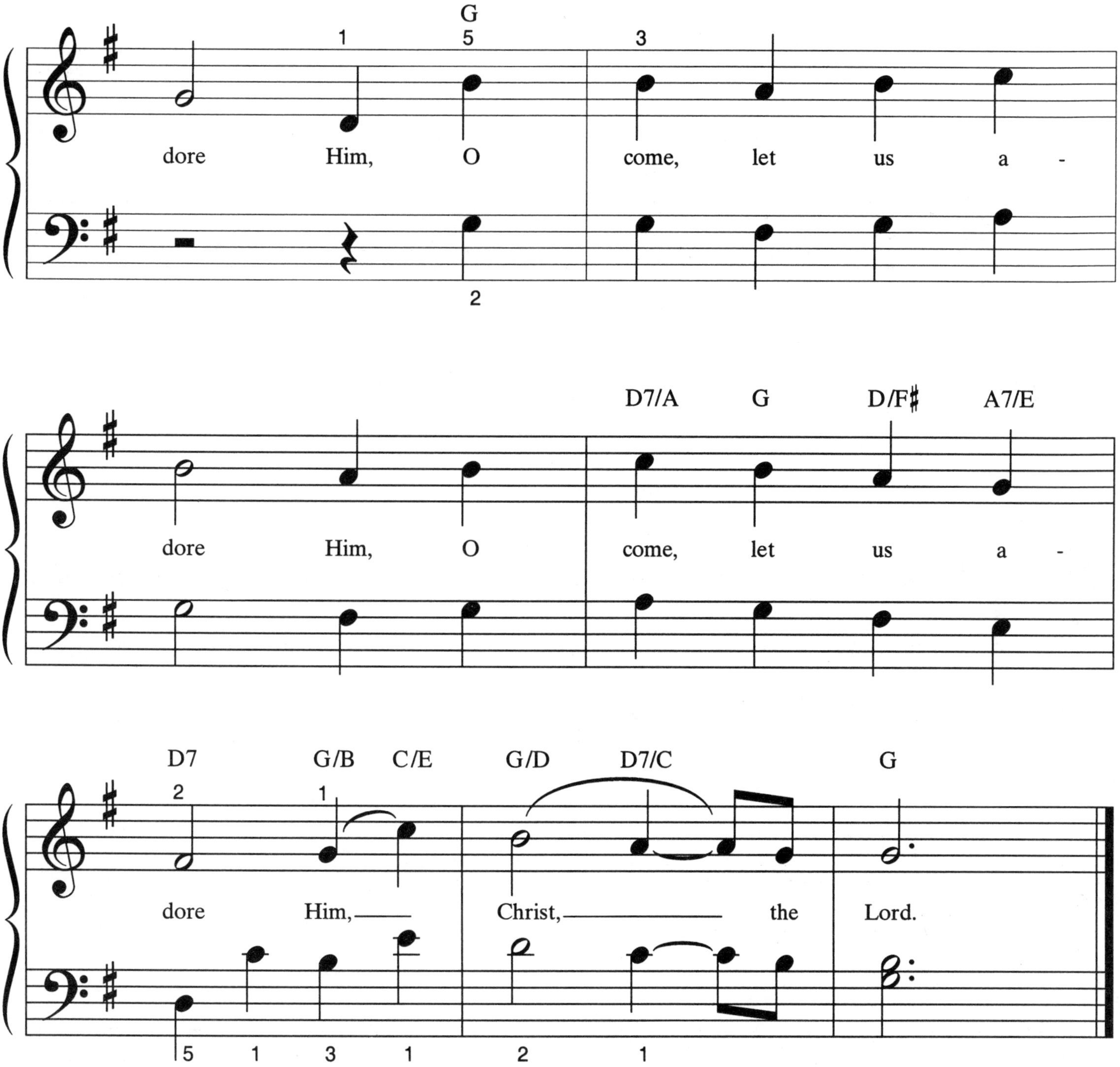
G
1 5 3
dore Him, O come, let us a -
2
D7/A G D/F♯ A7/E
dore Him, O come, let us a -
D7 G/B C/E G/D D7/C G
2 1
dore Him, Christ, the Lord.
5 1 3 1 2 1

Don't Save It All for Christmas Day

Words and Music by
PETER ZIZZO, RIC WAKE
and CELINE DION
Arranged by Richard Bradley

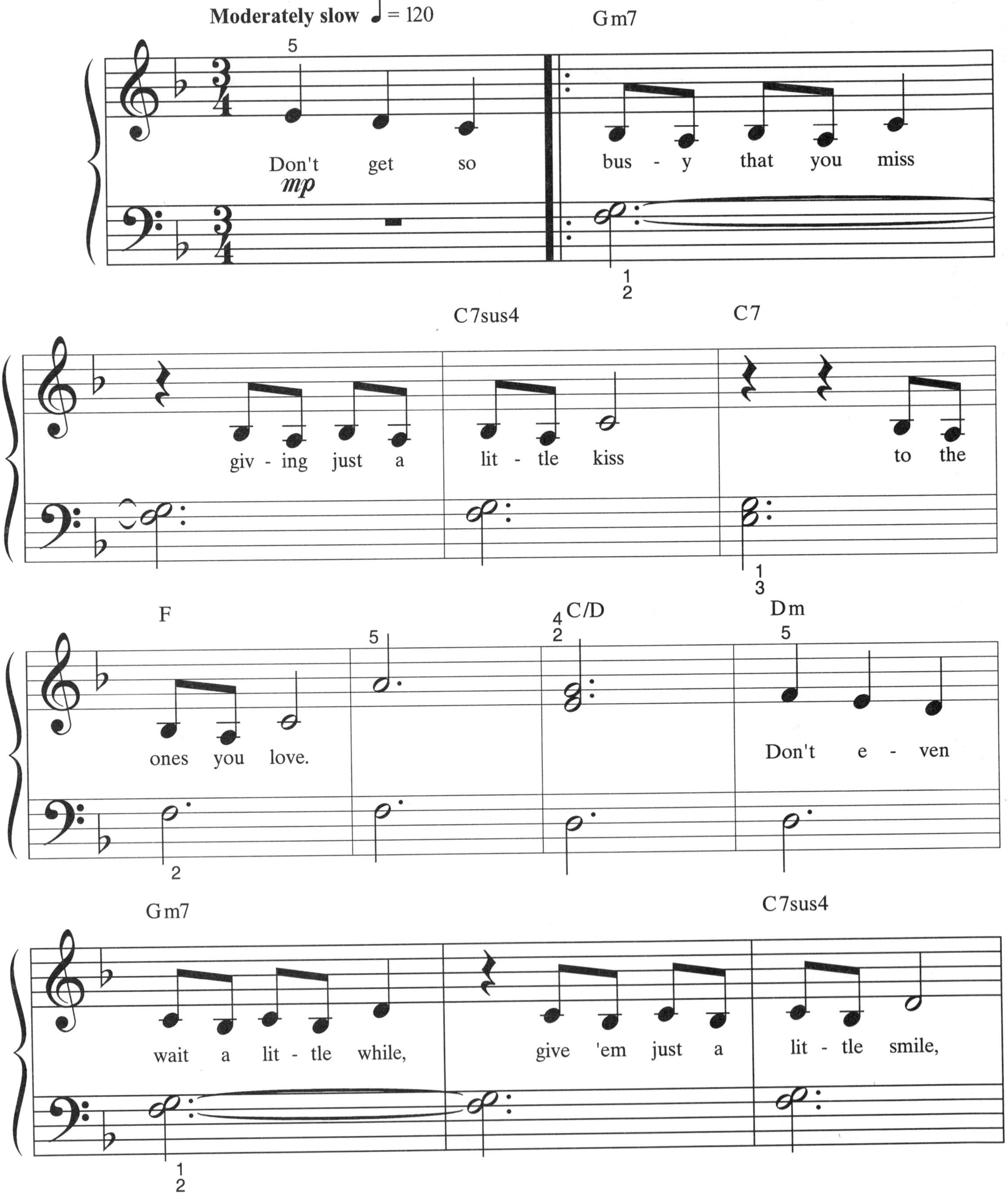
Moderately slow ♩ = 120
Gm7
C7sus4
C7
F
C/D
Dm
Gm7
C7sus4
5
mp
Don't get so busy that you miss
giv - ing just a lit - tle kiss to the
ones you love. Don't e - ven
wait a lit - tle while, give 'em just a lit - tle smile,

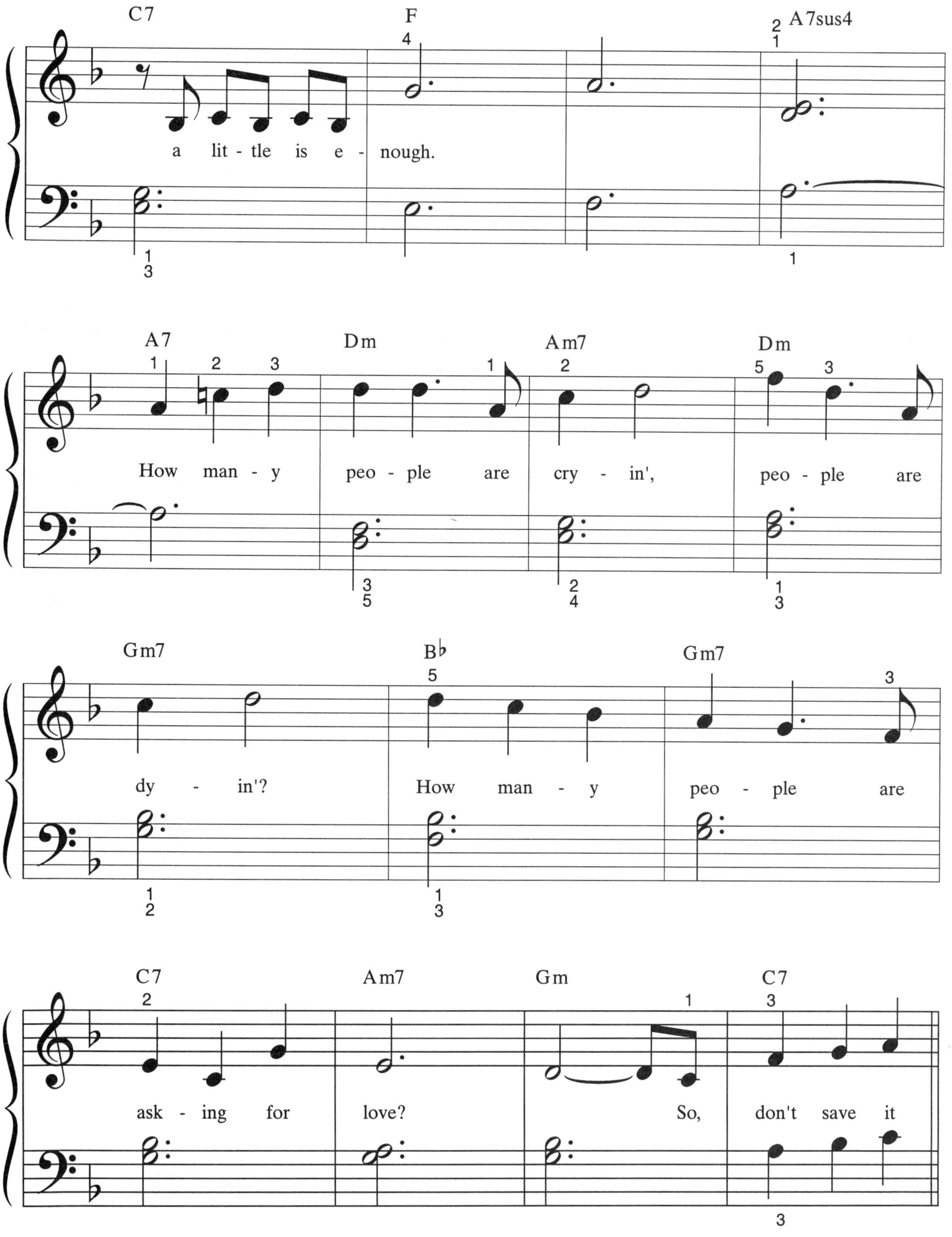
C7 F A7sus4
a lit - tle is e - nough.
A7 Dm Am7 Dm
How man - y peo - ple are cry - in', peo - ple are
Gm7 B♭ Gm7
dy - in'? How man - y peo - ple are
C7 Am7 Gm C7
ask - ing for love? So, don't save it

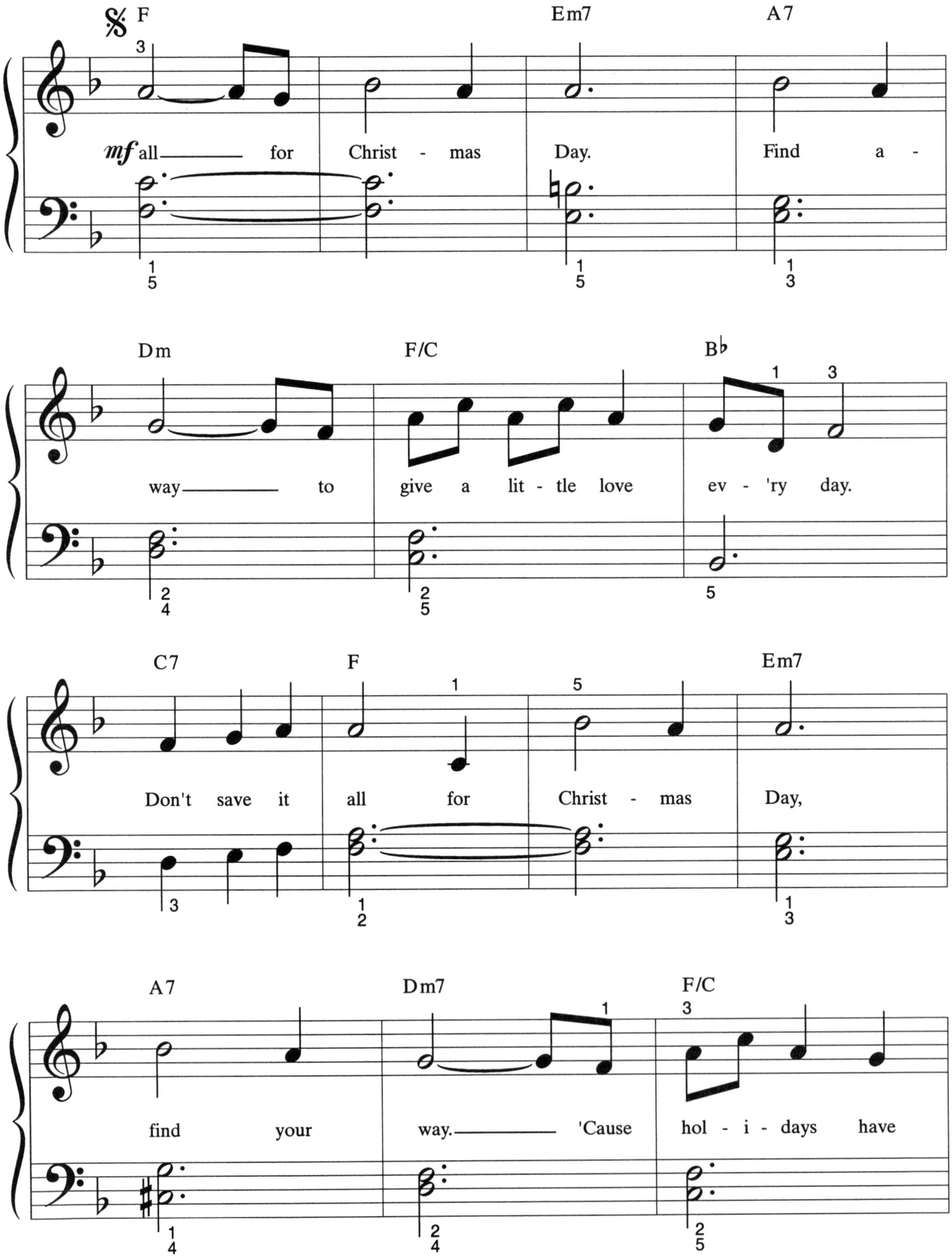
F Em7 A7
mf all for Christ - mas Day. Find a -
Dm F/C B♭
way to give a lit - tle love ev - 'ry day.
C7 F Em7
Don't save it all for Christ - mas Day,
A7 Dm7 F/C
find your way. 'Cause hol - i - days have

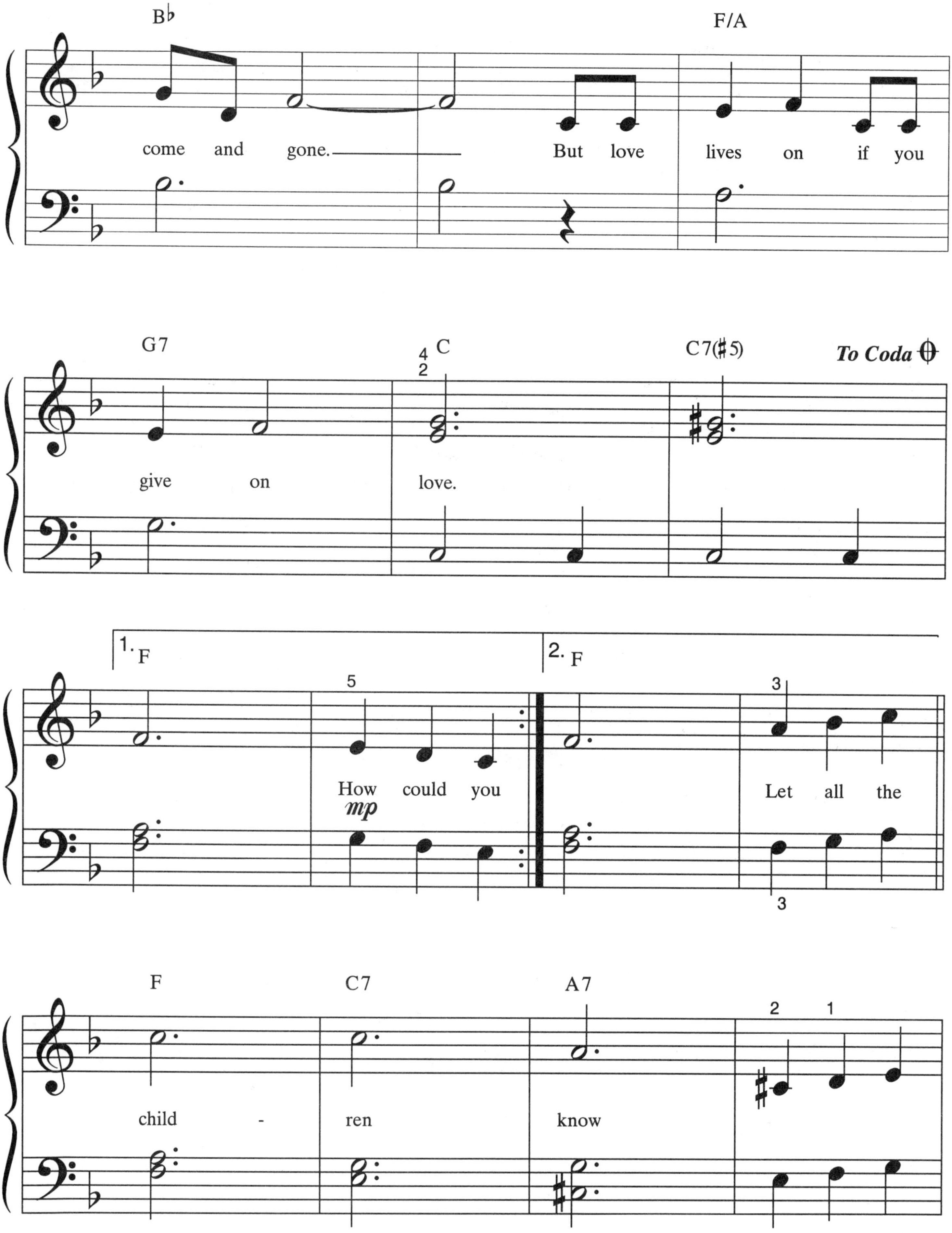
B♭
F/A
come and gone. But love lives on if you
G7
C
C7(♯5)
To Coda
give on love.
1. F
2. F
How could you
mp
Let all the
F
C7
A7
child - ren know

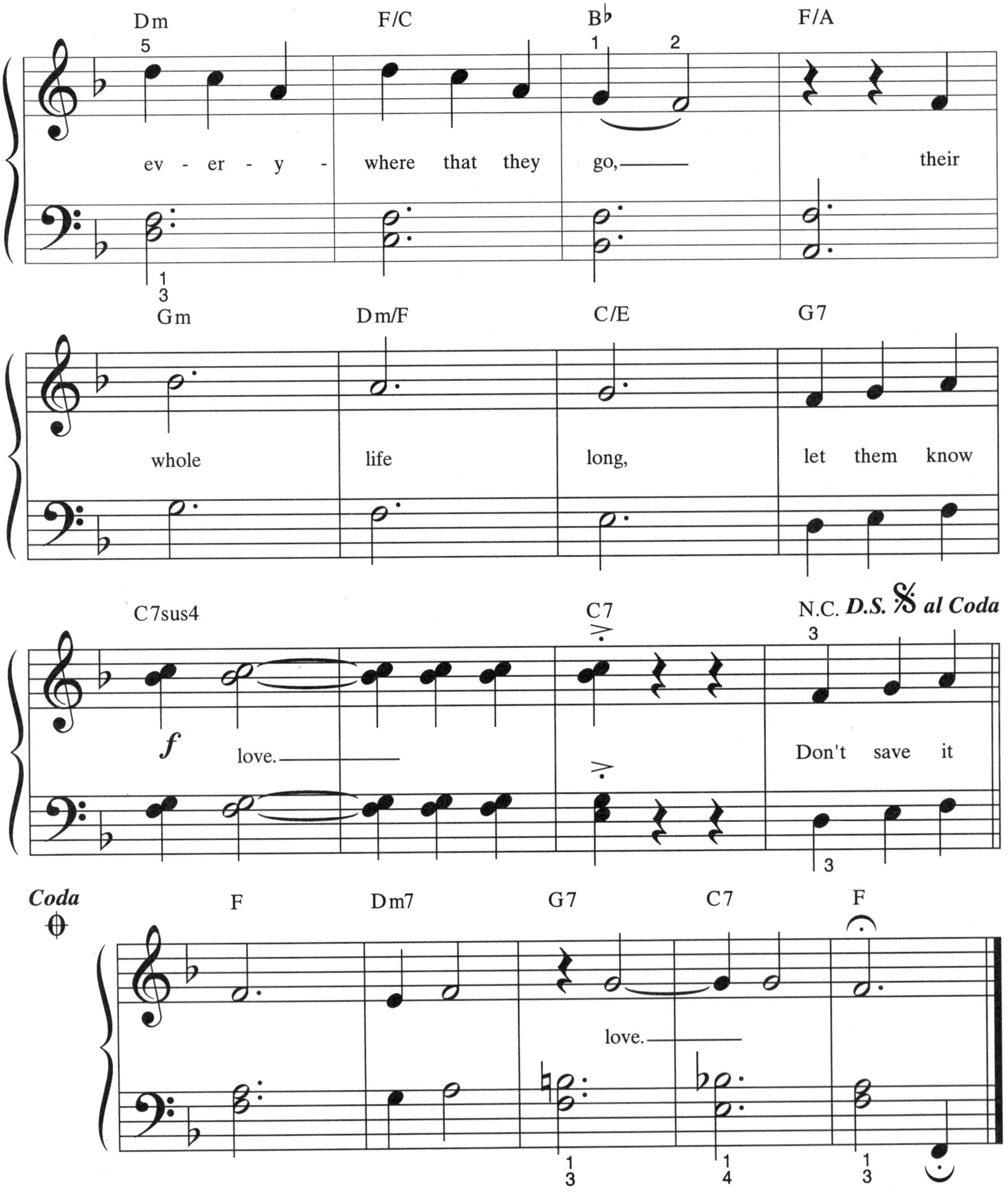
Dm F/C B♭ F/A
ev - er - y - where that they go, their
Gm Dm/F C/E G7
whole life long, let them know
C7sus4 C7 N.C. D.S. al Coda
f
love.
Don't save it
Coda
F Dm7 G7 C7 F
love.

Verse 2:
How could you wait another minute, a hug is warmer when you're in it. And, baby, that's a fact.
And saying I love you's always better. Seasons, reasons, they don't matter. So don't hold back.
How many people in this world, so needful in this world? How many people are praying for love?

Blue Christmas

Words by
JAY W. JOHNSON

Music by
BILLY HAYES
Arranged by Richard Bradley

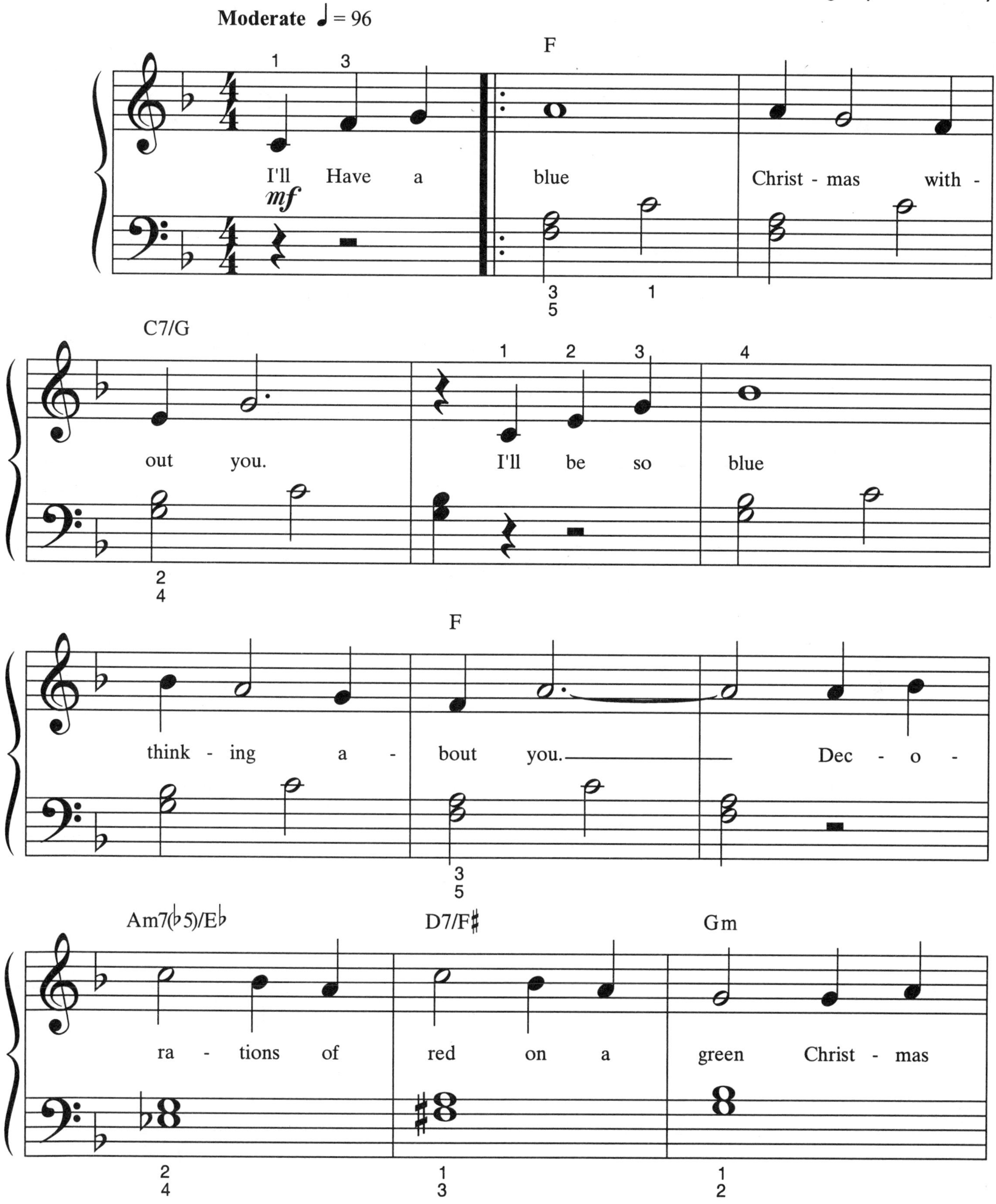
Moderate ♩ = 96
F
C7/G
F
Am7(♭5)/E♭
D7/F♯
Gm
mf
I'll Have a blue Christ - mas with - out you.
I'll be so blue
think - ing a - bout you.
Dec - o - ra - tions of red on a green Christ - mas

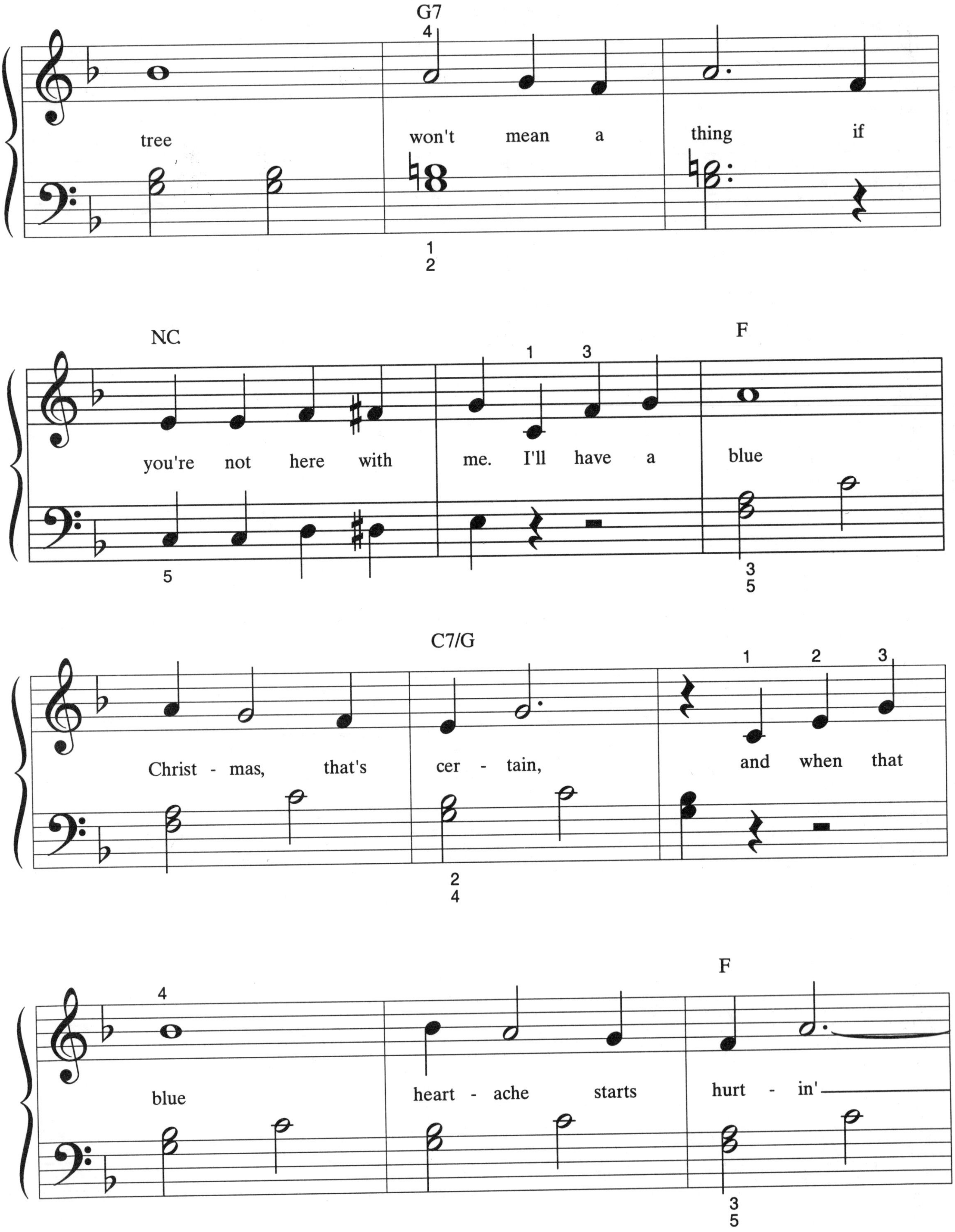
G7
tree won't mean a thing if
N.C.
F
you're not here with me. I'll have a blue
C7/G
Christ - mas, that's cer - tain, and when that
F
blue heart - ache starts hurt - in'

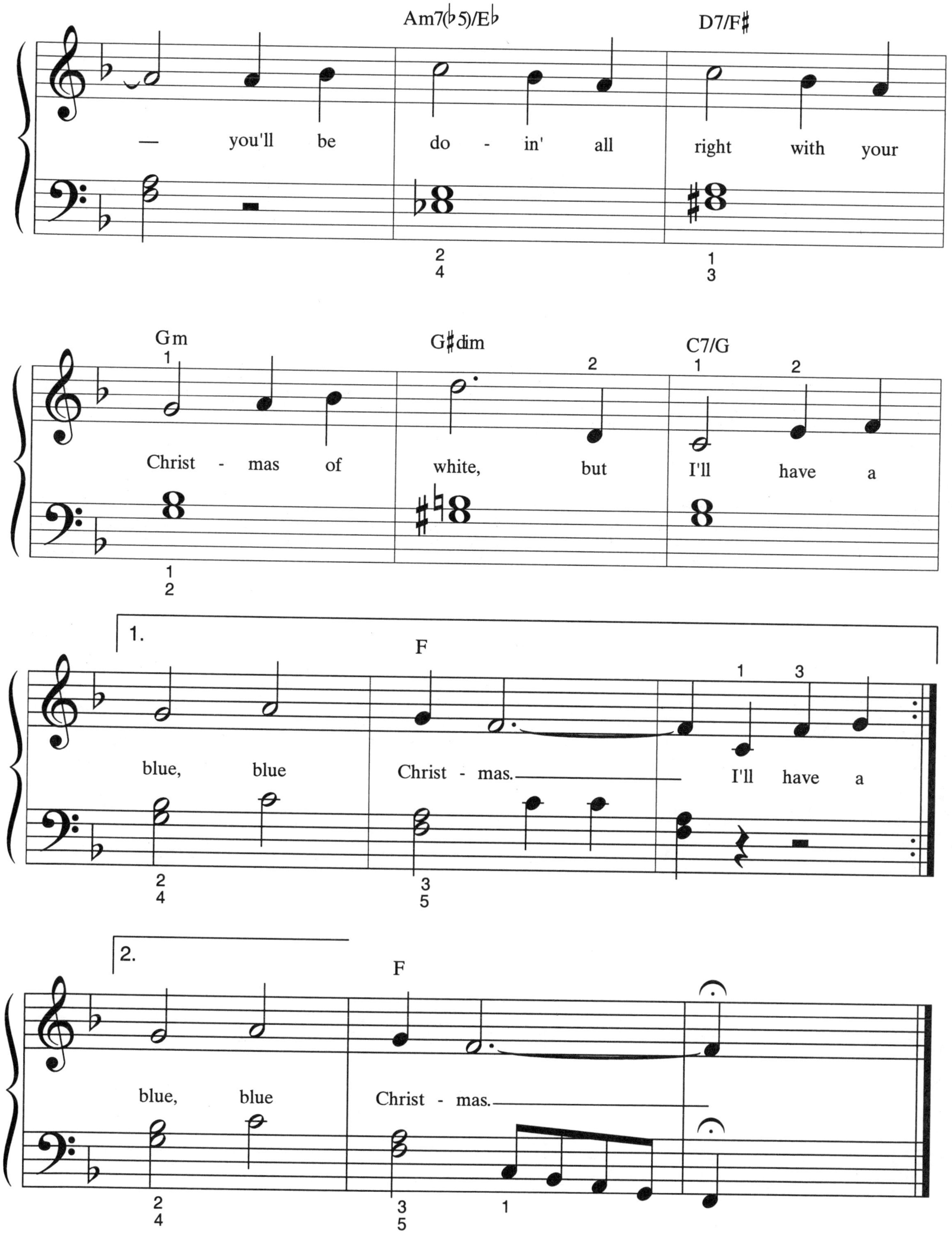
Am7(♭5)/E♭
D7/F♯
— you'll be do - in' all right with your
Gm
G♯dim
C7/G
Christ - mas of white, but I'll have a
1.
F
blue, blue Christ - mas. I'll have a
2.
F
blue, blue Christ - mas.

We Wish You a Merry Christmas

TRADITIONAL
Arranged by Richard Bradley

Joyfully ♩ = 154
C/E F
We wish you a Mer - ry Christ - mas, we
mf
D7/F♯ G E7/G♯
wish you a Mer - ry Christ - mas, we wish you a Mer - ry
Am D7/C G/D C/E
Christ - mas and a Hap - py New Year! Good
G/D D7/E G/B
ti - dings to you wher - ev - er you are; good

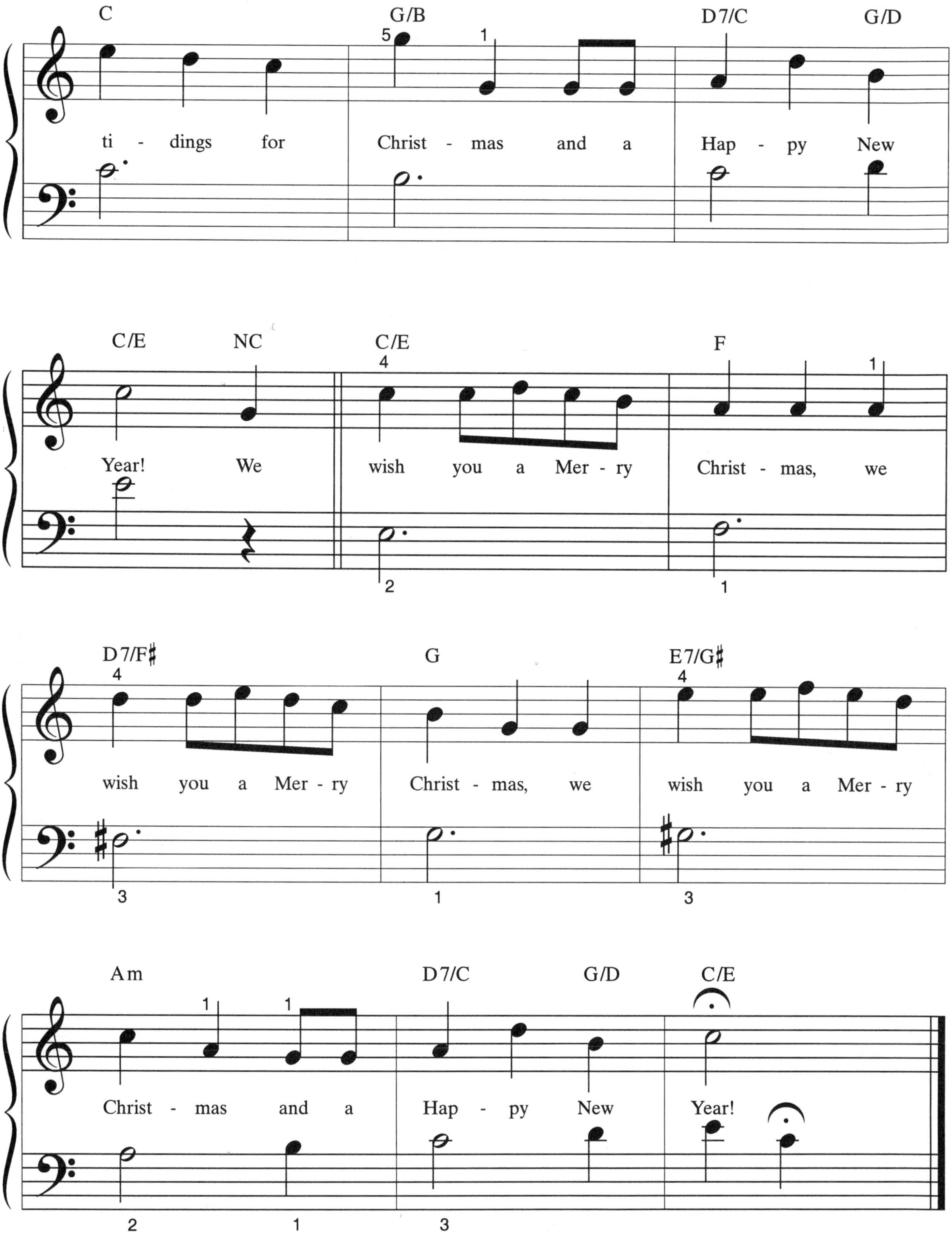
C G/B D7/C G/D
ti - dings for Christ - mas and a Hap - py New
C/E NC C/E F
Year! We wish you a Mer - ry Christ - mas, we
D7/F♯ G E7/G♯
wish you a Mer - ry Christ - mas, we wish you a Mer - ry
Am D7/C G/D C/E
Christ - mas and a Hap - py New Year!

It Came Upon the Midnight Clear

Words by
EDMUND H. SEARS

Music by
RICHARD S. WILLIS
Arranged by Richard Bradley

Moderately fast ♩ = 136
C F C
It came up - on the mid - night clear, that
mp
F D7 G G7
glo - ri - ous song of old, from
C F C
an - gels bend - ing near the earth, to
F G7 C NC
touch their harps of gold: "Peace

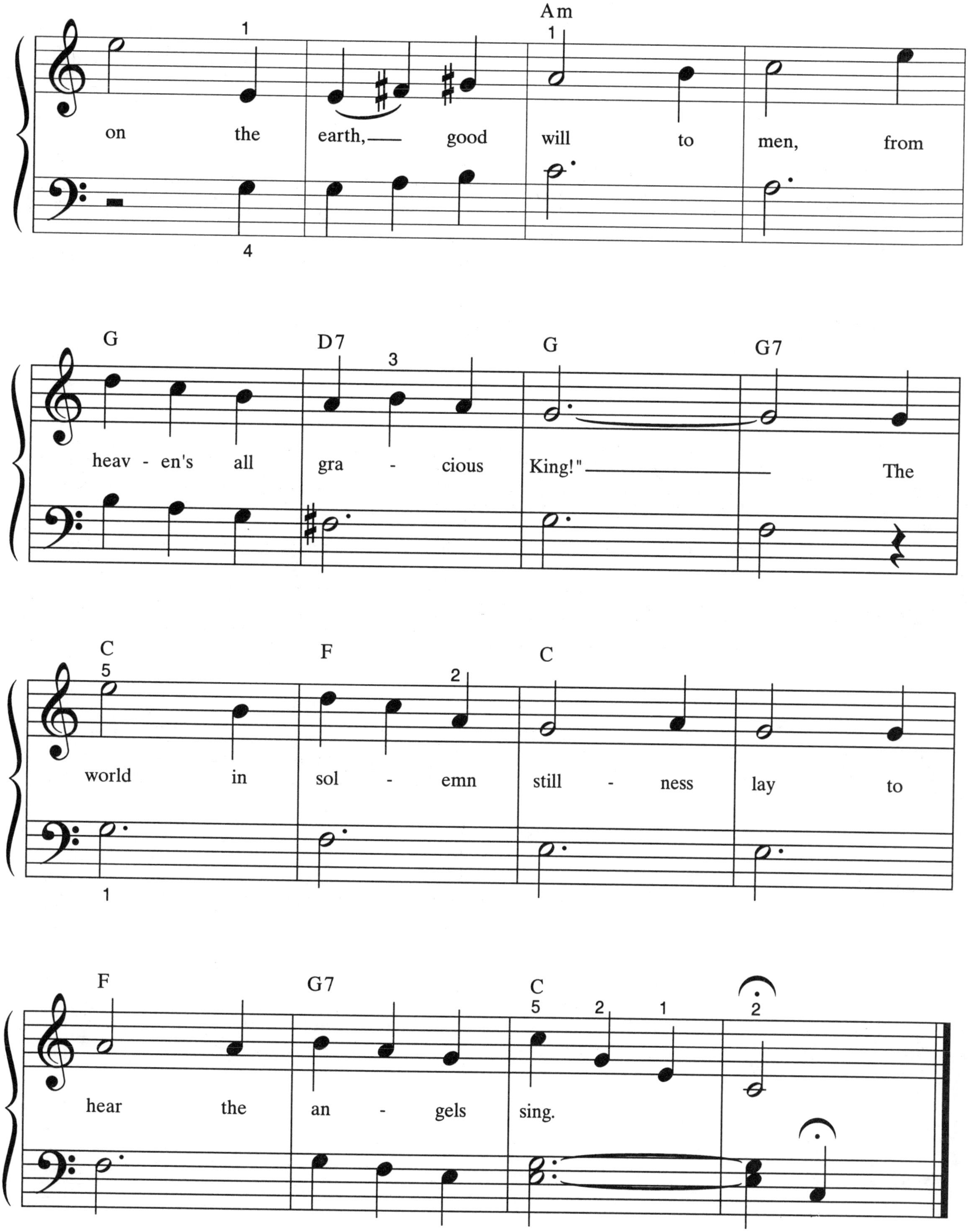
Am
on the earth, good will to men, from
G D7 G G7
heav - en's all gra - cious King!" The
C F C
world in sol - emn still - ness lay to
F G7 C
hear the an - gels sing.

God Rest Ye Merry, Gentlemen

TRADITIONAL
Arranged by Richard Bradley

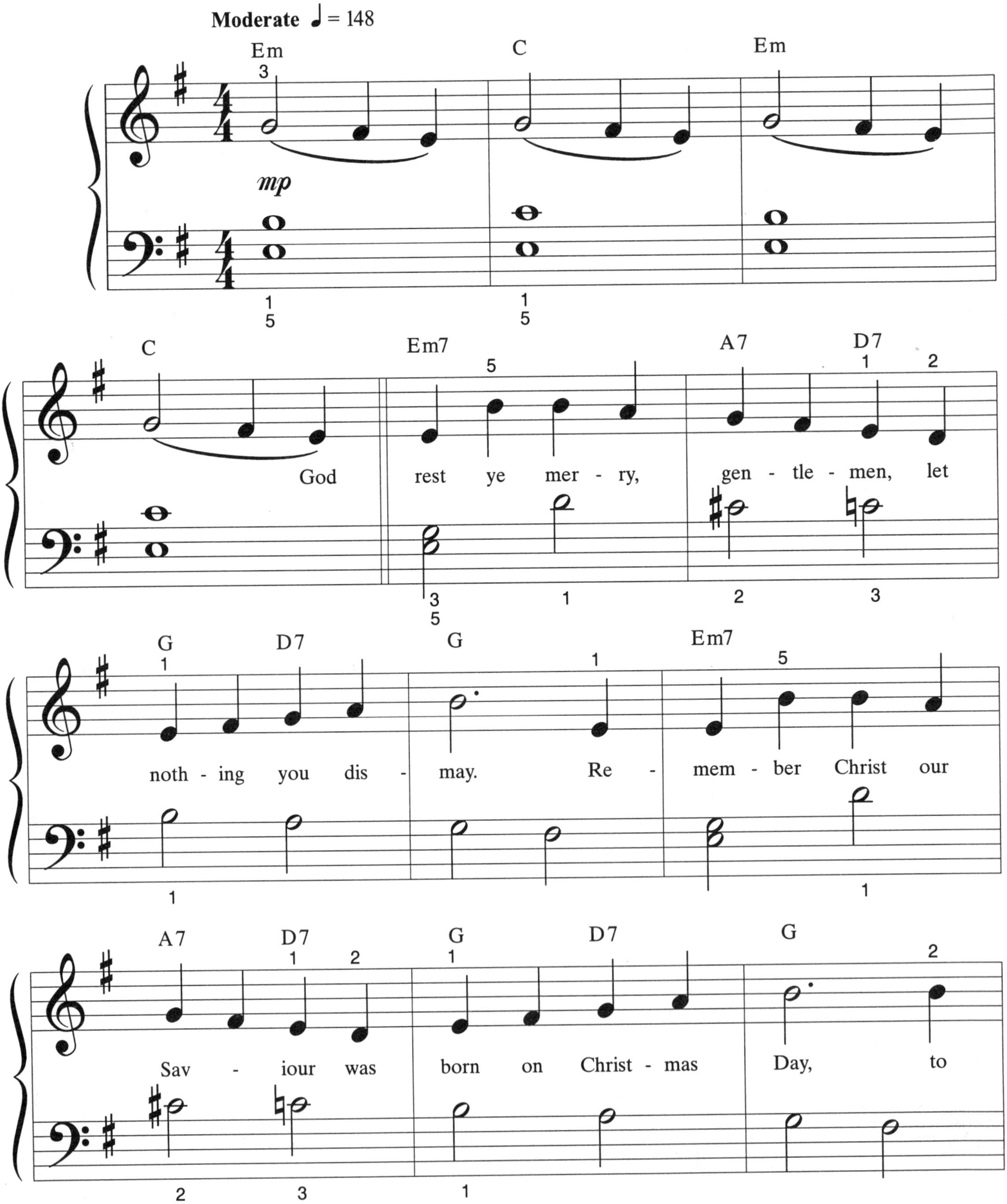
Moderate ♩ = 148
Em C Em
mp
C Em7 A7 D7
God rest ye mer - ry, gen - tle - men, let
G D7 G Em7
noth - ing you dis - may. Re - mem - ber Christ our
A7 D7 G D7 G
Sav - iour was born on Christ - mas Day, to

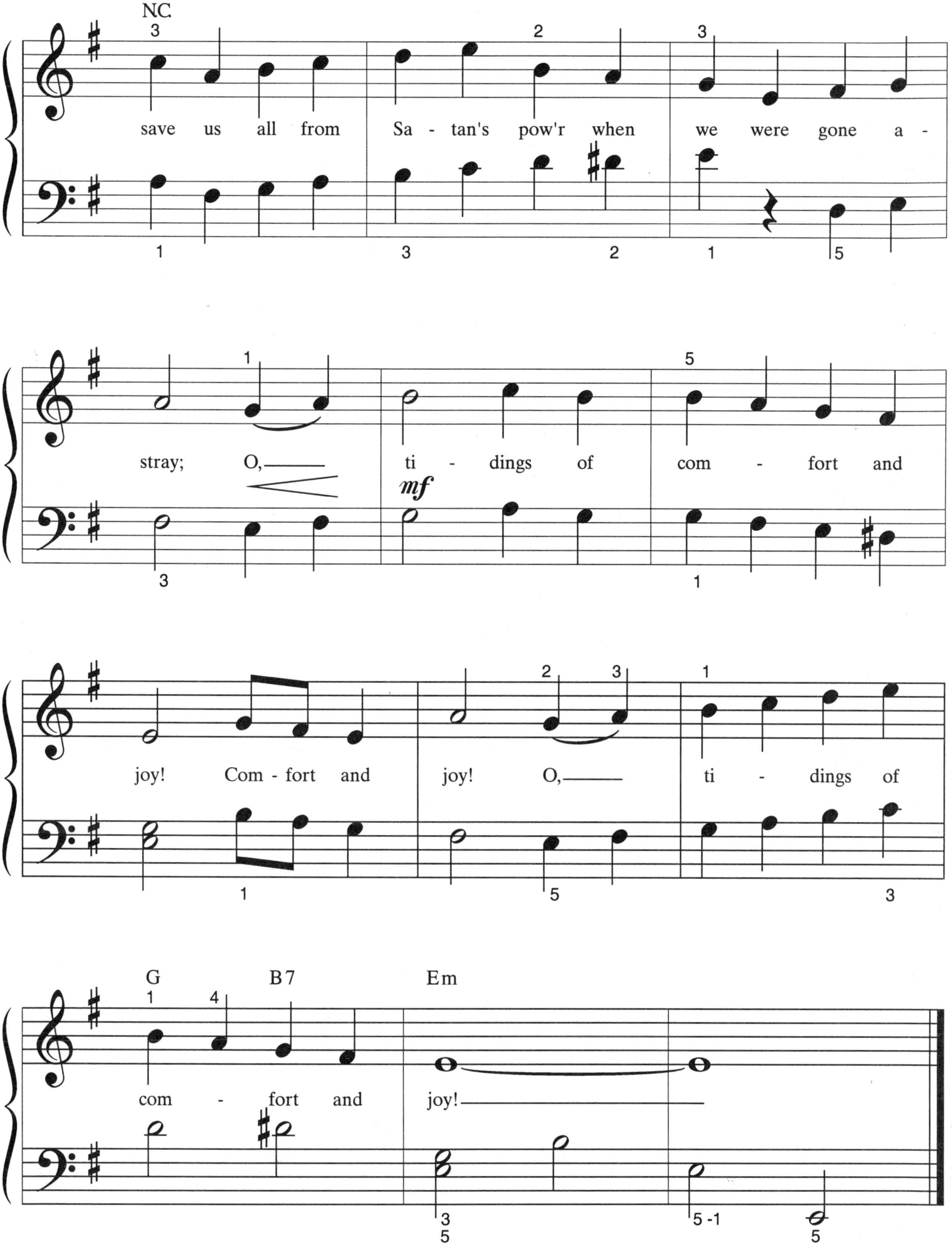
N.C.
save us all from Sa - tan's pow'r when we were gone a -
stray; O,
ti - dings of com - fort and
mf
joy! Com - fort and joy! O,
ti - dings of
G B7 Em
com - fort and joy!

Christmas Hymn

TRADITIONAL FRENCH CAROL
Arranged by Richard Bradley

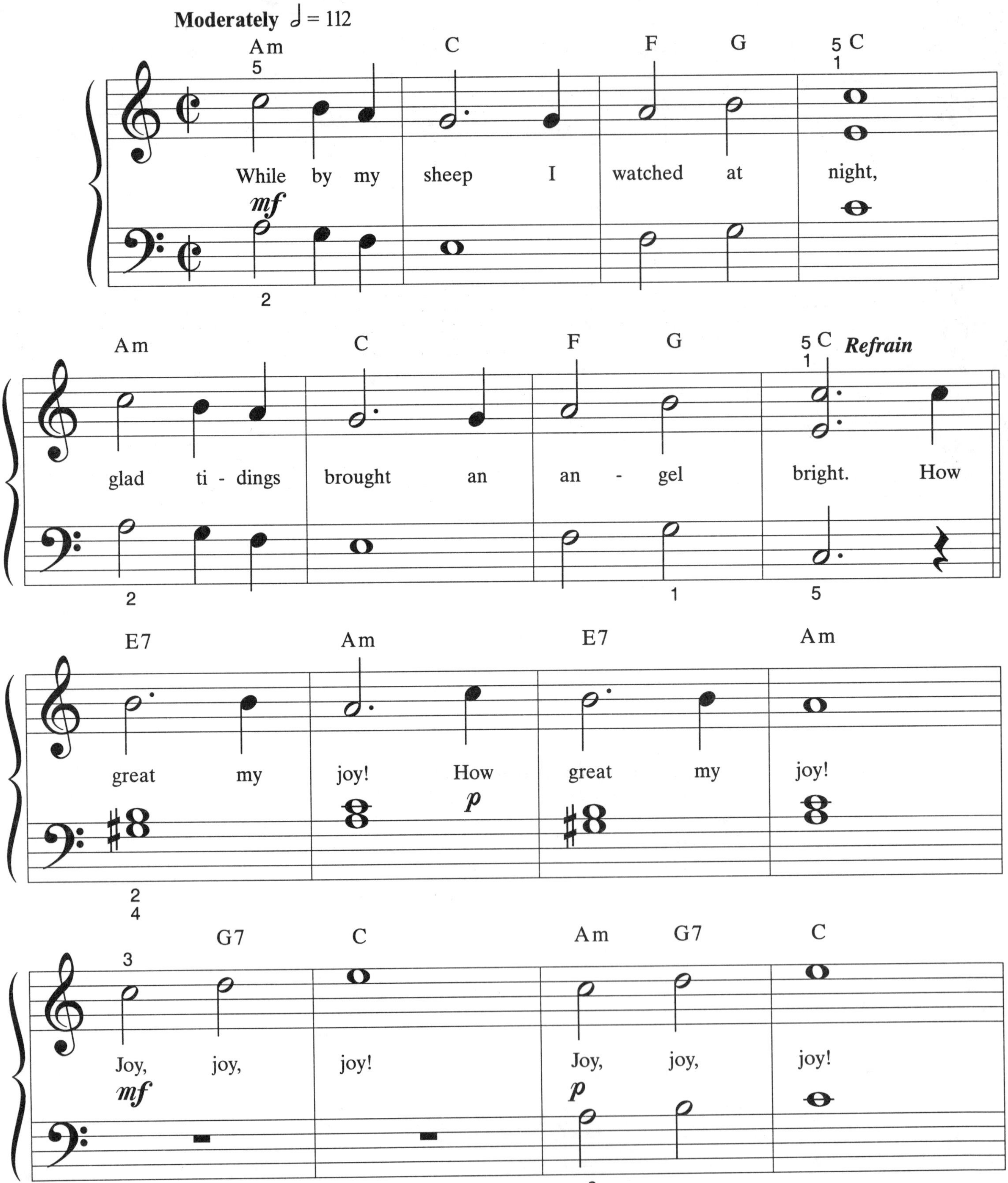
Moderately 𝅗𝅥 = 112
Am C F G C
While by my sheep I watched at night,
mf
Am C F G C
glad ti - dings brought an an - gel bright.
Refrain
How
E7 Am E7 Am
great my joy! How great my joy!
p
G7 C Am G7 C
Joy, joy, joy! Joy, joy, joy!
mf
p

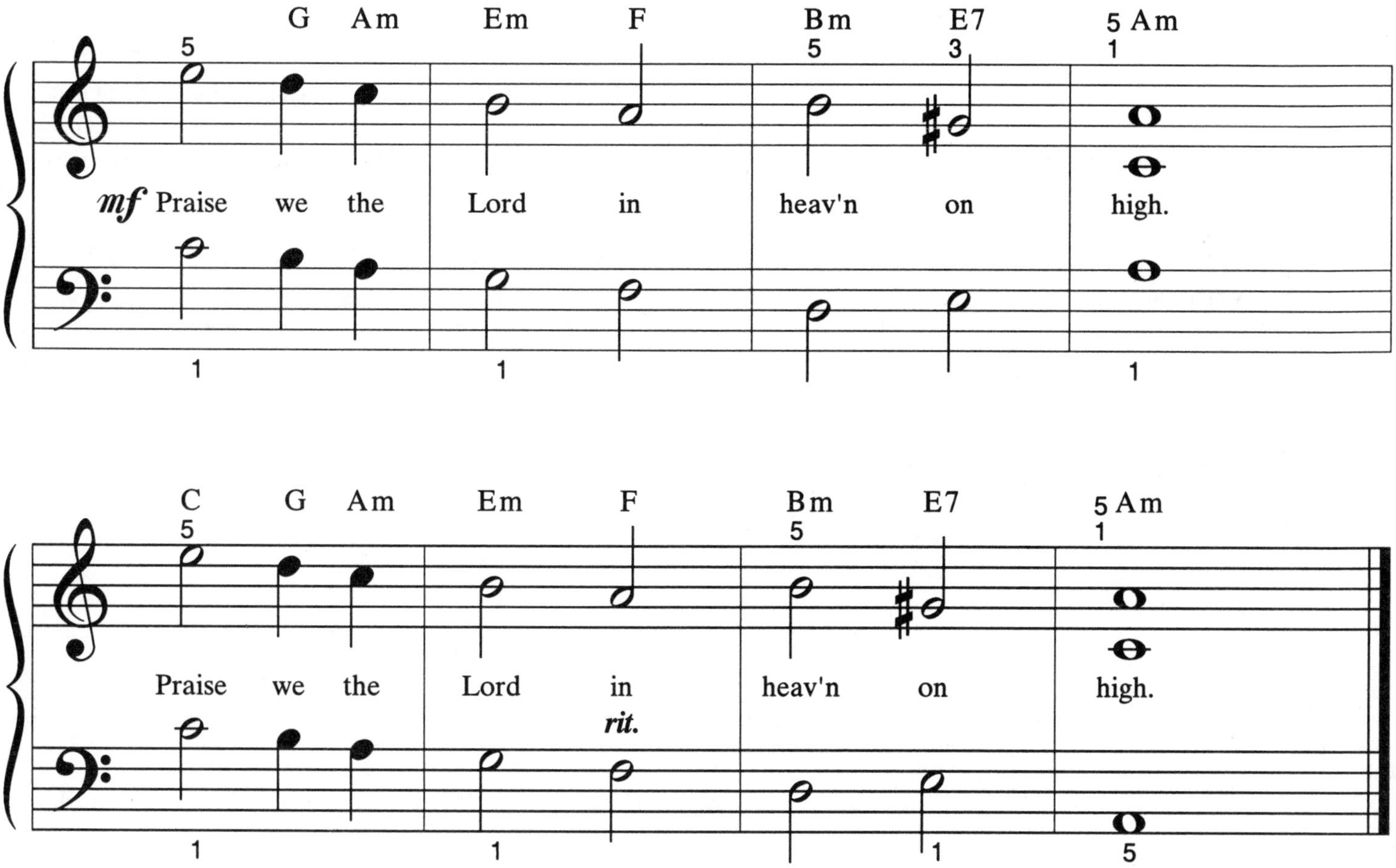
G Am Em F Bm E7 Am
mf Praise we the Lord in heav'n on high.
C G Am Em F Bm E7 Am
Praise we the Lord in heav'n on high.
rit.

Verse 2:
There shall be born, so he did say,
In Bethlehem a Child today. (Refrain)

Verse 3:
There shall He lie in manger mean,
Who shall redeem the world from sin, (Refrain)

Verse 4:
Lord evermore to me be nigh,
Then shall my heart be filled with joy. (Refrain)

Hark! The Herald Angels Sing

By
CHARLES WESLEY and
FELIX MENDELSSOHN
Arranged by Richard Bradley

Majestically ♩ = 124

F C
Hark! The her - ald an - gels sing,
mf
F B♭ F C F
"Glo - ry to the new - born King! Peace on earth, and
C G7 C
mer - cy mild God and sin - ners rec - on - ciled!"
NC F C7 F C7
Joy - ful, all ye na - tions rise,
f

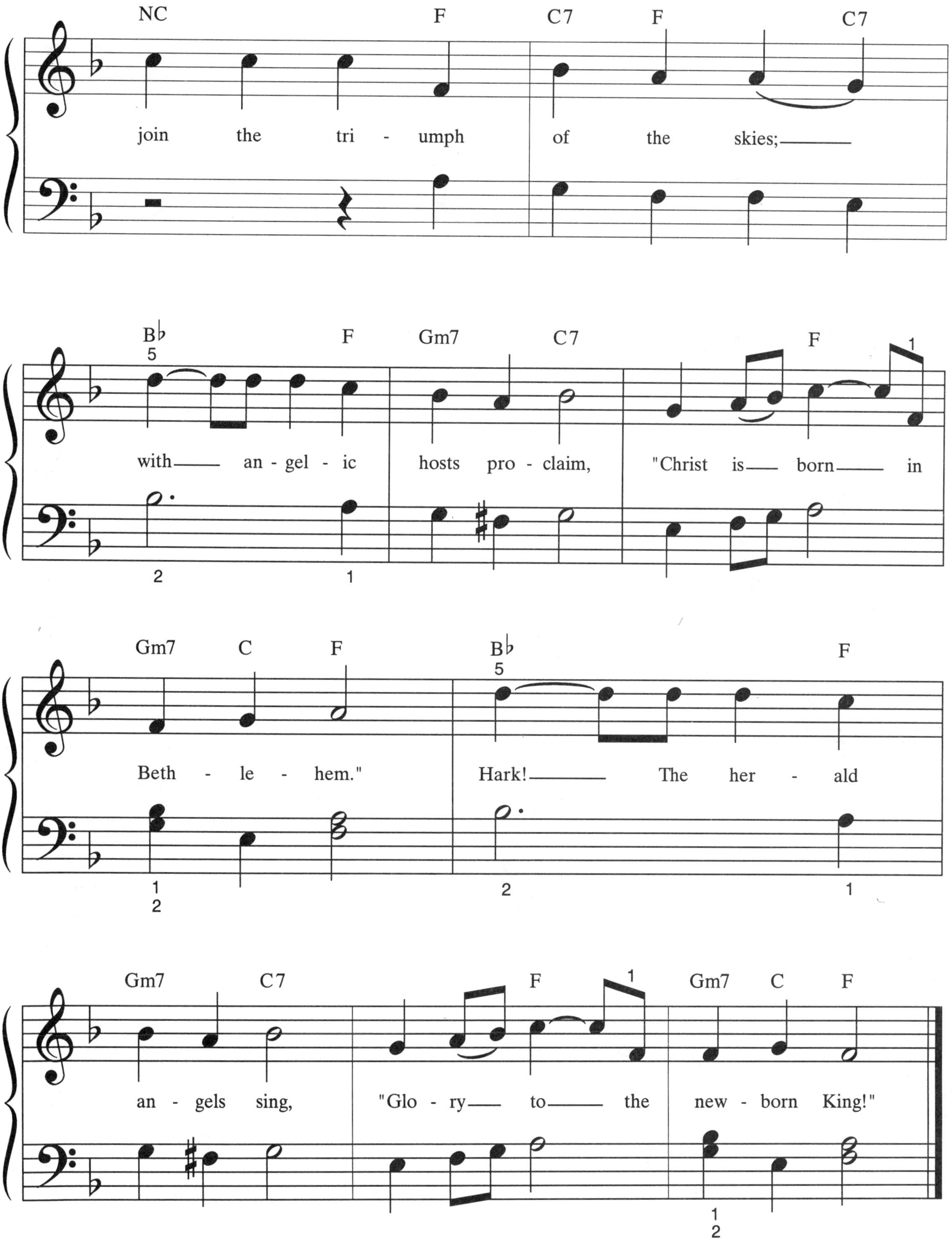
NC F C7 F C7
join the tri - umph of the skies;
B♭ F Gm7 C7 F
with an - gel - ic hosts pro - claim, "Christ is born in
Gm7 C F B♭ F
Beth - le - hem." Hark! The her - ald
Gm7 C7 F Gm7 C F
an - gels sing, "Glo - ry to the new - born King!"

Dance of the Sugar-Plum Fairy

(from *The Nutcracker Suite*)

PETER ILYICH TCHAIKOVSKY
Arranged by Richard Bradley

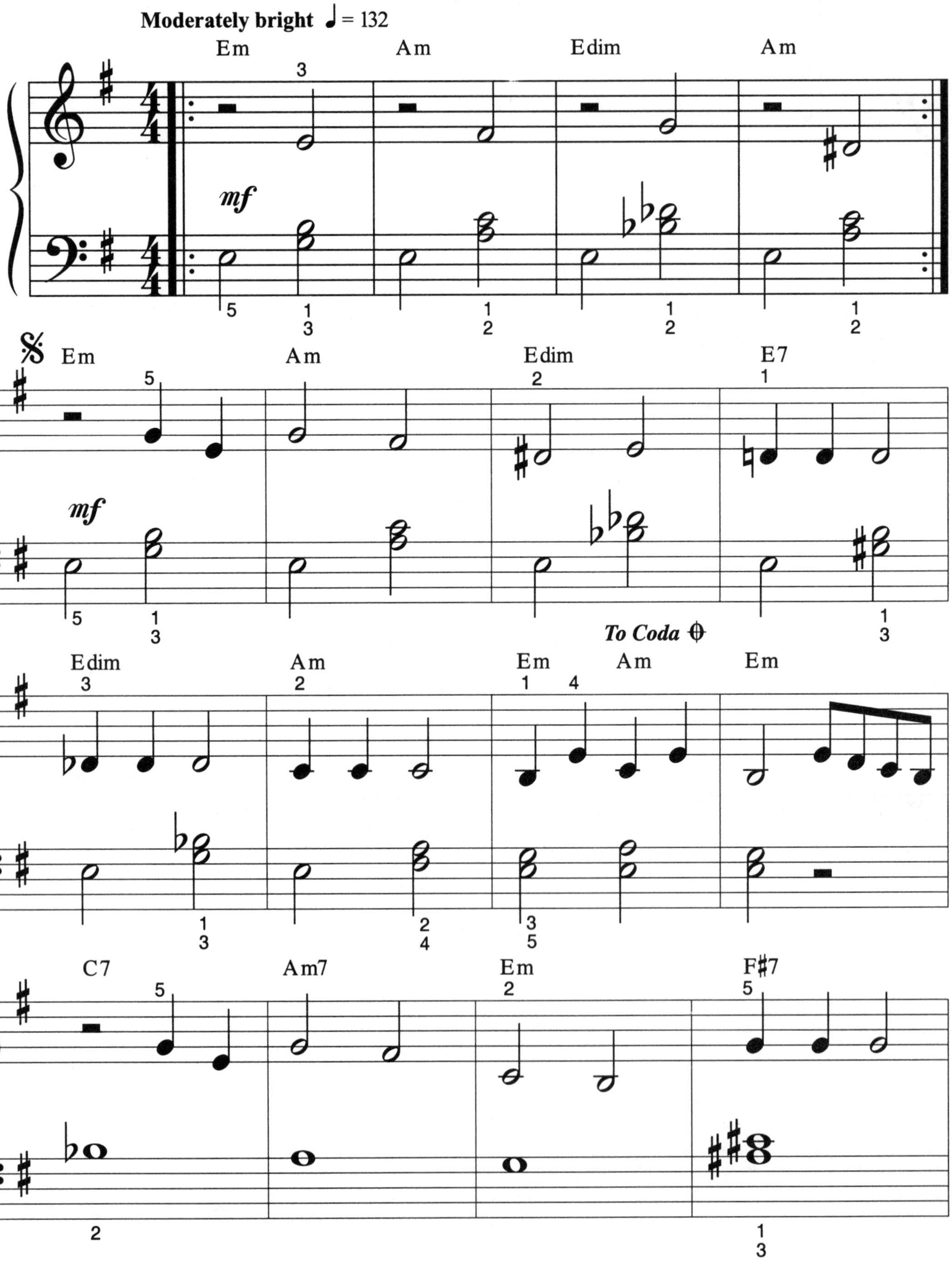

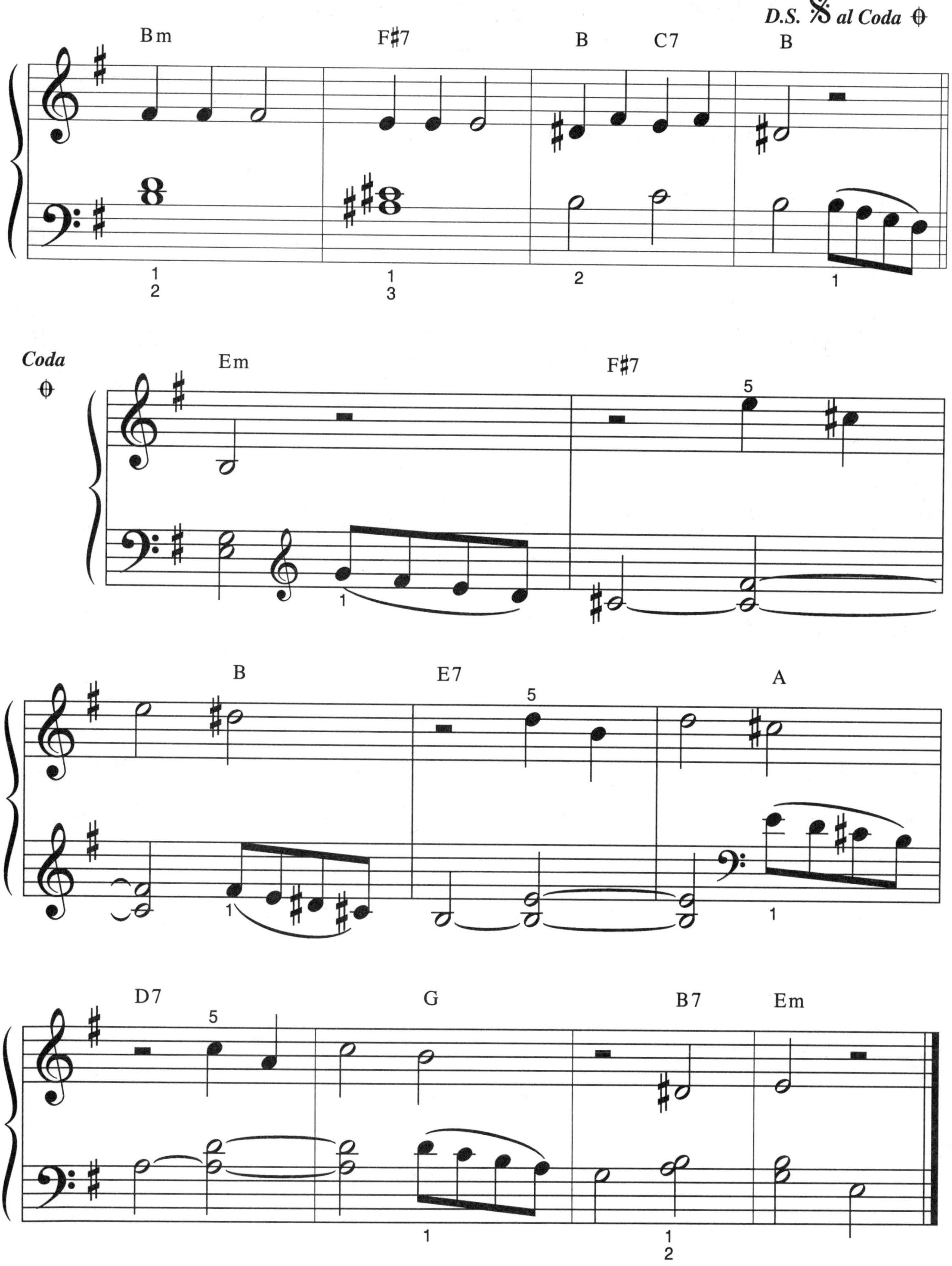
D.S. al Coda
Bm
F♯7
B
C7
B
Coda
Em
F♯7
B
E7
A
D7
G
B7
Em

Suzy Snowflake

Words and Music by
SID TEPPER and ROY BRODSKY
Arranged by Richard Bradley

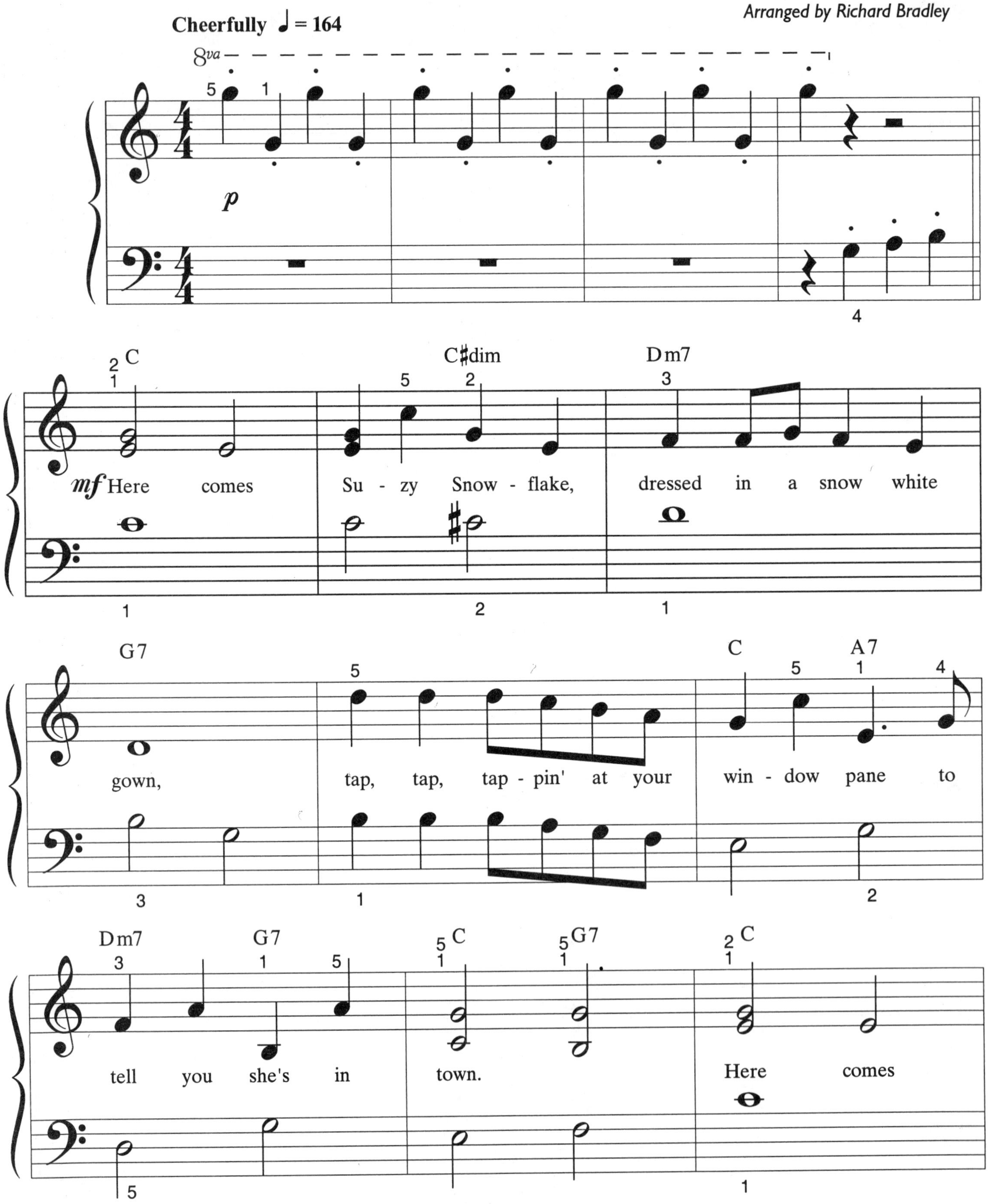
Cheerfully ♩ = 164
8va
p
C
C♯dim
Dm7
mf
Here comes Su - zy Snow - flake, dressed in a snow white
G7
C
A7
gown, tap, tap, tap - pin' at your win - dow pane to
Dm7
G7
C
G7
C
tell you she's in town. Here comes

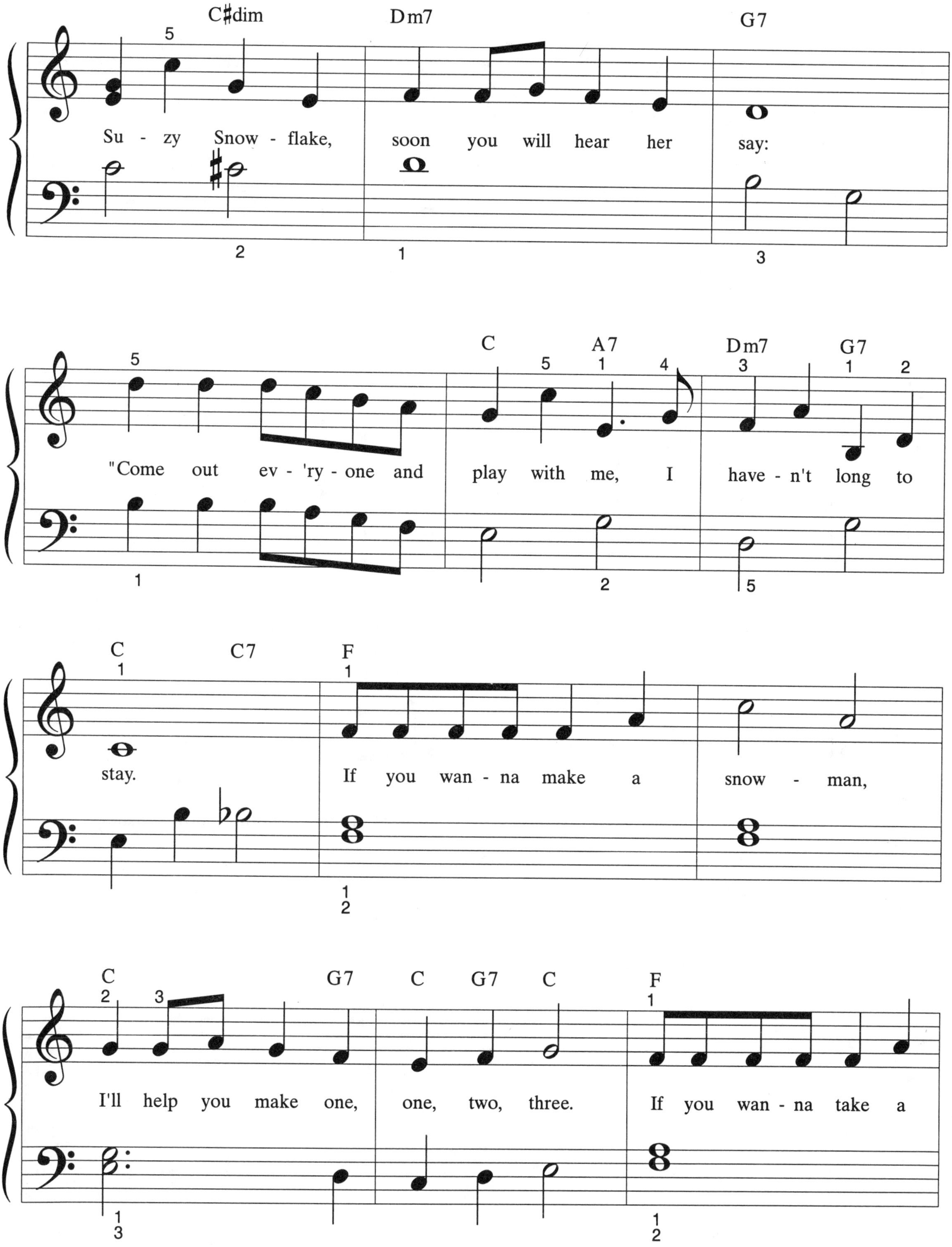
C♯dim Dm7 G7
Su - zy Snow - flake, soon you will hear her say:
C A7 Dm7 G7
"Come out ev - 'ry - one and play with me, I have - n't long to
C C7 F
stay.
If you wan - na make a snow - man,
C G7 C G7 C F
I'll help you make one, one, two, three.
If you wan - na take a

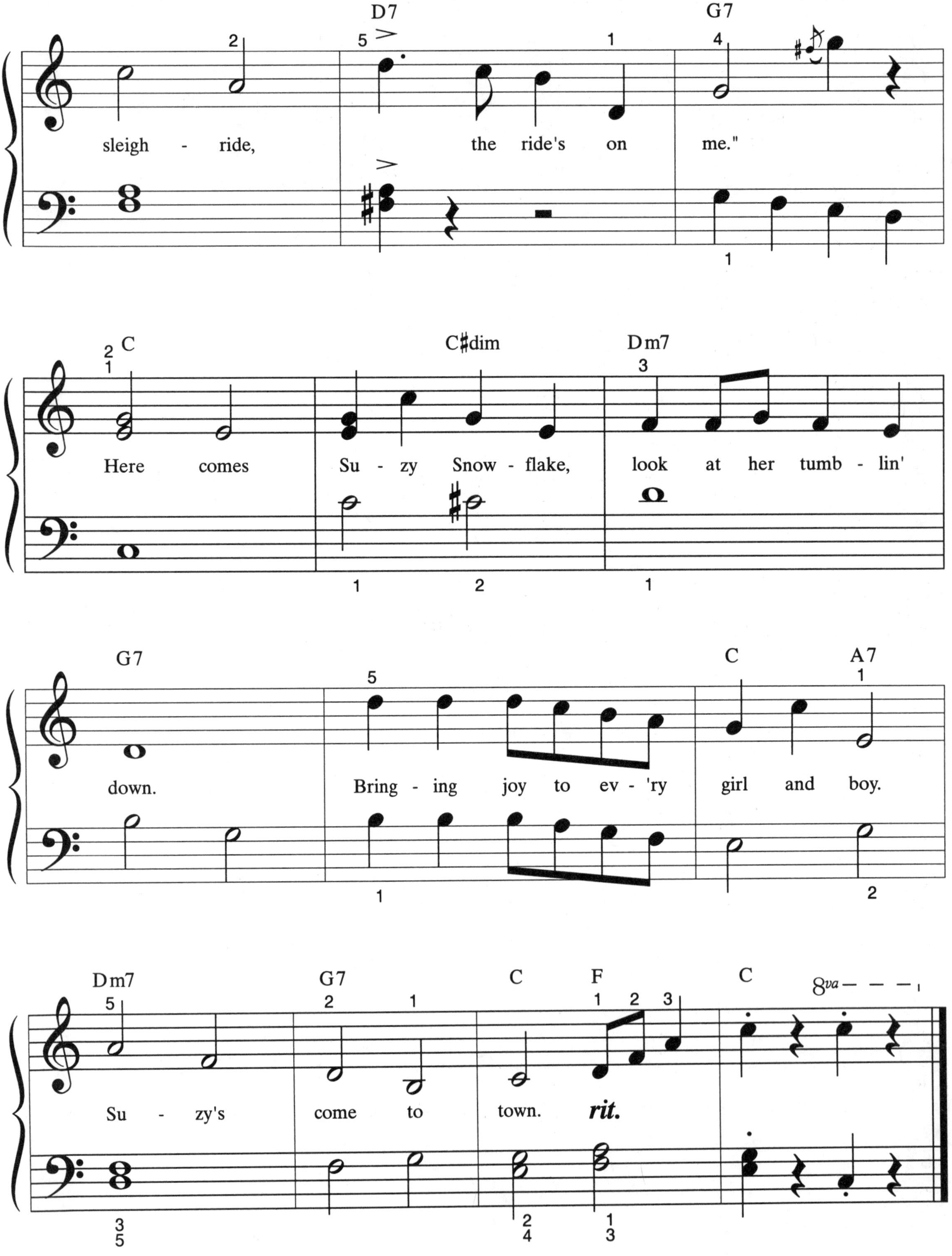
D7
G7
sleigh - ride, the ride's on me."
C
C♯dim
Dm7
Here comes Su - zy Snow - flake, look at her tumb - lin'
G7
C
A7
down. Bring - ing joy to ev - 'ry girl and boy.
Dm7
G7
C
F
C
8va
Su - zy's come to town.
rit.

Have Yourself a Merry Little Christmas

Words and Music by
HUGH MARTIN and RALPH BLANE
Arranged by Richard Bradley

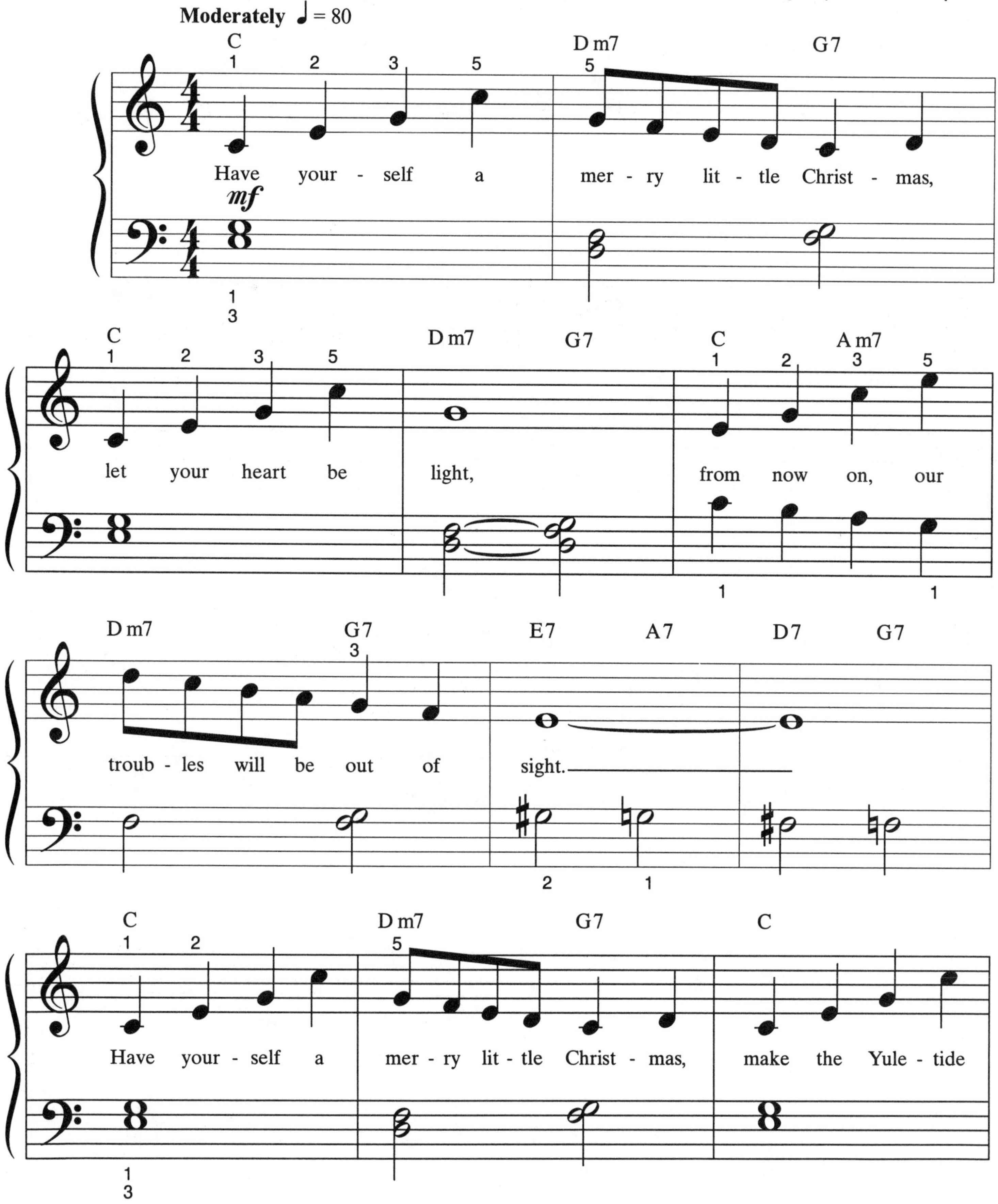
Moderately ♩ = 80
C Dm7 G7
Have your - self a mer - ry lit - tle Christ - mas,
mf
C Dm7 G7 C Am7
let your heart be light, from now on, our
Dm7 G7 E7 A7 D7 G7
troub - les will be out of sight.
C Dm7 G7 C
Have your - self a mer - ry lit - tle Christ - mas, make the Yule - tide

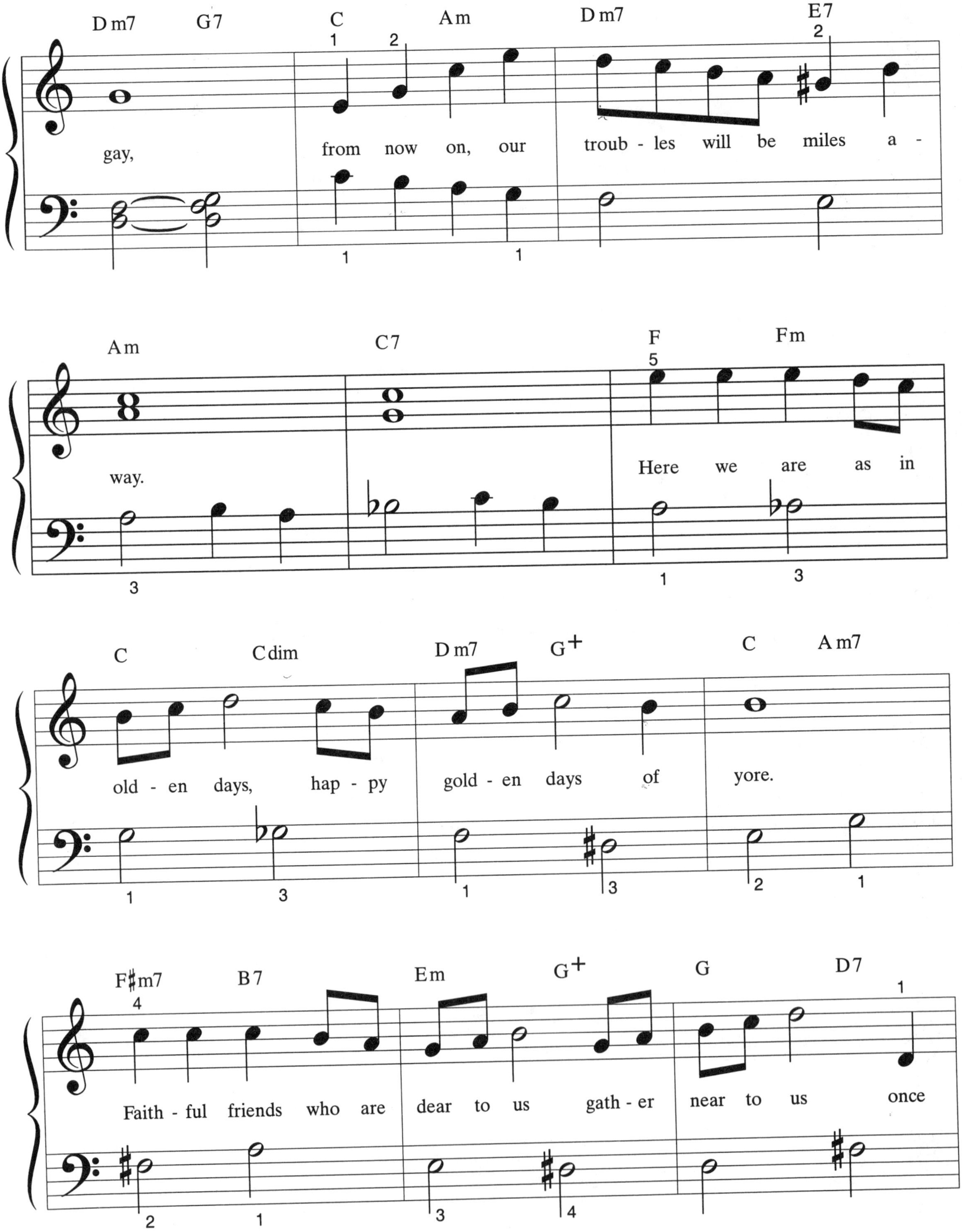
Dm7 G7 C Am Dm7 E7
gay, from now on, our troub - les will be miles a -
Am C7 F Fm
way. Here we are as in
C Cdim Dm7 G+ C Am7
old - en days, hap - py gold - en days of yore.
F♯m7 B7 Em G+ G D7
Faith - ful friends who are dear to us gath - er near to us once

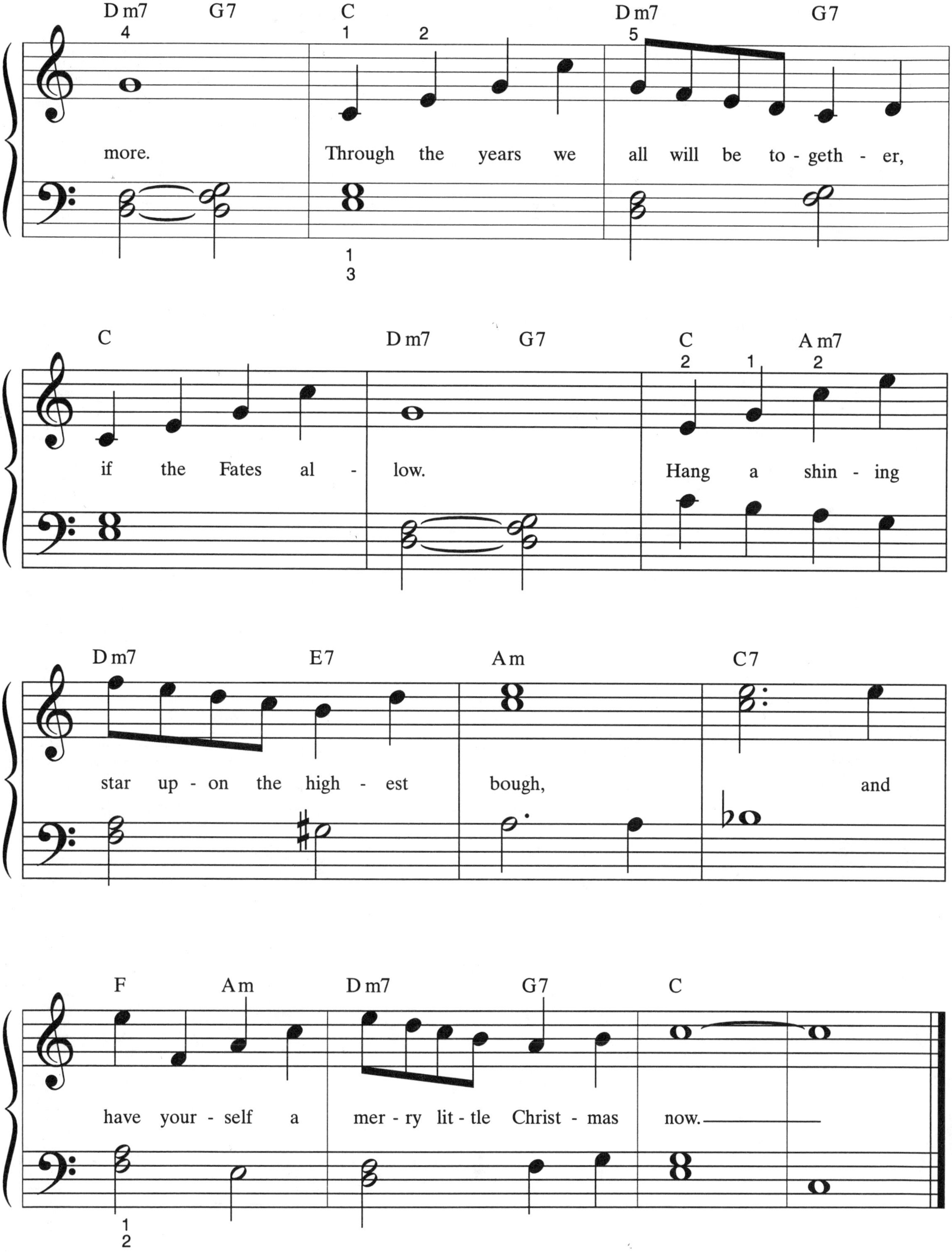
Dm7 G7 C Dm7 G7
more. Through the years we all will be to - geth - er,
C Dm7 G7 C Am7
if the Fates al - low. Hang a shin - ing
Dm7 E7 Am C7
star up - on the high - est bough, and
F Am Dm7 G7 C
have your - self a mer - ry lit - tle Christ - mas now.

(There's No Place Like)
Home for the Holidays

Words by
AL STILLMAN

Music by
ROBERT ALLEN
Arranged by Richard Bradley

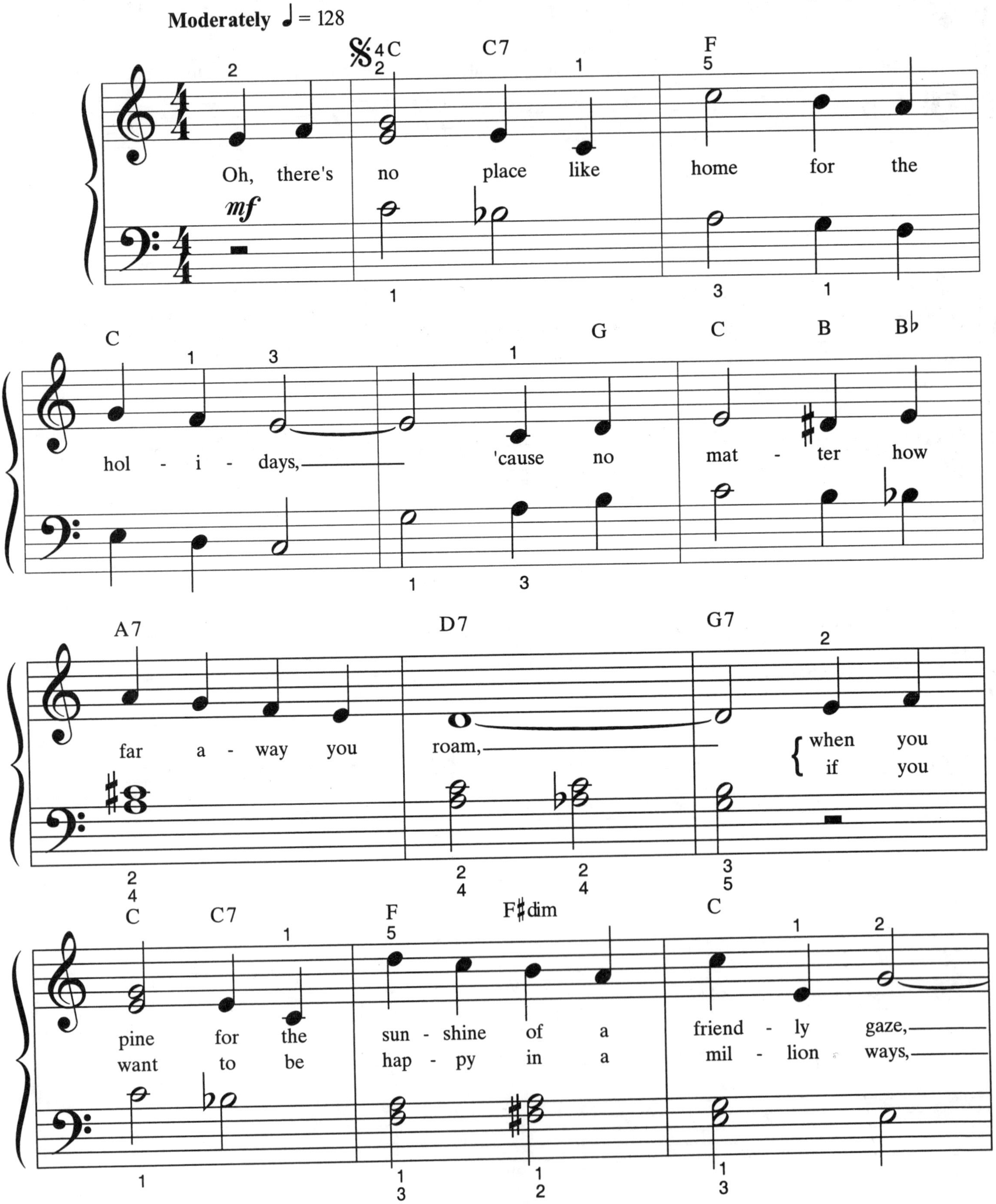
Moderately ♩ = 128
C C7 F
Oh, there's no place like home for the
mf
C G C B B♭
hol - i - days, 'cause no mat - ter how
A7 D7 G7
far a - way you roam, when you / if you
C C7 F F♯dim C
pine for the sun - shine of a friend - ly gaze,
want to be hap - py in a mil - lion ways,

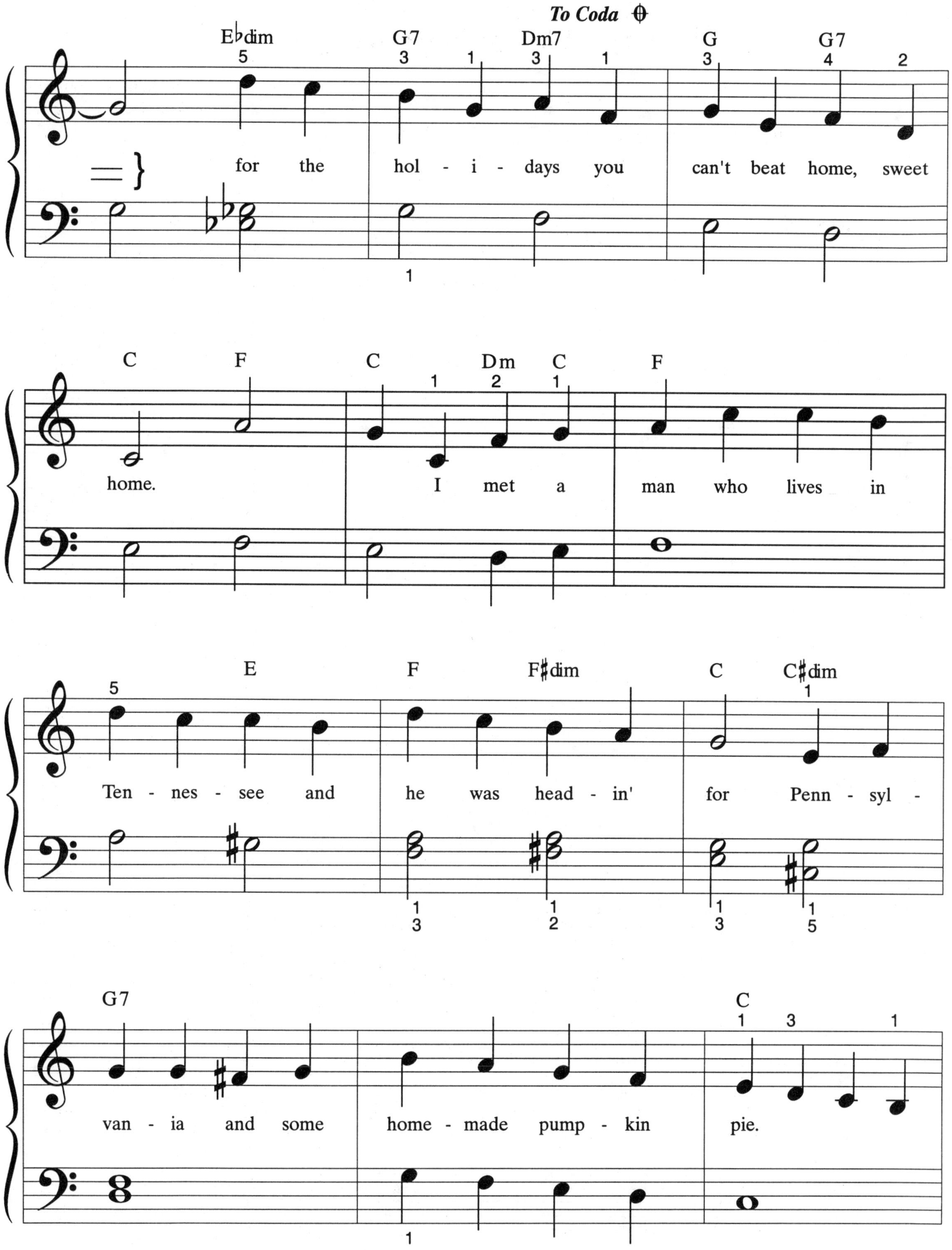

To Coda
E♭dim G7 Dm7 G G7
for the hol - i - days you can't beat home, sweet
C F C Dm C F
home. I met a man who lives in
E F F♯dim C C♯dim
Ten - nes - see and he was head - in' for Penn - syl -
G7 C
van - ia and some home - made pump - kin pie.

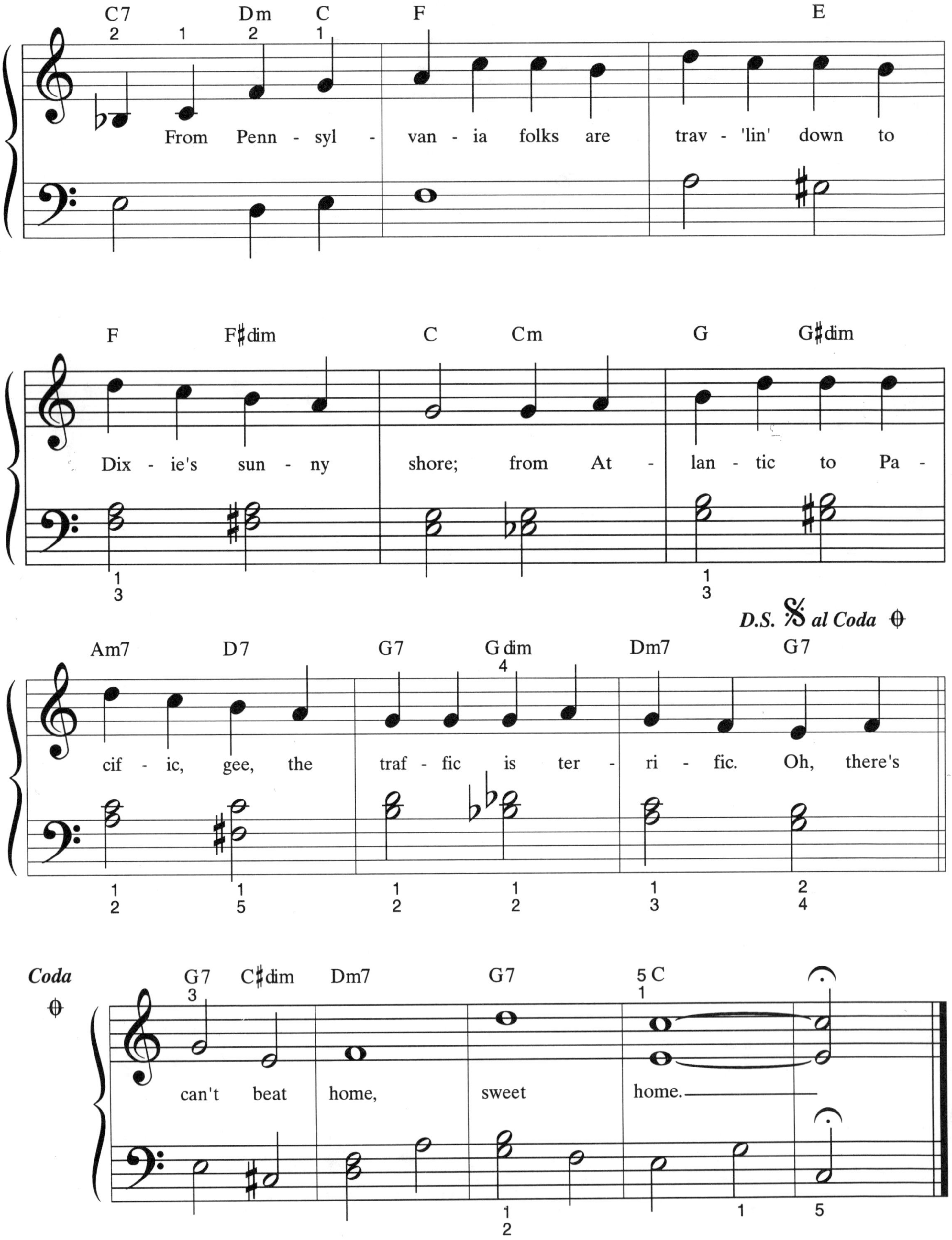
C7 Dm C F E
From Penn - syl - van - ia folks are trav - 'lin' down to
F F♯dim C Cm G G♯dim
Dix - ie's sun - ny shore; from At - lan - tic to Pa -
D.S. 𝄋 al Coda ⊕
Am7 D7 G7 G dim Dm7 G7
cif - ic, gee, the traf - fic is ter - ri - fic. Oh, there's
Coda ⊕
G7 C♯dim Dm7 G7 C
can't beat home, sweet home.